PERSONNEL POLICIES
FOR ENGINEERS AND SCIENTISTS

Other Major Studies Available
from the Industrial Research Unit

56. *The Objective Selection of Supervisors,* by Herbert R. Northrup, Ronald M. Cowin, Lawrence G. Vanden Plas et al. Manpower and Human Resources Studies No. 8, 1978; reprinted 1981, 1984. $25.00 (clothbound).

58. *Multinational Collective Bargaining Attempts: The Record, the Cases, and the Prospects,* by Herbert R. Northrup and Richard L. Rowan. Multinational Industrial Relations Series No. 6, 1979. $27.50 (clothbound).

59. *Union Violence: The Record and the Response by Courts, Legislatures, and the NLRB,* by Armand J. Thieblot, Jr., and Thomas R. Haggard. Labor Relations and Public Policy Series No. 25, 1983; reprinted 1984. $38.00 (clothbound).

60. *Collective Bargaining and the Decline of the United Mine Workers,* by Charles R. Perry, 1984. $30.00 (clothbound).

61. *The Decline of Annual Hours Worked in the United States Since 1947,* by Theresa Diss Greis. Manpower and Human Resources Studies No. 10, 1984. $30.00 (clothbound).

62. *Open Shop Construction Revisited,* by Herbert R. Northrup, 1984. $38.00 (clothbound).

63. *Personnel Policies for Engineers and Scientists: An Analysis of Major Corporate Practice,* by Herbert R. Northrup and Margot E. Malin. Manpower and Human Resources Studies No. 11, 1985. $30.00 (clothbound).

MANPOWER AND HUMAN RESOURCES STUDIES

No. 11

PERSONNEL POLICIES FOR ENGINEERS AND SCIENTISTS

*An Analysis of Major
Corporate Practice*

by

HERBERT R. NORTHRUP
and
MARGOT E. MALIN

INDUSTRIAL RESEARCH UNIT
The Wharton School, Vance Hall/CS
University of Pennsylvania
Philadelphia, Pennsylvania 19104
U.S.A.

Copyright © 1985 by the Trustees of the University of Pennsylvania
Library of Congress Catalog Card Number 85-60642
MANUFACTURED IN THE UNITED STATES OF AMERICA
ISBN: 0-89546-050-5
ISSN: 0149-080x

ISBN: 0-89546-053-X

Foreword

This study represents a continuation of my longtime interest in the subject of personnel policies for engineers and scientists, which began with a monograph and a series of articles completed during the late 1940s. The co-author, Ms. Margot E. Malin, received her bachelor of science in civil engineering from Tufts University, worked for two years as a sales engineer for a large manufacturing corporation, took a leave of absence to obtain the Master of Business Administration degree at the Wharton School, and is now with a New York City investment firm. She did most of the field interviews and wrote drafts of most of the chapters, which I then restructured and rewrote. Dr. Judith Sen, a research chemist, assisted with the field interviews.

Two Wharton graduate students, Ms. Cynthia Black, whose undergraduate degree is in chemical engineering, and Ms. Mary M. Halloran, a graduate computer scientist, assisted in the final research. Mr. O.P. Suri word processed the manuscript, and it was edited and the index developed by Ms. Barbara A. Kimmelman, associate editor, and Ms. Kate C. Bradford, chief editor. My secretary, Ms. Mary Jane Welsh, handled the voluminous correspondence and communications. Ms. Marthenia A. Perrin, the Industrial Research Unit's fiscal coordinator, and Ms. Margaret E. Doyle, former office manager, handled various administrative matters involved in the project. Ms. Sherrie L. Waitsman, administrative assistant, assisted in the preparation of some of the charts, and Ms. Sue A. Torelli, the Unit's librarian, found numerous data and publications that contributed to the study.

This study could not have been accomplished without the financial support of the Lilly Endowment, which provided a very generous two-year grant in March 1982. We are indeed very grateful to the trustees of the Endowment and to Mr. Gordon St. Angelo, senior program officer, whose sympathetic consideration, patience, and support were so essential to the work. Prior to the receipt of the Lilly grant, initial research was supported by a gift from International Paper Company through the courtesy of my former student, Mr. Ronald M. Cowin, director of organization planning and development; by unrestricted grants from the Gerstacker, Gulf, and General Mills Foundations; and by a grant from the Mobil Oil Corporation. The Hitachi Research Institute, through the courtesy of its director, Dr. Tsutomu Sato, and the Environmental Scanning Association later provided additional grants. Editing was underwritten by the

John F. Olin Foundation as part of the last of several grants in support of the publication program of the Industrial Research Unit. Publication was underwritten by the Lilly Endowment grant and by the Wharton Labor Relations Council.

This book is No. 11 in the Industrial Research Unit's Manpower and Human Resources Studies series which present the results of research in personnel training and development, as well as other human resource subfields. As in all Industrial Research Unit publications, the senior author is fully responsible for all opinions expressed, and in no case should such responsibility be attributed to any of the grantors to the project, to the University of Pennsylvania, or to any other organization with which either author is now, or was formerly, associated.

HERBERT R. NORTHRUP, *Director*
Industrial Research Unit
The Wharton School
University of Pennsylvania

Philadelphia
December 1984

TABLE OF CONTENTS

PART ONE
INTRODUCTION

CHAPTER

PART TWO
THE INSTITUTIONAL ENVIRONMENT

PART THREE
PERSONNEL POLICIES

PART FOUR
CONCLUDING REMARKS

APPENDIX

LIST OF TABLES

LIST OF FIGURES

PART ONE

Introduction

CHAPTER I

The Nature of the Study

Engineers and scientists (E/S) are a critical resource to industry and their role appears to be increasing. The decline in importance of the older manufacturing industries has been accompanied by the rise of high technology concerns. Moreover, intense competition, both domestic and foreign, has forced major manufacturing concerns to invest heavily in research and development (R&D) in order to improve old products and to develop new ones. Thus, E/S are a critical national resource. The strength of our nation's technological base is a major determinant of its economic health and is derived fundamentally from the cumulative knowledge base of E/S. A study of how industry manages these personnel, the problems which are encountered, and the solutions which have been developed in response to various pressures and to the needs both of E/S and of industrial management appeared both academically appropriate and practically useful.

The idea that personnel policies for E/S are deserving of special study is not a new one. There has long been a considerable amount of literature on various aspects of the subject, particularly in the technical journals but also in those concerned with personnel and human resource management. The senior author of this work has been interested in the subject for about forty years.[1] A number of considerations, however, led to the belief that an overall study for the 1980s would be appropriate.

The study was begun during the severe recession of 1981-1982. E/S and other professionals, as well as clerical and hourly workers, were suffering layoffs, downgradings, and salary and benefit reductions. The union movement, which has been only a minor factor

---

[1]See the following by Herbert R. Northrup: *Unionization of Professional Engineers and Chemists*, Industrial Relations Monograph No. 12 (New York: Industrial Relations Counselors, Inc., 1946); "Collective Bargaining by Professional Societies," in R. A. Lester and J. Shister, eds., *Insights into Labor Issues* (New York: Macmillan, 1948), pp. 134-62; "Industrial Relations with Professional Workers," *Harvard Business Review*, Vol. 26 (September 1948), pp. 543-59; "Personnel Administration for the Engineer," in *Unionization Among American Engineers*, Studies in Personnel Policy, No. 155 (New York: National Industrial Conference Board, 1956), pp. 52-55; and "Better Personnel Administration: A Key to the Engineering Crisis," *Personnel*, Vol. 24 (September-October 1957), pp. 60-66.

among E/S since World War II, was still failing to enroll E/S (as discussed in Chapter III and Appendix C) but coming closer than heretofore to winning National Labor Relations Board elections. The situation raised the question of whether corporate management was losing its relationship with professionals.

Answering this question required an intensive study covering a large sector of industry. Few such studies have been made because such work involves considerable time and expense, as well as access to key human resource personnel and technical executives managing E/S. The Wharton Industrial Research Unit has long had the access and, as explained in the foreword, was able to obtain the funding.

Finally, during the 1981–1982 recession much was heard about the "decline of industrial America." At the same time, high technology companies were mushrooming in Silicon Valley and elsewhere. Therefore, the effect of these industrial changes on human resources and the changes in emphasis occurring in the personnel management of E/S would be of interest. In particular, it was felt that innovative personnel policies should be implemented while those that seemed less effective could be examined for their shortcomings.

METHODOLOGY

The study began with a comprehensive literature search. From this an interview questionnaire was developed and tested with a series of interviews on the East Coast. (The outline for the questionnaire is presented in Appendix A.) Approximately one-hundred companies answered the questionnaire: about ten by mail and the rest through interviews, which were conducted during 1982 and the early part of 1983. Human resource executives were the most frequent respondents, but wherever possible, line executives involved in the management of E/S were also interviewed. Various levels of managers were included in the interviews, which ranged in length from two hours to two days.

In selecting companies for interviews, the authors made an effort to include those firms which were not high on the "desirable" list for E/S, as well as companies which employ the largest percentage of E/S and are considered the "in" or "sexy" places for E/S to work, such as those in the aerospace, electronics, communication, chemicals, and petroleum industries. Interviews were also arranged, therefore, with concerns in construction, paper manufacturing, steel, automobiles, farm equipment, and construction machinery. Many interviews occurred at a time of serious layoffs and cutbacks in which E/S were involved. The interviews also covered all major regions of the United States. The companies interviewed were, with few exceptions, *Fortune* "500" concerns. A few smaller high technology firms in Silicon Valley were also interviewed, but it was decided to leave them to a second study which is scheduled for release in 1986. This study, then, deals with the policies and programs of large corporations.

In addition to corporate executives, executives of four unions and six professional societies were interviewed. Prior to this study's inception, an analysis of the union role among E/S had been completed and published by Geoffrey W. Latta, a research specialist at the Wharton Industrial Research Unit.[2] It is reproduced in Appendix C. Therefore, the research for this study involving the union role among E/S was confined to developments that occurred following the publication of the earlier study. The role of professional societies is well documented by their own publications and is discussed in Chapter III and elaborated on in Appendix B.

It was originally planned to quantify the information received in the interviews much more than proved realistically possible. Policies under the same name varied so considerably that quantification concealed rather than enlightened. As a result, the bulk of the work uses descriptive analysis and practical samples to summarize and to discuss the findings. Variations in industry structure result in different approaches to personnel policies as do differences in the objectives of individual firms. The information, therefore, is presented in a manner which the authors believe does justice to the nature of the policies studied.

Engineers and scientists are defined, for the purpose of this study, by job function. This includes personnel working in areas of industrial and scientific research, design, development, manufacturing, and operations. Computer professionals whose workload concentration is scientific rather than business oriented are also included. Engineers and scientific professionals by training and education who currently hold management positions, or who have moved into nontechnical job functions such as human resources, sales, or finance are not included.

STUDY ORGANIZATION

This study is organized into four parts. Part Two deals with the external forces which determine to a large extent a company's key

---

[2]Geoffrey W. Latta, "Union Organization Among Engineers: A Current Assessment," *Industrial and Labor Relations Review,* Vol. 35 (October 1981), pp. 29–42. Reproduced by permission in Appendix C.

personnel policies: the labor market for E/S, the educational system, the role of the government, and the role of professional societies and unions. Part Three contains the main body of the work—a descriptive analysis of industry's personnel policies from recruiting to layoffs and measures dealing with obsolescence. This part concludes with chapters examining the special situation in research and development laboratories and the differences among key industries. Part Four contains the concluding observations.

PART TWO

The Institutional Environment

CHAPTER II

The Supply and Demand for Engineers and Scientists

In 1941, the United States Bureau of Labor Statistics (BLS) published a study entitled *Employment and Earnings in the Engineering Profession 1929 to 1934.*[1] It found that during the early years of the Great Depression, the nature of the engineering labor market changed dramatically. Whereas during the previous two decades a substantial number of entrants into the engineering professions did not hold degrees, during the depression years colleges were supplying as many engineers with degrees as were supplied from all sources in the 1920s. Moreover, although the number of persons considering themselves either trained for or working within the profession increased by 25.3 percent from 1929 to 1934, opportunities for engineering employment increased only by 4.4 percent. In contrast, in the 1920s the number of engineers had risen by 66.2 percent and the availability of job opportunities in that period is indicated by the large percentage of new engineers who were not college trained but were nevertheless working in the profession.[2]

The Great Depression caused considerable unemployment among engineers; many engineers migrated to other jobs. Only the large number of opportunities for engineers in New Deal-sponsored public works saved the profession from "disastrous" unemployment. Nevertheless, the unemployment rate exceeded 10 percent, and many individuals were out of work for well over one year, often several years, as nearly 40 percent of engineering graduates experienced unemployment.[3] The implications of the BLS study were clear: the engineering profession was overcrowded, and opportunities were severely limited.

No comparable period study exists for scientists, who were not employed in industry in large numbers at this time, but one can undoubtedly assume that many chemists, physicists, and other such

---

[1] Andrew Fraser, Jr., *Employment and Earnings in the Engineering Profession, 1929 to 1934,* Bulletin No. 682, Bureau of Labor Statistics, U.S. Department of Labor (Washington, D.C.: Government Printing Office, 1941).

[2] *Ibid.,* pp. 2, 36–40.

[3] *Ibid.,* pp. 7–9, 92–119.

professionals likewise found conditions severe in the 1930s. What is significant, however, is that by the time the BLS study was published, the labor market for engineers and scientists (E/S) had altered radically, and seemingly permanently. The pre-World War II defense build-up, followed by war production, greatly expanded the demand for engineers and scientists. Oversupply turned dramatically to shortages. Despite cyclical downturns, the trend toward increased demand has continued largely unabated into the 1980s. Today, engineers and scientists are at the forefront of industrial expansion and product development, and are the leaders in new high technology product development and company expansion.

In the remainder of this chapter, the supply and demand for E/S are examined. It will be seen that not only has the supply greatly expanded, but the composition of that supply in terms of race and sex has also been altered, although the percentages of women and minorities in the various fields generally remain far below those of their proportion in the labor force as a whole.

THE SUPPLY OF ENGINEERS AND SCIENTISTS

People qualify for employment as E/S in the United States by one of three routes: 1) by enrolling in a college or university and completing the required courses; 2) by working in jobs associated with E/S, learning the field, and doing what is necessary to acquire the knowledge beyond what is obtained by experience—for example, taking college courses and/or company development curricula while working; or 3) for non-natives, immigrating to the United States after professional training and/or experience abroad. The first method— formal education in the United States—is by far the most prevalent and has been so since the Great Depression.

Employment Trends Since 1940

The basic data on the supply of labor are found in the reports of the decennial census of the population. The census data reveal the overall trend toward increasing numbers of E/S in industry, but they have serious limitations for our purposes. First, the data are based upon individuals' conceptions of themselves. Employers or prospective employers may not agree that a self-designated title accurately describes a person's work. Individuals often exaggerate their status, or the importance of their jobs. Thus, the census may overestimate the number of E/S. Second, the census data do not clearly indicate whether those who term themselves E/S are in fact working as such, or if so, whether they are employed in industry. Because of these limitations, we have also utilized other sources, particularly, the National Science Foundation, the Bureau of Labor Statistics of the U.S. Department of Labor, the Scientific Manpower Commission, and data from various professional societies and industry associations. Since, however, census data are very useful for demonstrating trends over long periods, and in showing changes in the racial and sex composition of the labor supply, we shall begin the analysis therewith.

Table II-1 shows the number of experienced engineers by sex and race, as reported by the census, 1940–1980. The number of engineers reported increased by almost 5.5 times during this forty-year period and yet engineers are often (but because of cyclical factors, not always) in short supply. In all census years during this period, a majority of the engineers had four or more years of college, and that proportion has remained relatively stable—approximately 60 percent in 1940, 63 percent in 1980. Since our field studies indicated rather strongly that a very much smaller percentage of engineers in major industries do not have at least an undergraduate degree, it may well be that a sizable percentage of those who classify themselves as engineers for census purposes are not so classified by their employers. Since, however, the portion of those who do not have college degrees appears to be relatively constant over time, the trend value of the census data are probably not materially affected.

It is apparent also from Table II-1 that the engineering profession has historically been a province of white males. In 1940, females in the profession were too few to be counted and only 320 nonwhite males—.12 percent of the total—were found. By 1980, the numbers had substantially increased, but the percentages remained relatively small both for women and minorities. We shall explore the sex and racial composition in more detail below.

Table II-2 provides much the same information for engineers as does Table II-1, but it is divided into five principal subfields of engineering: chemical, electrical (including electronic), industrial, mechanical, and civil. Women have gained a larger share of the work in three of the fields over the years (their gains were not impressive in mechanical or civil engineering), but minorities, with the exception of Orientals, lag.

In science, the picture is somewhat different. Although the data for physicists are not entirely comparable (because in some census years other scientists are included), Table II-3 shows that physicists have experienced no such increased supply as have engineers. Minority and female physicists remain very few in number.

TABLE II-1
*Number of Experienced Civilian Engineers
by Sex and Race, 1940–1980*

	1940		1950		1960		1970		1980	
	Number	Percent[a]	Number	Percent[a]	Number	Percent[a]	Number	Percent[a]	Number	Percent[a]
Total engineers	255,480	100	527,190	100	869,716	100	1,256,935	100	1,400,973	100
Male engineers	255,480	100	520,530	98.7	862,002	99.1	1,236,160	98.3	1,336,164	95.4
White	255,160	99.9	517,800	98.2	849,807	97.7	1,199,811	95.4	1,232,918	88.0
Black	320[b]	0.1	1,620	0.3	4,174	0.5	14,198	1.1	31,499	2.2
Spanish[c]	n.a.	n.a.	n.a.	n.a.	n.a.	n.a.	17,237	1.4	29,834	2.1
Other[d]	n.a.	n.a.	1,110	0.2	8,021	0.9	18,777	1.5	63,938	4.6
Male engineers with four or more years of college	155,760	61.0	279,030	52.9	479,899	55.2	725,308	57.7	828,249	59.1[e]
White	155,580	60.9	277,710	52.7	472,513	54.3	n.a.	n.a.	754,330	53.8
Nonwhite	180	0.1	1,320	0.2	7,386	0.8	n.a.	n.a.	n.a.	n.a.
Black	n.a.	n.a.	n.a.	n.a.	n.a.	n.a.	6,989	0.5	15,058	1.1
Spanish	n.a.	n.a.	n.a.	n.a.	n.a.	n.a.	9,408	0.7	17,124	1.2
Other	n.a.	n.a.	n.a.	n.a.	n.a.	n.a.	n.a.	n.a.	54,668	3.9
Female engineers	n.a.	n.a.	6,660	1.3	7,714	0.9	20,775	1.7	64,809	4.6
White	n.a.	n.a.	6,510	1.2	7,552	0.86	19,697	1.6	56,603	4.0
Black	n.a.	n.a.	150	0.02	102	0.01	757	0.06	4,517	0.3
Spanish[c]	n.a.	n.a.	n.a.	n.a.	n.a.	n.a.	298	0.02	2,129	0.1
Other[d]	n.a.	n.a.	—	—	60	0.01	312	0.02	2,948	0.2
Female engineers with four or more years of college	n.a.	n.a.	2,640	0.5	2,830	0.3	9,069	0.7	28,454	2.0[e]
White	n.a.	n.a.	2,610	0.5	2,788	0.3	n.a.	n.a.	24,271	1.7
Nonwhite	n.a.	n.a.	30	0.01	42	0.004	n.a.	n.a.	n.a.	n.a.
Black	n.a.	n.a.	n.a.	n.a.	n.a.	n.a.	229	0.02	1,804	0.1
Spanish	n.a.	n.a.	n.a.	n.a.	n.a.	n.a.	84	0.01	692	0.04
Other	n.a.	n.a.	n.a.	n.a.	n.a.	n.a.	n.a.	n.a.	2,140	0.2

Sources: Derived from U.S. Department of Commerce, Bureau of the Census, *Sixteenth Census of the United States: 1940 Population, The Labor Force, Occupational Characteristics* (Washington, D.C.: Government Printing Office, 1943), pp. 59–70 *passim*, Table 3; *Census of Population:1950, Occupational Characteristics*, P-E No. 1B (Washington, D.C.: Government Printing Office, 1956), pp. 29, 107, 115, Tables 3, 10, 11; *Census of Population: 1960, Occupational Characteristics*, PC(2)-7A (Washington, D.C.: Government Printing Office, 1961), pp. 21, 116, 123, 130, 137, Tables 3, 9, 10; *Census of Population:1970, Occupational Characteristics*, PC(2)-7A (Washington, D.C.: Government Printing Office, 1973), pp. 12, 59, 73, 87, 101, Tables 2, 5, 6, 7; *Census of Population:1980, Detailed Population Characteristics*, U.S. Summary, PC80-2-D1-A, Section A: United States (Washington, D.C.: Government Printing Office, 1984), Tables 277 and 282.

Note: A dash represents zero or a percent which rounds to less than 0.1.

[a]All are percents of the total number of engineers.

[b]Only nonwhite data available.

[c]People of Spanish origin may be of any race; thus, all persons included here are also included in the race categories.

[d]American Indian, Japanese, Chinese, Filipino.

[e]1980 data for years of school completed by occupation is for employed persons.

n.a. = not available for these categories.

TABLE II-2
Number and Percentages of Women and Minorities in Five Subfields of the Engineering Labor Force 1970 and 1980

1970

Subfield	Total	Women No.	Women Per cent	Black No.	Black Per cent	Nat. American No.	Nat. American Per cent	Oriental No.	Oriental Per cent	Spanish[a] No.	Spanish[a] Per cent
Chemical	54,217	579	1.1	389	0.7	87	0.2	860	1.6	681	1.2
Electrical	290,185	4,948	1.7	4,130	1.4	238	0.1	5,373	1.9	4,102	1.4
Industrial	195,060	5,826	3.0	2,144	1.1	126	0.1	741	0.4	2,519	1.3
Mechanical	185,406	1,830	1.0	1,927	1.0	101	0.05	2,396	1.3	2,299	1.2
Civil	178,334	2,623	1.4	2,485	1.3	429	0.2	4,002	2.2	3,570	2.0

1980

Subfield	Total	Women No.	Women Per cent	Black No.	Black Per cent	Nat. American No.	Nat. American Per cent	Oriental No.	Oriental Per cent	Spanish[a] No.	Spanish[a] Per cent
Chemical	57,502	3,015	5.2	1,161	2.0	78	0.1	3,328	5.8	1,086	1.9
Electrical	322,874	16,179	5.0	9,576	3.0	805	0.2	14,804	4.6	7,866	2.4
Industrial	194,322	19,354	10.0	5,645	2.9	477	0.2	3,939	2.0	4,114	2.1
Mechanical	197,650	4,071	2.1	4,720	2.4	380	0.2	7,830	4.0	3,448	1.7
Civil	204,035	6,006	2.9	5,150	2.5	596	0.2	12,744	6.2	5,566	2.7

Sources: Derived from U.S. Department of Commerce, Bureau of the Census, *Census of Population: 1970, Occupational Characteristics,* PC(2A)-7A (Washington, D.C.: Government Printing Office, 1973), p. 12, Table 2; *Census of Population: 1980, Detailed Population Characteristics,* U.S. Summary, PC80-1-D1-A, Section A: United States (Washington, D.C.: Government Printing Office, 1984), p. 176, Table 277.

[a]People of Spanish origin may be of any race; thus, all persons included here are also included in the race categories.

Table II-4 shows that chemists encompass a far more numerous profession which doubled from 1940 to 1970, but remained relatively constant between 1970 and 1980. (The data of these two census years are not completely comparable because biochemists are excluded from the 1980 data.) The chemistry profession also has—and this is true historically—a substantially higher proportion of women in its ranks than most other E/S fields, Minorities, however, are not well represented.

Supply data for the biological and geological sciences are presented in Tables II-5 and II-6, for 1970 and 1980. These are specialties not utilized in many industries, but the significance of biological sciences for industrial research has greatly increased since 1970; the supply increased by 56 percent between 1970 and 1980. Women comprised one-third of the total in 1980, by far the highest proportion of any E/S classification. Minorities again were greatly underrepresented.

For geology and related fields, the jump in supply between 1970 and 1980 was even more dramatic—a gain of 120 percent—as petroleum and oil exploration firms vied for the services of earth scientists. When economic forces reasserted themselves over the OPEC cartel, the demand for such personnel dramatically receded, and presumably the supply, which was counted before the oil price decline, has also dropped. Women held about 11 percent of the geology jobs in 1980, but minorities held very few such positions.

Women and Minorities

The most complete current data for the supply of E/S, based upon educational and employment status, are published by the Scientific Manpower Commission and the National Science Foundation. The data from these organizations reveal substantial improvement in the status of women in E/S fields. Women earned 37 percent of the E/S bachelor's degrees granted in 1981 as compared with 27 percent in 1971. Women also made impressive gains at the doctoral level, earning 23 percent of the E/S doctorates granted in 1982 as compared with 11 percent ten years earlier.[4]

Despite these gains, Figure II-1 shows that women continue to be underrepresented in E/S fields, and particularly in engineering. Moreover, since the increased number of women in E/S fields is a relatively recent phenomenon, women have had comparatively less experience therein than have men, as shown in Figure II-2, and their rise in E/S and managerial hierarchies is considerably lower. Fur-

---

[4]*Women and Minorities in Science and Engineering* (Washington, D.C.: National Science Foundation, 1984), p. vii.

TABLE II-3

Number of Experienced Civilian Physicists
by Sex and Race, 1950–1980

Sex and Race	1950[a] Number	Per-cent[c]	1960 Number	Per-cent[c]	1970[b] Number	Per-cent[c]	1980 Number	Per-cent[c]
Physicists total	38,700	100.0	14,154	100.0	22,971	100.0	22,473	100.0
Male physicists	33,120	85.6	13,672	96.6	21,992	95.7	21,253	94.6
White	32,550	84.1	13,322	94.1	21,171	92.2	19,590	87.2
Black	420	1.1	142	1.0	237	1.0	320	1.4
Spanish[d]	n.a.	n.a.	n.a.	n.a.	350	1.5	324	1.4
Other	150	0.4	208	1.5	516	2.2	1,190	5.3
Male physicists with four or more years of college	23,280	60.2	11,880	83.9	19,850	86.4	18,346	81.6
White	23,100	59.7	11,530	81.5	n.a.	n.a.	n.a.	n.a.
Nonwhite	180	0.5	350	2.5	n.a.	n.a.	n.a.	n.a.
Black	n.a.	n.a.	n.a.	n.a.	189	0.8	n.a.	n.a.
Spanish	n.a.	n.a.	n.a.	n.a.	239	1.0	n.a.	n.a.
Other	n.a.	n.a.	n.a.	n.a.	n.a.	n.a.	n.a.	n.a.
Female physicists	5,580	14.4	482	3.4	979	4.3	1,220	5.4
White	5,340	13.8	422	3.0	869	3.8	1,121	5.0
Black	210	0.5	60	0.4	91	0.4	41	0.2
Spanish[d]	n.a.	n.a.	n.a.	n.a.	19	0.8	37	0.2
Other	30	0.1	—	—	19	0.8	40	0.2
Female physicists with four or more years of college	3,810	9.8	279	2.0	818	3.6	821	3.6
White	3,750	9.7	239	1.7	n.a.	n.a.	n.a.	n.a.
Nonwhite	60	0.1	40	0.3	n.a.	n.a.	n.a.	n.a.
Black	n.a.	n.a.	n.a.	n.a.	70	0.3	n.a.	n.a.
Spanish	n.a.	n.a.	n.a.	n.a.	19	0.8	n.a.	n.a.
Other	n.a.	n.a.	n.a.	n.a.	n.a.	n.a.	n.a.	n.a.

Sources: Derived from U.S. Department of Commerce, Bureau of the Census, *Census of Population: 1950, Occupational Characteristics,* P-E No. 1B (Washington, D.C.: Government Printing Office, 1956), pp. 29, 107, 115, Tables 3, 10, 11; *Census of Population: 1960, Occupational Characteristics,* PC(2)-7A (Washington, D.C.: Government Printing Office, 1961), pp. 21, 116, 123, 130, 137, Tables 3, 9, 10; *Census of Population: 1970, Occupational Characteristics,* PC(2)-7A (Washington, D.C.: Government Printing Office, 1973), pp. 12, 59, 73, 87, 101, Tables 2, 5, 6, 7; *Census of Population: 1980, Detailed Population Characteristics,* U.S. Summary, PC80-2-D1-A, Section A: United States (Washington, D.C.: Government Printing Office, 1984), Table 277; *Census of Population: 1980, Earnings by Occupation and Education,* PC-80-2-8B (Washington, D.C.: Government Printing Office, 1984), Table 1.

Note: A dash represents zero or a percent which rounds to less than 0.1.
[a]Data for 1950 is for natural scientists.
[b]Data for 1970 includes astronomers.
[c]All are percents of the total number of physicists.
[d]People of Spanish origin may be of any race; thus, all persons included here are also included in the race categories.
n.a. = not available for these categories.

thermore, women's interests within E/S fields are apparently quite different from those of men. Thus Figure II-3 shows, for example, that 61 percent of the employed male E/S, but only 15 percent of the employed female E/S, are engineers. On the other hand, 24 percent of the women but only 10 percent of the men are computer specialists. The tendencies of men and women to choose different E/S specialties affect affirmative action results and make it more or less difficult to meet hiring goals, depending upon the situation.

The various minorities, as the previously examined census data show, are also differently represented among E/S. Blacks are underrepresented in all E/S fields, native Americans are roughly proportionately represented, and the representation of Asians is disproportionately larger than their representation in the general U.S. labor force. Thus, despite considerable gains in college enrollment and graduation, blacks comprise only 2.6 percent of all employed E/S, as compared with 9 percent of the employed United States population and over 6 percent of all employed professionals, including teachers and ministers. Moreover, blacks remain underrepresented in professional and technical schools and achieve lower test scores, on average, in mathematics and science.[5]

There are wide variations in chosen fields among racial groups, as shown in Figure II-4. For example, blacks are heavily concentrated in social science, whereas Asians are concentrated more in the physical sciences. Figure II-5 shows that, as is the case with women, the newness of blacks to the E/S fields means they are less experienced than their white counterparts. Again these differences must be considered when companies design employment, upgrading, remuneration, and other human resource policies.

Hispanics comprise only about 2.2 percent of the employed E/S, roughly one-half of their proportion of all employed persons, but almost equal to their 2.6 percent representation among all professional and related workers.[6] On the other hand, the representation of Hispanics within the various E/S fields is not very different from their representation in the general E/S population, as shown by Figure II-6.

The sex and race data described above emphasize the underrepresentation of blacks, Hispanics, and, to a lesser extent, other minorities in the various E/S fields. Because of minority underrepresentation in training and educational institutions, it is a difficult task for companies to gain their share of available minority E/S graduates.

---

[5] *Ibid.*, pp. ix, 9.
[6] *Ibid.*, p. 12.

TABLE II-4
*Number of Experienced Chemists
by Sex and Race, 1940–1980*

	1940		1950		1960		1970		1980[b]	
	Number	Percent[a]	Number	Percent[a]	Number	Percent[a]	Number	Percent[a]	Number	Percent[a]
Total Chemists	55,900	100	76,590	100	82,109	100	111,790	100	102,239	100
Male chemists	55,900	100	69,540	90.8	75,414	91.8	98,470	88.1	81,699	79.9
White	55,640	99.5	68,340	89.2	72,986	88.9	91,831	82.1	72,000	70.4
Black	260[c]	0.5	870	1.1	1,533	1.9	3,350	3.0	3,642	3.6
Spanish[d]	n.a.	n.a.	n.a.	n.a.	n.a.	n.a.	2,029	1.8	1,794	1.8
Other	n.a.	n.a.	330	0.4	895	1.1	2,737	2.4	5,524	5.4
Male chemists with four or more years of college	32,680	58.5	43,800	57.2	53,094	64.7	71,608	64.1	64,356	62.9
White	32,620	58.4	43,110	56.3	51,280	62.4	n.a.	n.a.	n.a.	n.a.
Nonwhite	60	0.1	690	0.9	1,814	2.2	n.a.	n.a.	n.a.	n.a.
Black	n.a.	n.a.	n.a.	n.a.	n.a.	n.a.	2,259	2.0	n.a.	n.a.
Spanish[d]	n.a.	n.a.	n.a.	n.a.	n.a.	n.a.	1,166	1.0	n.a.	n.a.
Other	n.a.	n.a.	n.a.	n.a.	n.a.	n.a.	n.a.	n.a.	n.a.	n.a.
Female chemists	n.a.	n.a.	7,050	9.2	6,695	8.2	13,320	11.9	20,540	20.1
White	n.a.	n.a.	6,900	9.0	6,209	7.6	11,746	10.5	16,310	16.0
Black	n.a.	n.a.	150	0.2	266	0.3	595	0.5	1,475	1.4
Spanish[d]	n.a.	n.a.	n.a.	n.a.	n.a.	n.a.	275	0.2	792	0.8
Other	n.a.	n.a.	—	—	20	0.3	938	0.8	2,482	2.4
Female chemists with four or more years of college	n.a.	n.a.	4,800	6.3	4,741	5.8	10,053	9.0	14,806	14.5
White	n.a.	n.a.	4,680	6.1	4,418	5.4	n.a.	n.a.	n.a.	n.a.
Nonwhite	n.a.	n.a.	120	0.2	323	0.4	n.a.	n.a.	n.a.	n.a.
Black	n.a.	n.a.	n.a.	n.a.	n.a.	n.a.	377	0.3	n.a.	n.a.
Spanish[d]	n.a.	n.a.	n.a.	n.a.	n.a.	n.a.	132	0.1	n.a.	n.a.
Other	n.a.	n.a.	n.a.	n.a.	n.a.	n.a.	n.a.	n.a.	n.a.	n.a.

Sources: Derived from U.S. Department of Commerce, Bureau of the Census, *Sixteenth Census of the United States: 1940 Population, The Labor Force, Occupational Characteristics* (Washington, D.C.: Government Printing Office, 1943), pp. 59–70 *passim*, Table 3; *Census of Population:1950, Occupational Characteristics*, P-E No. 1B (Washington, D.C.: Government Printing Office, 1956), pp. 29, 107, 115, Tables 3, 10, 11; *Census of Population: 1960, Occupational Characteristics*, PC(2)-7A (Washington, D.C.: Government Printing Office, 1961), pp. 21, 116, 123, 130, 137, Tables 3, 9, 10; *Census of Population:1970, Occupational Characteristics*, PC(2)-7A (Washington, D.C.: Government Printing Office, 1973), pp. 12, 59, 73, 87, 101, Tables 2, 5, 6, 7; *Census of Population:1980, Detailed Population Characteristics*, U.S. Summary, PC80-2-D1-A, Section A: United States (Washington, D.C.: Government Printing Office, 1984), Table 277; *Census of Population: 1980, Earnings by Occupation and Education*, PC80-2-8B (Washington, D.C.: Government Printing Office, 1984), Table 1.

Note: A dash represents zero or a percent which rounds to less than 0.1.

[a]All are percents of the total number of chemists.

[b]1980 data does not include biochemists.

[c]Only nonwhite data available.

[d]People of Spanish origin may be of any race; thus, all persons included here are also included in the race categories.

n.a. = not available for these categories.

TABLE II-5
*Number of Experienced Biologists/Life Scientists
by Sex and Race, 1970 and 1980*

	1970[a]		1980	
	Number	Percent[b]	Number	Percent[b]
Total	29,546	100	46,079	100
Male biologists/life scientists	19,111	64.7	30,840	66.9
White	17,393	58.9	28,206	61.2
Black	782	2.6	885	1.9
Spanish[c]	368	1.2	541	1.2
Other[d]	933	3.2	1,559	3.4
Male biologists/life scientists with four or more years of college	16,836	57.0	27,956	60.7
White	n.a.	n.a.	n.a.	n.a.
Black	451	1.5	n.a.	n.a.
Spanish[c]	268	0.9	n.a.	n.a.
Other[d]	n.a.	n.a.	n.a.	n.a.
Female biologists/life scientists	10,435	35.3	15,239	33.1
White	9,422	31.9	13,224	28.7
Black	641	2.2	817	1.8
Spanish[c]	129	0.4	439	0.9
Other[d]	372	1.3	1,106	2.4
Female biologists/life scientists with four or more years of college	7,396	25.0	12,210	26.5
White	n.a.	n.a.	n.a.	n.a.
Black	314	1.1	n.a.	n.a.
Spanish[c]	55	0.9	n.a.	n.a.
Other[d]	n.a.	n.a.	n.a.	n.a.

Sources: Derived from U.S. Department of Commerce, Bureau of the Census, *Census of Population: 1970, Occupational Characteristics,* PC(2)-7A (Washington, D.C.: Government Printing Office, 1973), Tables 2, 5, 6, 7; *Census of Population: 1980, Detailed Population Characteristics,* U.S. Summary, PC80-1-D1-A, Section A: United States (Washington, D.C.: Government Printing Office, 1984), Table 277; *Census of Population: 1980, Earnings by Occupation and Education,* PC 90-2-8B (Washington, D.C.: Government Printing Office, 1984), Table 1.
[a]1970 data is for biologists only.
[b]All are percents of the total number of biologists/life scientists.
[c]People of Spanish origin may be of any race; thus, all persons included here are also included in the race categories.
[d]American Indian, Japanese, Chinese, Filipino
n.a. = not available for these categories.

Virtually all companies interviewed for this study had active affirmative action programs, and spent great sums on recruiting, as discussed in Chapter IV. Despite these serious efforts, and numerous affirmative action programs undertaken by the professions,

TABLE II-6
*Number of Experienced Geologists/Geodesists
by Sex and Race, 1970 and 1980*

	1970		1980	
	Number	Percent[a]	Number	Percent[a]
Total	20,943	100	46,127	100
Male geologists/geodesists	20,182	96.7	40,985	88.8
White	19,949	95.2	39,519	85.7
Black	40	0.2	488	1.1
Spanish[b]	170	0.8	776	1.7
Other[c]	130	0.6	716	1.6
Male geologists/geodesists with four or more years of college	18,228	87.0	36,228	78.5
White	n.a.	n.a.	n.a.	n.a.
Black	40	0.2	n.a.	n.a.
Spanish[b]	170	0.8	n.a.	n.a.
Other[c]	n.a.	n.a.	n.a.	n.a.
Female geologists/geodesists	761	3.6	5,142	11.1
White	744	3.5	4,829	10.5
Black	17	0.1	205	0.4
Spanish[b]	—	—	63	0.1
Other[c]	—	—	101	0.2
Female geologists/geodesists with four or more years of colelge	571	2.7	3,515	7.6
White	n.a.	n.a.	n.a.	n.a.
Black	17	0.1	n.a.	n.a.
Spanish[b]	—	—	n.a.	n.a.
Other[c]	n.a.	n.a.	n.a.	n.a.

Sources: Derived from U.S. Department of Commerce, Bureau of the Census, *Census of Population: 1970, Occupational Characteristics,* PC(2)-7A (Washington, D.C.: Government Printing Office, 1973), Tables 2, 5, 6, 7; *Census of Population: 1980, Detailed Population Characteristics,* U.S. Summary, PC80-1-D1-A, Section A: United States (Washington, D.C.: Government Printing Office, 1984), Table 277; *Census of Population: 1980, Earnings by Occupation and Education,* PC 90-2-8B (Washington, D.C.: Government Printing Office, 1984), Table 1.
Note: A dash represents zero or a percent which rounds to less than 0.1.
[a]All are percents of the total number of geologists/geodesists.
[b]People of Spanish origin may be of any race; thus, all persons included here are also included in the race categories.
[c]American Indian, Japanese, Chinese, Filipino.
n.a. = not available for these categories.

industry, and government,[7] the underrepresentation of blacks and Hispanics will probably continue for many years. As late as 1969–

[7]These programs are described in the relevant chapters for the various E/S fields in Stephen A. Schneider, *The Availability of Minorities and Women for Professional and Managerial Positions, 1970–1985,* Manpower and Human Resources Studies, No. 7 (Philadelphia: Industrial Research Unit, The Wharton School, University of Pennsylvania, 1977).

FIGURE II-1
Employed Women as a Percent of
All Employed Engineers and Scientists

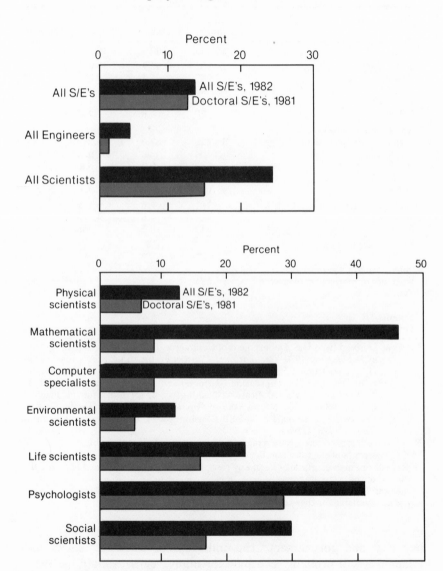

Source: *Women and Minorities in Science and Engineering* (Washington, D.C.: National Science Foundation, 1984), p. 3.

FIGURE II-2

Proportion of Engineers and Scientists with Less Than Ten Years of Professional Experience by Field and Sex, 1982

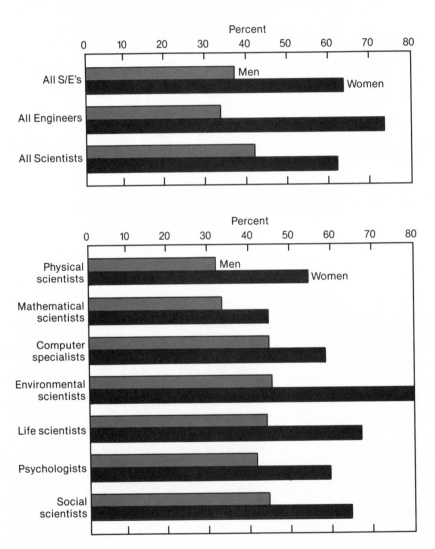

Source: *Women and Minorities in Science and Engineering* (Washington, D.C.: National Science Foundation, 1984), p. 5.

FIGURE II-3

Employed Engineers and Scientists by Sex and Field, 1982

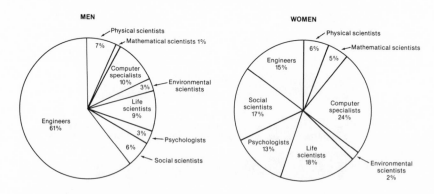

Source: *Women and Minorities in Science and Engineering* (Washington, D.C.: National Science Foundation, 1984), p. 4.

1970, blacks represented only 2.8 percent of the engineering students, and 45 percent of black graduates in 1970 were from predominantly black schools where facilities and training were likely to be somewhat less advanced than those required in major industries.[8] The situation for science students was even more exaggerated.[9] Yet black students who did obtain E/S degrees had little difficulty in finding jobs by 1978.[10] Clearly, increasing the supply of qualified minority E/S, although a long and difficult task, is the only real solution to the problem.

THE DEMAND FOR ENGINEERS AND SCIENTISTS

Industry must compete with other sectors of the economy for E/S. As shown in Table II-7, educational institutions, the federal government, and other governmental and nonprofit institutions compete for the supply. In 1980, business and industry employed 59.4 percent of all E/S, including psychologists and social scientists, but a much

---

[8]The classic work on blacks in engineering for this and earlier periods was done by Robert Kiehl. See, e.g., his *Opportunities for Blacks in the Profession of Engineering* (Newark, N.J.: Foundation for the Advancement of Graduate Study in Engineering, 1970). For his discussion of enrollments, see pp. 16–24.

[9]For a general discussion of these problems, see Schneider, *Availability of Minorities and Women,* pp. 15–73, 163–209.

[10]See Kiehl, *Opportunities for Blacks in the Profession of Engineering,* pp. 52–53, 55–57.

FIGURE II-4
Field Distribution of Engineers and Scientists by Race, 1982

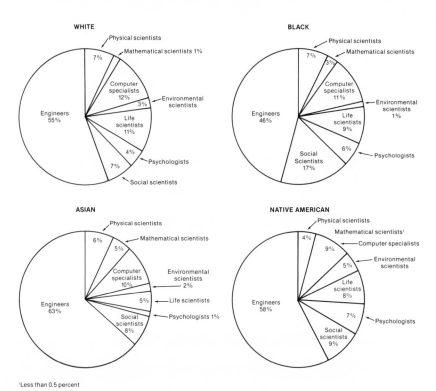

'Less than 0.5 percent

Source: *Women and Minorities in Science and Engineering* (Washington, D.C.: National Science Foundation, 1984), p. 10.

larger percentage of engineers and computer scientists (77.2 percent and 73.9 percent, respectively).

Within industry, there is a wide diversity of utilization and demand among E/S fields. Most engineers are employed in industry, ranging from 88.0 percent of all chemical engineers to about 60 percent of all civil engineers. Among the sciences, industry's needs are concentrated in relatively few fields, including especially computer scientists and chemists. Industry employs 73.9 percent of the former and 61.1 percent of the latter. In contrast, industry employs a relatively small minority of mathematicians, psychologists, and social scientists. Figure II–7 shows the percent distribution of E/S in industry by field for 1981.

FIGURE II-5
*Proportion of Engineers and Scientists with Less Than Ten Years of
Professional Experience by Race, 1982*

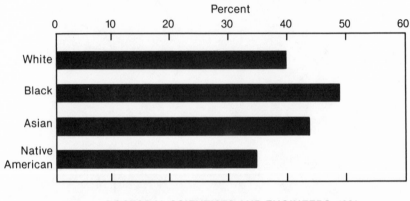

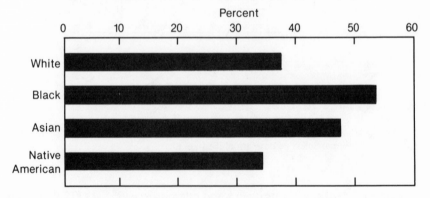

Source: *Women and Minorities in Science and Engineering* (Washington, D.C.:
National Science Foundation, 1984), p. 11.

Since the latter one-half of the 1970s, industry's demand for E/S
has risen considerably. As a result, employment of E/S in industry
increased 47 percent between 1976 and 1981, more than three times
the 15 percent rise in total industrial employment during this period.
This dramatic increase in E/S employment is attributable to the
expansion of the high technology industries, increased defense
expenditures, increased industrial research and development, and

FIGURE II-6
*Field Distribution of Employed Engineers and Scientists
by Hispanic Status, 1982*

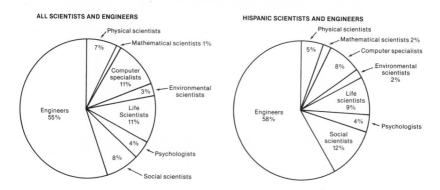

Source: *Women and Minorities in Science and Engineering* (Washington, D.C.:
National Science Foundation, 1984), p. 13.

rapid technological change.[11] As these developments occurred, the
older mass production industries were declining, thus exacerbating
the contrast between the more highly technical industries in which
E/S are concentrated and the more mature industries with heavy
concentrations of blue-collar workers. The adoption of new technologies in the mature industries has created additional recruiting challenges for them.

Since the mid-1970s, industry demand has been especially heavy
for electrical and civil engineers, although demand for the latter
dropped during the 1981–82 recession because construction was
hard hit. More than one-quarter of the total growth in engineering
employment was the result of increased demand for electrical engineers,[12] whom our field work found still in short supply. Among scientists, the demand for computer specialists has yet to peak, and the
discussion in the following chapters will feature problems of recruiting, retaining, and compensating talented individuals in this field.

Type of Industry and Demand for E/S

Because of their needs and structure, various industries have
quite different E/S requirements. The nature of the product, the rela-

---

[11]National Science Board, National Science Foundation, *Science Indicators 1982*,
NSB–83–1 (Washington, D.C.: Government Printing Office, 1983), p. 87.
[12]*Ibid.*

TABLE II-7
Scientists and Engineers by Field and Type of Employer, 1980

	Total	Business & Industry		Educational Institutions		Federal Government		Other[a]	
		Total	Percent	Total	Percent	Total	Percent	Total	Percent
Total, all fields	2,873,700	1,706,800	59.4	505,700	17.6	248,400	8.6	412,900	14.4
Physical scientists	220,500	116,900	53.0	55,900	25.4	19,600	8.9	28,100	12.7
Chemists	141,800	86,600	61.1	26,900	19.0	9,100	6.4	19,200	13.5
Physicists/astronomers	58,800	22,400	38.1	24,100	41.0	6,600	11.2	5,700	9.7
Other	19,900	7,900	39.7	4,800	24.1	3,900	19.6	3,400	17.1
Mathematical scientists	118,700	42,000	35.4	52,200	44.0	12,600	10.6	11,900	10.0
Mathematicians	83,800	28,100	33.5	42,800	51.1	6,400	7.6	6,500	7.8
Statisticians	34,900	13,900	39.8	9,400	26.9	6,200	17.8	5,400	15.5
Computer specialists	345,500	255,300	73.9	36,600	10.6	21,500	6.2	32,200	9.3
Environmental scientists	92,000	46,500	50.5	17,000	18.5	14,400	15.6	14,200	15.4
Earth scientists	71,500	40,500	56.6	12,500	17.5	9,200	12.9	9,200	12.9
Oceanographers	3,000	500	16.7	1,100	36.7	700	23.3	800	26.7
Atmospheric scientists	17,500	5,400	30.9	3,500	20.0	4,500	25.7	4,100	23.4

Engineers	1,387,000	1,070,800	77.2	64,500	4.6	101,600	7.3	150,100	10.8
Aero/astronomical	46,600	30,500	65.5	1,800	3.9	8,000	17.2	6,300	13.5
Chemical	72,400	63,700	88.0	4,000	5.5	2,000	2.8	2,900	4.0
Civil	187,300	111,300	59.4	5,600	3.0	17,800	9.5	52,500	28.0
Electrical/electronics	255,800	202,900	79.3	14,000	5.5	22,900	9.0	15,900	6.2
Mechanical	233,100	197,700	84.8	12,600	5.4	14,100	6.0	8,800	3.8
Other	591,900	464,800	78.5	26,500	4.5	36,800	.6.2	63,800	10.8
Life scientists	377,100	107,000	28.4	153,200	40.6	50,400	13.4	66,600	17.7
Biologists	190,100	39,300	20.7	95,200	50.0	16,200	8.5	39,300	20.7
Agricultural scientists	147,400	63,400	43.0	31,600	21.4	32,100	21.8	20,400	13.8
Medical scientists	39,600	4,300	10.9	26,400	66.7	2,100	5.3	6,900	17.4
Psychologists	123,000	19,300	15.7	49,000	39.8	2,800	2.3	51,800	42.1
Social scientists	209,900	49,000	23.3	77,400	36.9	25,500	12.1	58,000	27.6
Economists	70,300	24,500	34.8	23,200	33.0	13,500	19.2	9,200	13.1
Sociologists/anthropologists	54,900	9,100	16.6	25,200	45.9	3,700	6.7	17,000	31.0
Other	84,600	15,500	18.3	29,000	34.3	8,300	9.8	31,800	37.6

Source: Original data from *U.S. Scientists and Engineers 1980*, National Science Foundation, NSF 82-314, reprinted in Betty M. Vetter, *Professional Women and Minorities*, 4th ed. (Washington, D.C.: Scientific Manpower Commission, 1983), p. 93, Table 4-32.

Note: Percent may not add due to rounding.

[a]Includes nonprofit organizations; military; state, local, and other governments; and "no reports."

FIGURE II-7

*Percent Distribution of Scientists and Engineers in
Industry by Field, 1981*

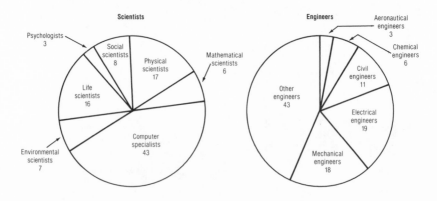

Source: National Science Board, National Science Foundation, *Science Indicators
1982*, NSB-83-1 (Washington, D.C.: Government Printing Office, 1983), p. 88.

tive pace of technological change, the commitment to research and development, and a host of other factors determine an industry's demand for E/S. The aerospace, electrical and electronic, chemical, and petroleum industries are the largest employers of E/S.

For many years, the aerospace industry[13] has employed approximately 20 percent of all research and development engineers in industry, as shown by Table II-8. As will be seen in Chapter XI, this industry, followed closely by electrical and electronic equipment, spends the most on research and development. The chemical, pharmaceutical, and petroleum industries also feature large expenditures of this nature, as does, perhaps surprisingly to many, the motor vehicle industry. These industries, therefore, employ large numbers of E/S.

Geographical Location and Demand for E/S

The labor market for E/S is a national one; the classified ads in the Sunday *New York Times* and *Los Angeles Times* or in the *Wall Street Journal* make this very clear. E/S are, of course, concentrated where the jobs are. California has the largest share of aerospace and high technology companies, and these sectors are expanding in Texas and the Pacific Northwest. Hence these areas have heavy concentra-

---

[13]Defined here as standard industrial classifications (SIC) Nos. 372 and 376.

Table II-8

Employment and Cost of R&D Scientists and Engineers
All Industries and Aerospace Industry
1972-1983

Year	Employment[a] All Industries[b] (Thousands)	Aerospace[c] (Thousands)	Aerospace as a Percent of All Industries	Cost per R&D Scientist and Engineer[d] All Industries[b]	Aerospace[c]
1972	350.2	70.8	20.2%	$ 55,300	$ 69,200
1973	357.7	72.1	20.2	59,200	70,800
1974	360.0	70.6	19.6	63,300	76,400
1975	363.3	67.5	18.6	66,500	85,100
1976	364.4	66.9	18.4	72,200	91,300
1977	382.8	72.0	18.8	75,800	91,300
1978	404.4	82.0	20.3	80,400	89,400
1979	423.9	86.5	20.4	87,400	93,300
1980	450.6	85.9	19.1	94,900	101,600
1981	487.8	95.2	19.5	103,900	128,400
1982	509.8	91.1	17.9	112,800	147,400
1983	535.6	99.5	18.6	n.a.	n.a.

Source: *Aerospace Facts and Figures 1984/1985* (Washington, D.C.: Aerospace Industries Association of America, Inc., 1984), p. 150.

[a]Employment as of January. Scientists and engineers working less than full time have been included in terms of their full time equivalent number.

[b]All manufacturing industries and those non-manufacturing industries known to conduct or finance research and development.

[c]SIC codes 372 and 376.

[d]The arithmetic mean of the numbers of R&D scientists and engineers reported for January in two consecutive years, divided into the total R&D expenditures of each industry during the earlier year.

n.a. = Not available.

tions of E/S. The Northeast still boasts the great research laboratories of American Telephone & Telegraph, General Electric, E.I. du Pont de Nemours, Westinghouse, Merck, and many other major companies, and the Detroit area, those of the automobile companies. As plants have been established in the Sunbelt, opportunities for E/S have expanded there. Many companies have also established manufacturing facilities and laboratories in the Southeast or Southwest, in order to provide attractive settings to aid in the recruitment of E/S, thus extending the geographical range of the E/S population.

Location, however, must meet structural constraints. A paper company must build its facility where wood is available in abundance, and must find E/S who are willing to live in sparsely populated areas. The personnel policies related to such problems are discussed in Part III of this study.

CONCLUSION

The supply of E/S has increased dramatically since World War II, but the demand has increased faster, despite some dips during several years. As a result, E/S in industry have suffered relatively little unemployment, as discussed in Chapter X. Industry's personnel policies for E/S will be shown in future chapters to be heavily oriented toward recruiting, retaining, developing, and compensating its E/S in order to ensure a relatively satisfied and productive labor force.

The E/S labor supply remains largely male and white. Women and minorities have made considerable progress in recent years, but the historic underrepresentation of minorities in these fields means that it will take many years of affirmative action to increase significantly the proportion of minorities, particularly blacks, in the E/S labor supply. As a result, minority E/S employment remains a key problem for designers of company personnel policies.

Projections concerning the supply-demand equation for E/S indicate shortages in some subfields, but oversupply in others.[14] Such predictions are fraught with potential error as conditions change rapidly. The structure of scientific and engineering education can affect supply, and both the supply and demand may influence corporate personnel policies, as discussed in later chapters. Despite potential demand-supply imbalances, the BLS has suggested that recent alarm concerning this problem has exaggerated its severity:

> Employers complain that they cannot find the engineers they need; the Defense Department doubts that enough engineers will be available in the future to meet defense needs, and others fear that the United States will be unable to compete economically with other countries unless we produce more engineers. Even though the 1981–82 recession dampened the demand for engineers in most specialties, many observers continue to believe that future shortages will endanger national defense and hinder the technological and economic competitiveness of the United States. Contrary to these expressions of anxiety, however, actual shortages in the past few years have been limited to a few specialties; and the latest BLS projections indicate an overall balance between supply and requirements for the rest of the 1980's.[15]

The supply-demand situation for scientists is similar. Shortages usually involve a few specialized areas and are not severe. Moreover, as Figure II–8 shows, fears that the United States is not producing

---

[14]See, e.g., Fred Landis and Joseph A. Svestka, "The Demand for Engineers—Projections Through 1987," *Management Science,* Vol. 29 (April 1983), pp. 455–64.

[15]Douglas Braddock, "The Job Market for Engineers: Recent Conditions and Future Prospects," *Occupational Outlook Quarterly,* Vol. 27 (Summer 1983), p. 2.

FIGURE II-8

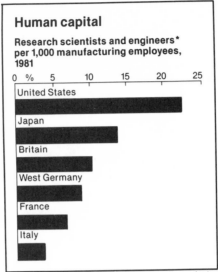

Human capital

Research scientists and engineers*
per 1,000 manufacturing employees,
1981

*Including university graduates

Source: Data originally compiled by the Organization for Economic Cooperation
and Development; chart reprinted by
permission of the publisher from *The
Economist*, Vol. 293 (November
24–30, 1984), p. 96.

its share of research E/S in comparison with other countries do not
seem to be based on the evidence.

The supply-demand equation for E/S has another elastic aspect
which must be considered. The United States remains by far the
favorite destination for persons, including professionals, who seek
opportunity outside their native lands. Immigration regulations can
be, and indeed are, administered with the supply-demand situation
as part of the process. Shortages can, therefore, sometimes be
addressed in this manner.[16]

---

[16]Vinod B. Agarwal and Donald R. Winkler, "Migration of Professional Manpower
to the United States," *Southern Economic Journal*, Vol. 50 (January 1984), pp. 814–30.
See also "High Percentage of Foreign Students Enrolled in U.S. Graduate Engineering," *Civil Engineering-ASCE*, Vol. 52 (May 1982), p. 18.

CHAPTER III

External Constraints: Education, Government, Professional Societies, and Unions

Personnel policies designed for engineers and scientists (E/S) are subject to numerous outside pressures and constraints. In this chapter, we deal briefly with four of these—education, government, professional societies, and unions. The purpose is to provide a background for the discussion of personnel policies in the chapters that follow rather than to extensively cover these subjects. Further information on professional societies and unions is found in the appendices.

EDUCATION

The educational pipeline constitutes the major inflow to the E/S labor pool. Thus, the state of the educational system can be considered an external force acting on a company. When this pipeline is allowed to degenerate into a state of disrepair, its radius effectively decreases and consequently fewer qualified graduates emerge. This creates recruiting and retention problems for industry. The lack of qualified E/S can stifle a firm's growth and ultimately its competitiveness.

The E/S educational process serves to instill professional values in a student. These values become integrated with the individual's career expectations and are carried beyond the university into industry. Professionalism contributes to the needs for recognition and reward of E/S in industry. It may also create organizational-professional conflicts. In addition, the content of academic E/S training may not entirely conform to the demands of industry. Corporations often complain that the gap between the theoretical knowledge attained in a university and the practical knowledge required for a job is too large. Educational programs with the potential to prepare students for industrial settings, such as cooperative experience and summer employment programs, as well as the problems involved and the solutions devised, are discussed in later chapters.

The educational process responds to change slowly. For example, a shortage of earth scientists existed in 1979. By 1983, when those who had entered this field as freshmen in 1979 were graduated, the shortage had disappeared and had been transformed into an over-supply. Often during an economic downturn, engineering enrollment has declined, but an upsurge is generally experienced both in the economy and in the demand for engineers long before enrollments can be converted into graduates.

In Chapter II, it was noted that the supply-demand equation had remained in rough equilibrium despite occasional shortages or gluts over the years, and that this situation appeared likely to continue throughout the 1980s. There are, however, some disquieting situations in E/S education which could adversely affect the supply. These include the declining number of doctoral students; the quality of equipment in institutions of learning; and, because of competition from industry, a potential decline in the number and quality of E/S faculty.

The Problems Analyzed

In 1980, the proportion of recent doctorates—those holding their degrees for seven years or less—on the full-time faculties of E/S departments in Ph. D.-granting institutions was 21 percent, as compared with 28 percent in 1974 and 39 percent in 1968. Meanwhile, the proportion of tenured faculty in these institutions increased about 5 percent on average between 1974 and 1980. Between these later two years faculty shifts to nonacademic employment accounted for about 20 percent of all departures from these faculties.[1]

Salary differentials among various potential E/S employers help explain these developments. Although it will be shown in Chapter VII that doctorate holders earn considerably more than those with bachelors' degrees, entry salaries for E/S with bachelor's degrees have risen so substantially that the incentives to pursue doctorates have declined. Moreover, industrial research laboratories compete vigorously with universities for the services of E/S with Ph.D. degrees. Meanwhile, during the 1970s universities were forced to retrench as a result of declining overall enrollments; fewer newer faculty were employed, and an increasing proportion of faculty became tenured, making it difficult for new, younger faculty members to gain that status. These less desirable aspects of academic life left about 10 percent of E/S faculty positions unfilled in 1980. (See Table

---

[1]National Science Foundation, *Young and Senior Science and Engineering Faculty 1980: Characteristics, Appointments and Departures, and Research Activities,* Special Report NSF 81-319 (Washington, D.C.: Government Printing Office, 1981), p. viii.

TABLE III-1
Reasons for Departures of
Full-Time Science/Engineering Faculty
Who Left Their 1978/79 Positions
(Percent)

Field	Total	Retire-ment	Illness or death	Another academic position	Non-academic position	Other	Failure to receive tenure	Other
				Voluntary resignation			Involuntary resignation	
All selected fields	100	20	4	34	20	6	12	5
Engineering	100	23	5	32	28	6	5	1
Physical sciences	100	27	6	21	23	8	13	3
Biological sciences	100	23	4	32	14	6	16	6
Mathematical/ computer sciences	100	11	5	39	20	5	12	9
Social sciences	100	19	3	39	13	6	14	7
Psychology	100	12	2	42	21	3	17	3

Source: *Young and Senior Science and Engineering Faculty 1980*, Special Report NSF81-319 (Washington, D.C.: National Science Foundation, 1981), p. 8.

III-1.) Moreover, almost 25 percent of the junior faculty received their bachelor's degrees outside of the United States.[2] Although the latter are often very qualified, some may lack sufficient understanding of United States engineering and scientific practices.

As a result of financial problems, many engineering and science departments during the 1970s permitted their equipment to deteriorate. The situation was exacerbated by the fast pace of technological development which demanded expensive new processes and equipment. Fortunately, this problem has been clearly recognized and at least somewhat ameliorated by gifts from industry, foundations, and government. The problem demands continuing attention and funding, however, because of the speed with which technology renders equipment and processes obsolete.

---

[2]"Engineering Colleges Report 10% of Faculty Positions Vacant in Fall 1980," *Science Resources Studies Highlights* (National Science Foundation, NSF 81-3212), November 2, 1981, p. 1. See also on this subject such more popular articles as Carolyn Phillips, "Campus Glitch: Universities in U.S. Are Losing Ground in Computer Education," *Wall Street Journal*, January 14, 1983, pp. 1, 15; "How Industry Is Draining University Sciences," *Business Week*, November 17, 1980, pp. 170D, 170H; Jeremy Main, "Why Engineering Deans Worry a Lot," *Fortune*, January 11, 1982, pp. 84–90; and Roger Lowenstein, "Two-Edged Sword: Surge in Engineering Enrollments Begins to Ease Industry's Shortages but Stirs Trouble at Colleges," *Wall Street Journal*, August 20, 1981, p. 46.

Even if equipment is thoroughly current, major problems develop when faculty expertise is not. The increasing proportion of E/S faculty which has tenure, the smaller proportion that are young, and the resultant narrower opportunities for the latter could have profound long-term effects. It could, for example, dampen creativity or transfer a higher proportion of that creativity from the academic campus to the industrial research laboratory. As will be discussed in Chapter XI, there is a considerable movement for increased industry-university cooperation to the mutual advantage of both parties which is especially helpful in supporting faculty research and in ameliorating academic financial difficulties.

Despite recognition of the problem, companies find it difficult not to recruit faculty when a particular need is felt and, as noted, a significant portion of faculty respond affirmatively. The problem would seem to lie in the personnel policies of universities. It seems very clear, first, that universities often regard professional schools as sources of income to support programs in deficit-ridden departments that could well be reduced in scope without educational disadvantage. Academic administrators apparently find it difficult to acknowledge that liberal arts faculties often promote graduate programs which grant degrees in fields with little prospects of jobs.

Second, universities too often are inhibited from paying faculty salaries that reflect the market for the professional field involved. Many universities are dominated by liberal arts departments for which, except in the sciences, the supply of potential faculty members greatly exceeds the demand—in part again because doctorates continue to be produced in spite of the lack of demand and in spite often of less qualified applicants. Because the salaries of such personnel are depressed by oversupply, some universities find it difficult to pay what the market demands for teachers in engineering, science, and in other fields in which industry competes with academia. The net effect is to encourage some of the young, talented teachers and researchers to seek a nonacademic career.

It should also be emphasized that the technical and scientific problem does not begin at the universities. Too often, high school students are insufficiently prepared in mathematics and science, and potentially talented students are later turned away from careers as E/S because of poor preparation.[3] Business and industry leaders

---

[3]On this point, see the remarks of Dr. George A. Keyworth II, Director, Office of Science and Technology Policy, Executive Office of the President, to the National Engineering Action Conference, New York, April 7, 1982. Declining test scores reflect this problem.

have recognized this problem, but it remains a serious one for the long run, although as yet there is no evidence either of a shortage or a decline in quality of those who receive E/S degrees.

GOVERNMENT

Government activities, regulations, support, and customer orders play a major role in all industrial personnel policies and are extremely important for those involving E/S. As we shall note in Chapter XI, the federal government is a major underwriter of research and development, supporting thousands of E/S working on government-funded projects. The federal government is the biggest customer of the aerospace industry, which employs about 20 percent of all research and development E/S, and is also a sizable customer of many large companies in other industries. It, therefore, follows that not only do policies and actions of the federal government affect large numbers of E/S, but also these policies will have a strong influence on the companies employing E/S.

A large government contract can mean that a company will hire hundreds, or even several thousand, E/S; the cancellation of a contract, or the failure to win one, can mean layoffs and downgrading for as many. Government regulations in regard to company reimbursement for training, retraining, seminars, professional association membership, etc., can determine company policies in these matters.

EEO

Perhaps in no area of personnel policies is regulation so important as in equal employment opportunity (EEO) matters. Title VII of the Civil Rights Act of 1964, as amended, forbids discrimination on the basis of race, color, creed, national origin, or sex. The Age Discrimination in Employment Act (ADEA) of 1967, as amended in 1974 and 1978, outlaws discrimination on the basis of age for those between forty and seventy years of age, and forbids compulsory retirement of employees prior to age seventy. The Rehabilitation Act of 1973 precludes discrimination against handicapped personnel by organizations that receive federal funds. Numerous laws have also been passed over the years protecting job rights of armed services veterans. Special laws governing Vietnam-Era and disabled veterans strengthened their rights to nondiscrimination in jobs with organizations which, like most major industries, are federal contractors.[4]

   Other laws pertain to EEO issues as well. The Equal Pay Act of
1963 forbids different pay for equal work if based upon sex. Numerous state laws supplement the federal ones. Moreover, for age discrimination and equal pay matters, if the state law is more favorable
to the employee, the federal law provides that the state law shall
prevail. This is very important in age discrimination matters since a
growing number of states, including California, New York, and Massachusetts, now outlaw all compulsory retirement without an age
limit.

   The Equal Employment Opportunity Commission (EEOC) administers Title VII of the Civil Rights Act and, as a result of a Carter
administration reorganization, the ADEA and the Equal Pay Act as
well. The Rehabilitation Act and the Vietnam-era veterans' legislation are administered by the Office of Federal Contract Compliance
Programs (OFCCP) of the U.S. Department of Labor, which also
administers Executive Order 11246. This executive order in effect
carries nondiscrimination one step further by requiring that government contractors actively seek to increase the proportion of minorities, women, and other protected groups. Goals and timetables must
be set by the government contractors to achieve these results. The
effect is perilously close to quota arrangements and favoritism for
protected groups.[5] Yet it cannot be denied that affirmative action
has achieved results that might not otherwise have been possible.[6]
Certainly, the strong push by defense contractors to employ minority and female E/S is clearly apparent and has been so for many
years. Yet, as we noted in the previous chapter, the road is long
because of the few minorities who entered—or were permitted to
work if they did enter—these professions.[7]

---

[4]For an explanation of the history and background of the ADEA, the Rehabilitation
Act, and Vietnam-Era veteran legislation, see James P. Northrup, *Old Age, Handicapped, and Vietnam-Era Antidiscrimination Legislation*, rev. ed., Labor Relations
and Public Policy Series No. 14 (Philadelphia: Industrial Research Unit, The Wharton
School, 1980).

[5]For a case study in which affirmative action was in fact a quota arrangement, see
Herbert R. Northrup and John A. Larson, *The Impact of the AT&T-EEO Consent
Decree*, Labor Relations and Public Policy Series No. 20 (Philadelphia: Industrial
Research Unit, The Wharton School, University of Pennsylvania, 1979).

[6]See, e.g., Jonathan S. Leonard, "The Impact of Affirmative Action on Employment," *Journal of Labor Economics*, Vol. 2 (October 1984), pp. 439–63.

[7]In 1966, twenty-one companies, which then accounted for about two-thirds of the
aerospace industry's total employment, were surveyed. Only 0.8 percent of their professional (mostly E/S) employees were black. Yet these companies employed more
than 40 percent of all black professionals in the manufacturing industry which
reported to the EEOC. See Herbert R. Northrup et al., *Negro Employment in Basic
Industry*, Studies of Negro Employment, Vol. I (Philadelphia: Industrial Research
Unit, The Wharton School, University of Pennsylvania, 1970), pp. 726–27.

The ADEA has both changed industry policy and opened up new challenges and problems. Prior to its enactment, older E/S were hard hit by layoffs during downturns as management sought to weed out unproductive and obsolete E/S—a state that has been frequently, and not always correctly, assumed to be highly correlated with age. The situation has now changed. Management must show that its older E/S are in fact less productive and more deserving of layoffs, or face charges of discrimination and potentially heavy backpay and damage awards. Indeed the situation is so reversed that any professional over forty years of age who is laid off is likely seriously to consider filing a charge. In Chapters IX and X, the difficult problems of layoffs and obsolescence are discussed, as are some innovative policies designed to deal constructively with these problems.

Policies affecting older workers are becoming increasingly significant because the average age of the population is increasing, the result of declining birthrates since 1960 and reduced mortality rates. By 1990, over 39 million Americans will have reached or passed age sixty, forming a group about equal in size to the number of Americans in their twenties and thirties.[8] Not only do many of these older persons desire to work, but it may well be that industry will increasingly turn to them to meet its labor force requirements. This accentuates the need for continual retraining and upgrading if obsolescence is to be avoided.

NLRB and OSHA

The National Labor Relations (Taft-Hartley) Act, as amended, governs conduct (not substance) in the relations between management and unions, and in the relations of both with employees, and provides the mechanisms for determining whether employees desire a union bargaining agent. Section 9(b) of this law precludes the National Labor Relations Board (NLRB), which administers the Act, from including professional and nonprofessional employees in the same bargaining unit unless the professionals vote to be included in such a unit. Section 9(b) was added to the law as part of the Taft-Hartley amendments at the request of professional societies.[9]

As will be discussed below, unions are not a powerful force among

---

[8] Gordon F. Bloom and Herbert R. Northrup, *Economics of Labor Relations*, ninth ed. (Homewood, Ill.: Richard D. Irwin, Inc., 1981), pp. 16–17.

[9] For the law and cases on this aspect of the Taft-Hartley Act, including the NLRB's definition of the term "professional employee," see John E. Abodeely et al., *The NLRB and the Appropriate Bargaining Unit*, rev. ed., Labor Relations and Public Policy Series No. 3 (Philadelphia: Industrial Research Unit, The Wharton School, University of Pennsylvania, 1981), pp. 210–16.

professionals and represent only about 2 percent of the E/S in private industry. Their influence is somewhat greater than their representation suggests, however, because in the desire to avoid unionization, managements give due regard to the impact of their policies on E/S.

Industries like aerospace are relatively "clean," with excellent safety records. The chemical industry also has a fine safety record, but often involves exposure to substances that can materially affect health and company liability.[10] The Occupational Safety and Health Act (OSHA), administered by the U.S. Department of Labor, brought the federal government into the workplace to a degree heretofore unknown. It also created new industrial positions for E/S, and responsibilities to devise equipment, develop processes and materials, and otherwise contribute to safety and health.

Information, Research, and Competition

In addition to being a customer and regulator of American industry, the federal government conducts scientific research on its own. The National Institutes of Health, the U.S. Bureau of Standards, and a host of other agencies both engage in research and development and provide grants for others to do so. Thus, as noted in Chapter II, the government is a competitor to industry in the labor market. In addition, the National Science Foundation and numerous statistical agencies provide important information about E/S. Obviously, there are few human resource policies for E/S that are not directly or indirectly affected by the federal government.

PROFESSIONAL SOCIETIES

Professional societies play an important role in the fields of science and engineering. The general concerns of the many societies are similar, encompassing technical, professional, and educational objectives which are aimed at advancing theory and practice in their specific fields. Each society also has its own constitution, policies, and goals, and attempts in various ways to support the "fair treatment" of members on the job. In this section the interaction of professional societies and industrial corporations will be explored. Specific attention will be paid to the pressures which professional societies exert

---

[10]See Herbert R. Northrup, Richard L. Rowan, and Charles R. Perry, *The Impact of OSHA*, Labor Relations and Public Policy Series No. 17 (Philadelphia: Industrial Research Unit, The Wharton School, University of Pennsylvania, 1978). This study examines OSHA's impact on the aerospace, chemical, and textile industries.

TABLE III-2
Key Professional Societies and Their Abbreviations

1. American Association of Engineering Societies (AAES)—an umbrella organization of engineering societies.

2. American Biological Society (ABS)

3. American Chemical Society (ACS)

4. American Association of Petroleum Geologists (AAPG)

5. American Institute of Chemical Engineering (AIChE)

6. American Institute of Mining, Metallurgical, and Petroleum Engineers (AIME)

7. American Physical Society (APS)

8. American Society of Civil Engineers (ASCE)

9. American Society of Mechanical Engineers (ASME)

10. Geological Society of America (GSA)

11. Institute of Electrical and Electronic Engineers (IEEE)

12. National Society of Professional Engineers (NSPE)

For a full listing of professional societies, see *Encyclopedia of Associations*, 19th ed. (Detroit: Gale Research Company, 1984), Vol. 1, Section 4, "Scientific, Engineering, and Technical Organizations," pp. 459–574.

on corporations. Those societies which will be referenced or discussed are listed in Table III–2. A fuller discussion of the policies of key societies is found in Appendix B.

Professional societies have historically taken primarily a technical orientation through activities such as sponsoring continuing education programs, publishing technical journals, organizing symposiums, setting standards, and preparing policy statements. They provide various means by which an engineer or scientist can maintain currency in a particular field, including participation in professional development programs or other events. They thus fulfill an important role in combating obsolescence.

In addition to strictly technical activities, professional societies have periodically become involved in other issues pertinent to science and engineering. After the passage of the National Labor Relations (Wagner) Act, several societies became involved in organizing engineering unions as a means of securing separate bargaining units for professionals.[11] Other issues which continue to receive attention today include professional ethics, industrial employment practices (which sometimes involve conflicts with corporations), and legisla-

---

[11]The collective bargaining activities of the societies in this era are discussed in Herbert R. Northrup, *Unionization of Professional Engineers and Chemists*, Industrial Relations Monograph No. 12 (New York: Industrial Relations Counselors, Inc., 1946). Following the inclusion of the "professional proviso" in the Taft-Hartley Act in 1947, the societies discontinued this activity. A large increase in unionization would likely see them reenter the representation for collective bargaining field.

tion pertinent to E/S as individuals and to their chosen fields of employment. Recently, professional societies have also become involved in cooperative efforts between industry, academia, and the government to strengthen the nation's technological infrastructure. They support the formation of "partnerships" between these sectors aimed at sharing resources and improving educational conditions.

Pressure on Companies

Because of the diversity of their activities, professional societies often exert direct external pressure on companies. The publication and distribution of employment guidelines throughout various industries constitute one component of this external pressure. As discussed in Appendix B, these guidelines have not received a warm reception in industry because companies are not willing to permit professional societies to determine their human resources policies or practices. In addition, internal forces are applied indirectly through company employees who are professional society members. These internal forces can take many forms. For example, employees may learn about innovative programs at a competitor's facility from attendance at a conference. An individual's need for recognition and reward on the job may increase through participation in professional society activities.

Limiting Factors

The arenas in which the various professional societies are involved are many, but there are several factors which limit the range and effectiveness of their activities. Although superficially a professional society unites individuals with field of interest and, perhaps, type of education in common, beneath the cohesive front the societies are composed of individuals working in different sectors: professors, technical managers, those employed by industry, those employed by government, self-employed individuals, etc., all with differing viewpoints and personal objectives. This diversity of membership has created internal conflicts when professional societies have attempted to determine their appropriate roles and/or positions on specific topics, their involvement in certain issues, and their future direction. For this reason, the societies' involvement in professional activities, especially employment practices, has been considerably less than some members would like. In other words, the magnitude and direction of the forces which professional societies attempt to exert on corporations represent a compromise drawn from the opinions of the collective membership.

Lobbying

Since professional societies need assets to operate, they must register with the U.S. Internal Revenue Service (IRS) as an organization or association. Their revenue comes from membership dues, standards testing, sale of publications, and other related areas. The tax status the society selects dictates the amount of lobbying in which it can engage, and thus influences its activities. The ACS, ASCE, AIChE, and ASME have all selected a tax status of 501(c)(3) which limits the extent of their lobbying activities. The NSPE and IEEE have selected a tax status of 501(c)(6) which allows them actively to influence legislation.

The major impact of tax status classification on an organization is to determine whether the majority of activities funded are technical or political. No substantial funds can be used to influence legislation by 501(c)(3) societies. The programs which they sponsor to influence legislation dealing with unions, pensions, or employment conditions for their members are effectively limited. Both the NSPE and IEEE have offices in Washington, D.C. and employ lobbyists. Professional society representatives interviewed for this study quickly pointed out that they are not "bargaining units" when the collective bargaining issue was raised. They do not want the NLRB to challenge their activities or attempt to classify them as a "labor organization."

Collective Bargaining

In general, the professional societies now take a "middle-of-the-road" attitude toward collective bargaining. The diversity of their membership contributes to this position. As previously indicated, the societies include a broad spectrum of individuals spanning owners of firms, managers of corporations, and employed engineers. The ACS membership also includes scientists. The IEEE has a special membership grade for technicians. Many of the societies also have student chapters. On one hand, the variety in the membership can be an asset to a society because it encourages interaction among individuals with all levels and fields of experience. Role models and support are built in for younger members, while older members have an opportunity to advise, teach, and lead. On the other hand, this diversity has an obvious impact on the position a society may take on controversial issues.

Using collective bargaining as an example, one finds that some of the members feel that the professional societies should be more outspoken on this subject, while others feel that it is not the societies' place, and that they should, therefore, be less active in this area. A noted exception to this is the NSPE, which has been a consistently strong voice against unionization for engineers. Collective bargaining and employment conditions are two of the most controversial issues in which the professional societies have become involved. The lack of cohesiveness resulting from a diverse membership becomes apparent when heated debates on these topics arise among members. It is likely, however, that most society members feel that unionization is probably "unprofessional."

Organization and General Activities

Local chapters throughout the United States are affiliated with the national unit of each society. (Some of the societies also have international representation but in this study only domestic units are examined). Local chapters sponsor general meetings and special lectures and often include technical sections organized to explore a particular topic. The national unit employs staff members, with various responsibilities including education, membership, public relations, etc., who offer seminars and conferences on particular topics at a national level. Some societies have very active standards and testing groups whose results are published and used throughout industry. In certain cases, task forces are organized to explore a particular issue and make policy recommendations to the board of directors. Members of the task force are volunteers, and their efforts are usually supported by a national staff member. Task forces and subcommittees often publish reports and recommendations. Each society publishes a monthly magazine and/or newspaper. Conference proceedings are often made available.

Many professional societies also have active student chapter programs. Through these programs, students are introduced to working E/S, as well as to applications of the theories which they have learned in school. Student chapters perform an important service by helping to bridge the gap between industry and academia. Students who actively participate in local chapters can develop a more realistic view of the workplace. The student chapters also contribute to the development of professional standards, and encourage a student to understand how these standards may be applied to the workplace. The societies also encourage interaction between student chapters of different schools through activities such as design competitions and paper presentations. This prepares the student for continued participation after graduation.

A new program (developed jointly by several societies) has created a limited number of summer internships for engineering students in Washington, D.C. The students selected as interns have the opportunity to interact with government officials. The program's intent is to increase students' awareness of the government sector, specifically the activities involved in policy formulation.

Opportunities for continuing education are varied and include lectures, technical study groups, update courses, etc. Participation in professional society activities is one method by which a diligent engineer can combat obsolescence, as discussed in Chapter X. Many of the professional societies encourage licensing and registration. Some offer study courses to prepare individuals for the required tests.

The professional societies collectively represent a wealth and breadth of technical knowledge. They are often asked by Congress for assistance in preparing policy statements or reports on technical subjects. In addition, members may be called upon to testify as professional witnesses on technical issues. Through activities such as these, E/S have important opportunities to exercise social responsibilities and influence policy.

Industry Response

Although the professional societies exert forces on industry, this should not imply that the forces are necessarily hostile, or that industry response is necessrily negative. Many corporations encourage their E/S employees to participate in professional society activities. Indeed, some provide an incentive to participate by paying membership dues either partially or completely. In additon, E/S are usually granted time and given expenses to attend pertinent technical conferences. As noted, participation in professional society activities can help an individual combat obsolescence. Current research and design techniques are discussed at technical meetings. For E/S unable to attend the meetings, information is often available in proceedings published by the societies. Interaction with peers provides an opportunity for professional recognition.

It is also likely that some conflict between professional and organizational loyalty is fueled by participation in professional societies. If this is true, it would be most detrimental to those firms which offer no internal opportunities for intangible rewards. Encouraging participation in society activities can supplement a company's intangible rewards but, as discussed in Chapter VII, is no substitute for a well-constructed reward and recognition program. Corporate interviews conducted for this study indicated that industry views the professional societies as providing an important technical service. They do not object *per se* to professional development activities. They object only when they infringe upon areas that have traditionally been exclusively under management's control. It seems that through cooperative partnerships new symbiotic relationships can be formed between the two groups. This will involve a clearer understanding on the part of the bureaucracies of the societies that they cannot expect industry to follow employment guidelines which the societies have developed without regard to the needs or practices of individual firms. Appendix B provides further details concerning the employment guidelines of key societies and related matters.

UNIONS

Most E/S unions date from the late 1940s, when E/S in the aerospace industry had seen a sharp build-up of staff during World War II and sharp cutbacks thereafter. The fear of a return to the depression conditions of the 1930s and the failure of some companies to treat E/S as professionals led to the formation of unions. In addition, some unions were sponsored by professional societies as a means of keeping professionals out of collective bargaining units dominated by blue-collar workers prior to the enactment of the Taft-Hartley amendments to the National Labor Relations Act.

Following the passage of the Taft-Hartley Act in 1947, with its proviso requiring professionals to determine for themselves whether they desire a separate bargaining unit, professional societies in E/S fields dropped their interest in creating bargaining units. Soon thereafter, defense expenditures were greatly increased as a result of the Korean War, and the interest of E/S in unionization began a secular decline. Moreover, companies employing E/S had by then begun to develop integrated human resource policies to deal with problems of their E/S employees and thus discourage unionization.

A problem of the E/S unions is that their leaders and their constituencies have never been able to agree upon their relationship to subprofessionals and to the general labor movement. Proposals concerning whether to include subprofessionals in E/S unions and whether to affiliate with the AFL-CIO or with one of the major national unions have split and weakened E/S unions since the early 1950s. During this period, a number of E/S bargaining units have been decertified, and few new units won. Today, most E/S unions are composed of engineers rather than scientists, and are found chiefly in the aerospace industry, although there are a few key unions in the electrical-electronics industry on the East Coast—RCA and Leeds & Northrup in the Philadelphia area, and Sperry on Long Island, New York. Nearly all the important engineering unions are independent, the one at Sperry being a major exception. Table III-3 lists some of the key engineering unions and their memberships.

TABLE III-3
Key Engineering and Science Unions

Company and Area	Union	Size of Bargaining Unit	Union Membership in Unit
Aerospace Corporation, Los Angeles	Aerospace Professional Staff Association (APSA)	2,000	n.a.
Boeing Company, Seattle, Houston, and Oak Ridge, Tennessee	Seattle Professional Engineering Employees Association (SPEEA)	19,848	10,708
Boeing Company, Wichita, Kansas	Wichita Engineering Association (WEA)	1,800	1,000[a]
Leeds & Northrup, Philadelphia	Programmers, Engineers and Scientists Association (PESA)	241	n.a.
Lockheed California, Los Angeles	Engineers and Scientists Guild (ESG)	2,525	1,110[a]
McDonnell-Douglas, Los Angeles	Southern California Professional Engineering Association (SCPEA)	2,400	1,400
RCA, Moorestown, N.J. (Philadelphia Area)	Association of Scientists & Professional Engineering Personnel (ASPEP)	1,600	1,300
Tennessee Valley Authority, Chattanooga, Tennessee	TVA Engineering Association, Inc. (TVAEA)	8,400	7,300

Source: *SPEEA Spotlight,* Vol. 26 (September 1984), pp. 5–6.
[a]Authors' estimates from other published reports.
n.a. =not available.

The AFL-CIO does have an engineering affiliate, the International Federation of Professional and Technical Engineers (IFPTE), but its 23,000 members include only 5,000 in the private sector.[12] There is also a loose-knit coordinating body, the Council of Engineers and Scientists Organizations (CESO) to which many key independent E/S unions are affiliated. During 1980 and 1981, CESO and IFPTE officials worked with AFL-CIO staff for eighteen months to create a national union constitution to which appropriate organizations would presumably affiliate, but most independent union memberships voted down this latest in a number of attempts to create a national E/S union.[13]

In Appendix C, there is reproduced a thorough study of E/S

[12]"Politics, Merger, Union's Constitution and Finances Dominate IFPTE Convention," *White Collar Report,* Vol. 56 (August 15, 1984), p. 204.
[13]"CESO Unions Reject Constitution for National Engineers Union," *White Collar Report,* No. 1334 (December 17, 1982), pp. A–1–2.

unions, their problems, and their prospects based upon an earlier Wharton Industrial Research Unit research project. Although this study found the prospects of unionization poor for E/S, it also appeared that unions, while losing NLRB elections, were gaining a higher percentage of employee votes. The severe recession of 1981–82 and consequent layoffs of E/S appeared to afford unions an opportunity, but the only successes in this period involved small units of E/S employed by the Boeing Company in Houston, Texas, and Oak Ridge, Tennessee. They were unionized by the Seattle Professional Engineering Employees Association (SPEEA), which represents Boeing E/S in Seattle.

CONCLUSION

In the first study of E/S unionization made by the senior author of this work in 1946, it was estimated that about 5 percent of engineers were union members.[14] Since then these unions have not only failed to keep pace with the growth of the E/S labor force, but have actually lost bargaining rights at a number of companies, including General Dynamics, Western Electric, General Electric, and Honeywell. Today, it is likely that such unions represent about 2 or 2.5 percent of their potential and have as members only about one-half of those that they actually represent. The academic preparation of E/S introduces a strong sense of professionalism, which is maintained through participation in specialty societies. Because of their loyalty to professional ideals, E/S generally have shown low interest in unions, which remain today, as described in the 1950s, at best "a constructive irritant."[15] Their existence reminds management that E/S require sound human resource policies, and that if management does not develop and administer such policies, they could become a subject of collective bargaining—something that E/S have given repeated demonstrations that they do not desire under ordinary circumstances.

---

[14]Northrup, *Unionization of Professional Engineers and Chemists*, p. 3.
[15]Herbert R. Northrup, "Better Personnel Administration: A Key to the Engineering Crisis," *Personnel,* Vol. 24 (September/October 1957), p. 60.

PART THREE

Personnel Policies

CHAPTER IV

Recruiting

Industry spends enormous sums of money to recruit engineers and scientists (E/S). The individual expertise of each engineer and scientist contributes to the firm's competitiveness, well-being, and profitability in this technologically oriented world. The development of a successful recruiting program is, therefore, a difficult but important task which requires all the elements of any successful management project: careful planning, organization, and execution, plus the integration and cooperation of management functions. Business and human resources planning, personnel development, and succession planning all must by synchronized if recruitment is to be successfully managed and achieve its purpose: to find, evaluate, hire, and orient additional human resources in order to staff positions necessary to the functioning of the organization.

RECRUITING PHILOSOPHY

The first person whom a prospective employee typically meets is a company recruiter or personnel staff member. Before the meeting takes place, the prospect may have preconceptions about the company as a place to work which may or may not be realistic, but which are based upon the company's "image." Such images are grounded in a host of factors, including the company's products, newspaper and magazine stories about the company and its officials, the company's advertising and promotional materials, comments and rumors about its personnel and administrative practices, and other fact and fiction which may find its way into the media. The market's perception of the company, which may also differ from reality, is also a strong determinant of its attractiveness to prospective employees. Thus, the size of the potential employee pool may at least partially be determined by perceptions built up over time in a variety of ways that are not fully controllable by the company.

Successful recruiting of E/S is a difficult task in a competitive environment. The market is nationwide and, in some areas, even worldwide. The Sunday *New York Times*, for example, carries several pages of recruiting advertisements for E/S jobs all over the United States and in foreign countries as well. Many engineers and scientists have skills that are relatively easy to transfer to another company or industry. Successful recruiting must be complemented by policies which induce E/S to remain with a company after employment if the recruiting task is to be efficient and ultimately profitable.

Successful recruiting is thus a key aspect of the general personnel policies affecting a company's human resources. Behind these policies must stand a soundly developed, effective image based upon such factors as good product performance, effective company advertising, increased visibility on key university campuses, and other such factors. The various methods of direct contact selected by a firm must be refined so that the particular message a company desires to convey to an applicant is, in fact, received in that form.

In this chapter, recruiting techniques employed by the various firms participating in the study are discussed. First, the general qualities sought in technical personnel are noted. Next, direct approaches to recruiting are described. Several factors are discussed which can determine whether a company will ultimately be successful in hiring the individuals they have selected.

QUALITIES SOUGHT IN TECHNICAL PERSONNEL

The qualities considered important in an employee vary with the nature of the task to be performed, the advancement opportunities related to the specific job, and the promotional philosophy of the firm. For those E/S employed in production facilities, working relationships are important. "People skills" were mentioned by almost every company describing manufacturing positions. One manager stated: "I have never seen an engineer fail in this company from lack of technical skills. Failure results from deficiency in interpersonal skills."[1] On the other hand, for E/S involved in research, academic achievement is most highly valued.

Several additional items were mentioned frequently as indicators of outstanding future performance. These include superior past performance and a strong work ethic. No apparent consensus exists concerning grade point averages, since job skill requirements vary within a single company, as well as between companies and industries. Whether high grades, top schools, or advanced degrees ensure superior performance on the job has not been conclusively demonstrated. Nevertheless, many companies expressed a distinct preference for candidates with better-than-average academic performance. Universities at which they recruit are carefully selected.

---

[1]West Coast company, interview with company representatives, May 1982.

Industry has in the past relied heavily on the assumption that our institutions of higher learning effectively train, educate, and ultimately graduate an employable product possessing a reasonable expectation of succeeding in the individual world. Inherent in this reliance is an almost unquestioned acceptance of the performance criteria of academic institutions as indicators of future potential success in the work environment. Selection, placement, and levels of compensation are strongly influenced by the academic achievement of the new employee and by the relative ranking of the university attended.[2]

One major aerospace company interviewed initiated a study to determine if several of the variables usually considered important in college recruiting could be related to employee success as measured by retention and salary progression. Two variables commonly believed to be most important—academic achievement and quality of the academic institution attended—were found to be poor predictors of employee retention. Furthermore, they failed to predict an individual's salary progression once on the job. These results were contrary to the expectations of both the employer who initiated the study and the students interviewed.[3] Although this analysis was performed only for a single firm, the results are interesting and raise questions concerning the exclusive reliance of firms generally on schools, grades, and class position to recruit college graduates for a variety of positions.

Many companies mentioned their interest in recruiting individuals with "realistic goals." Often they felt that this attribute was acquired through some prior industry experience such as participation in cooperative programs or summer internships. Other companies recruit college graduates for training programs rather than hiring them for specific jobs. With this system, a balance must be achieved between the number of individuals completing their training and the number of slots opening in permanent positions. A company with a training program of this type requires an efficient human resources planning and monitoring system. Real economic growth may differ markedly from the expectations upon which a company bases its hiring quota decisions; thus, the number of people emerging from a six-month to two-year training program may exceed or fall short of actual opportunities. This certainly occurred during the recession of the early 1980s, when companies first recruited too many trainees for their needs, and then recruited too few for their requirements during the sharp upturn that followed.

---

[2]G. J. Schick and B. F. Kunnecke, "Do High Grades, Top Schools, or an Advanced Degree Lead to Job Security and Extraordinary Salary Progression?" *Interfaces,* Vol. 12 (February 1982), p. 9.

[3]*Ibid.,* pp. 10–18.

The search for individuals who satisfy specific company criteria, including some of the general qualities outlined above, is complicated by regulation and legislation, as discussed in Chapter III. Particularly, companies must demonstrate that they have conformed with affirmative action requirements. Therefore, even within a stringent company hiring qualification framework, additional requirements are imposed to guarantee equal opportunity for all classes. Given the characteristics of the E/S labor pool, particularly the low representation of minorities and women, these requirements complicate the search for qualified technical personnel, and in some cases undoubtedly lead to different standards in judging and recruiting candidates for E/S positions, as many companies interviewed quite freely admitted.

DIRECT APPROACHES TO RECRUITING

There are two major sources from which a company may recruit: individuals just graduating from universities, and experienced engineers and scientists. The mix between the two is primarily a function of company philosophy: should the company follow the "promotion from within" doctrine? Several companies interviewed adhered strictly to this practice. This requires investment in training and education, and exposure of recent graduates to a broad variety of work assignments, ultimately leading to the development of capable professionals and managers from within. The danger is that other companies will capitalize upon that investment through pirating. On the other hand, the decision to hire experienced people to fill open positions can result in lower levels of company loyalty. A company may acquire a reputation as a temporary stopover for talented workers. Lower employee expectations may result, producing high turnover. This problem seems typical of new or marginal organizations which do not have resources to invest in training or career planning.

The mix between college graduates and experienced hires is also affected by other factors. (See Table IV-1.) The size and maturity of both the company and the industry influence this decision. An emerging industry typically hires recent university graduates with knowledge of current advances in a field and only those experienced individuals who possess state-of-the-art knowledge acquired through research and development in competitors' laboratories. The anticipated growth rate of the company, industry, and economy also enter into this decision. A company growing quickly will have many promotional opportunities, which may be further enhanced by a rapidly growing industry. The optimal mix of new graduates and experi-

TABLE IV-1
Factors Which Enter the Optimal Mix Employment Decision
New Graduates Versus Experienced Hires

I. Company Philosophy
A. Promotion from within
B. Infusion with outside talent

II. Growth
A. Company
B. Industry
C. Economy

III. Maturity
A. Products
B. Company
C. Industry

enced hires is dynamic and likely to change annually, and even during the recruiting year as environmental forces interact. For example, the aerospace industry, suffering a downturn in the 1970s, cut back its E/S recruiting. Expansion in the 1980s increased opportunities for more experienced E/S to fill key positions and train new hires from universities, and aerospace firms have been forced to recruit from other industries to fill such positions.

College Recruiting

Once the decision is made concerning the number of individuals to employ from each category, a variety of recruiting approaches are used to identify and review candidates who are most closely matched with the particular needs of their corporation. Most companies employ campus coordinators or representatives to organize university recruiting. There are various methods of deploying these representatives. For example, regional territories may be assigned, or alumni may be sent to recruit at their alma maters, etc. Interviews are frequently scheduled by these coordinators. The individual who actually performs the interviewing may be a corporate professional recruiter, or a line manager, depending upon company size and philosophy. Students are eligible to sign up for interviews based upon a coordination of university rules and company requests. Nearly all companies interviewed cited summer internships and cooperative programs as beneficial in identifying candidates. Two aerospace companies found that part-time jobs offered to students during the year helped them to identify prospective employees and increased their corporate visibility on campus. Work experience is generally recognized as contributing to more realistic expectations on the part of graduates.

The campus interview is usually followed by a field visit. At this stage in the recruiting process interviews are usually performed exclusively by line management, although arranged by personnel departments. One company which recruits individuals for its training program uses a seminar approach. Since exact field locations or positions are not yet known during the interview process, candidates are invited to a conference held at a hotel, where they are familiarized with the company, the structure and intent of its training program, and a variety of possible positions.

After the interview process is complete, formal employment offers are made to candidates. Each company adjusts the number of offers that it extends by a factor, based on past experience, accounting for individuals who will pursue alternative employment opportunities. During a recession, the number of offers received per candidate generally declines so that the acceptance rate may be higher than anticipated. Thus, this factor must also be adjusted for different economic environments.

Surprisingly, few companies participating in this study engaged in "post offer follow-up." In the two- to three-month period during which a candidate evaluates offers from various firms, follow-up can be extremely helpful for a firm that wants to demonstrate its interest. This follow-up can take a variety of forms. It may be a simple telephone call asking "Do you have any questions?", or a dinner to which a corporate representative invites several students from a particular region. The cost of this extra effort is low, and the potential gain is high, especially when one considers the overall costs involved in identifying key recruits. Once the candidate makes a decision, several firms mentioned that they follow up with questionnaires to determine the reasons behind the applicant's acceptance or rejection of their job offer. The information obtained from such surveys, however, has not been especially useful to these companies, particularly because those who accept the offer refrain from any negative remarks and those who do not accept usually do not respond unless they want to keep their options open for the future, and therefore are most circumspect in their replies.

Experienced E/S Recruitment

Since experienced E/S are generally working, they are more difficult to identify, and thus a variety of recruiting techniques are used. Such personnel are generally hired for a specific position, rather than for an internship or a training program. The selection criteria are usually concentrated more heavily on actual work experience and contribution to an organization, rather than on the broad range of intangibles or "predictors" used to evaluate college graduates. Table IV-2 summarizes the diversity of methods used by companies in recruiting experienced technical personnel. An earlier study done by Deutsch, Shea & Evans showed that although the method most frequently used to recruit such personnel was the employment agency, the quality of the applicants provided by most agencies was poor. The next most frequently used method was newspaper advertising. The success of this technique was considered average.[4]

Newspaper advertising, however, is today becoming a more sophisticated technique utilizing the methodology developed by consumer and advertising agencies.[5] Company advertising of this nature not only stresses its needs, but paints a picture of the company and what it does or makes. An examination of the E/S recruiting advertisements in the Sunday *New York Times* and the *Wall Street Journal* demonstrates what appear to be effective recruiting advertising and image portrayal by many companies.

TABLE IV-2
Methods Used to Recruit Experienced Technical Personnel

Employment agencies
Manpower advertising
Employee referrals
Technical journal advertisement
Subscription to computerized job banks
Headhunter (executive search)
Job fairs/field recruiting trips
Résumé banks—data base of previously received résumés
Walk-ins
Mail-ins
General corporate advertising
Recontacting former employees
Technical conventions
Recalling employees who have been working under industry assist agreements
Job shoppers
Contacting firms that are currently laying off
Alumni placement centers
Professional society placement
Direct mail

Sources: Personal interviews; Deutsch, Shea and Evans, Inc., *Technical Manpower Recruitment Practices,* Fifth in a Series of Studies (New York: Deutsch, Shea and Evans, Inc., 1969), pp. 8–15.

Note: Ordering is random and does not indicate usage frequency.

---

[4]Deutsch, Shea and Evans, Inc., *Technical Manpower Recruitment Practices,* Fifth in a Series of Studies (New York: Deutsch, Shea and Evans, Inc., 1969), pp. 8–15.

[5]Margaret Nemec, "Recruitment Advertising—It's More Than Just 'Help Wanted,'" *Personnel Administrator,* Vol. 26 (February 1981), p. 58.

Employee referral programs were used by over one-half of the study respondents. Those who used this method reported the quality of response superior to that obtained either by advertising or by the use of employment agencies. Some companies have tried to improve the yield of this technique by instituting "add-a-friend" bonuses. Technical journal advertisements are another method that has proved successful for many companies, which found that they produce a flow of candidates over a three- to four-month period which may be helpful in filling positions which open regularly over time.

Our interviews found that computerized services typically yield poor results because data bases are not kept current. Such job banks do, however, have potential if properly maintained. Several services have designed their data bases so that they may be accessed by a variety of attributes, such as type of degree or nationality. One chemical company sees job banks as a good supplement to campus recruiting programs and similar efforts. Personal contact may be an important aspect of recruitment, however, and many companies have recently initiated job fairs in depressed locations with high unemployment hoping to attract technical personnel to other geographic areas.

Individuals who initiate contact with a company's personnel office through personal letters constitute an often overlooked potential source of technical talent. Typically, résumés are reviewed strictly with current openings in mind and are subsequently "filed." This practice raises an important consideration: if a qualified individual is rejected upon initial application because of the lack of opportunities, would that individual ever reapply assuming that an appropriate position eventually develops? One company interviewed was especially sensitive to the fact that care must be taken in the wording of a rejection letter because a large pool of individuals who would not consider reapplication effectively reduces the company's future hiring ability. Another company has developed a computer system to facilitate résumé retrieval by attribute.

Recruiting for scientific and engineering skills is likely to remain competitive. While techniques discussed in this section are traditional, advertising will become more innovative and sophisticated as companies compete for limited technical personnel resources. Electronic advertising, for example, has potential as communications costs decline and cable networks and video display terminals become more common.

PROBLEMS IN ATTRACTING CANDIDATES

There are a variety of factors which may affect a company's ability to attract qualified individuals. These factors, and programs which have been developed in response to them, are described below.

Economic Factors

The cyclical nature of the economy in general, and more specifically of various individual sectors, creates an uncertain climate in which human resources projections must be developed and hiring decisions must be made. When the economy is booming, jobs for E/S are plentiful, and new graduates receive multiple offers. During a recession, however, fewer offers are extended and consequently the average individual has fewer options from which to choose. Thus, an offer extended during a period of economic adversity will more likely be accepted, and the company that continues to hire during such a period is more likely to employ its target candidates. For example, the downturn of the aerospace industry during the 1970s made it considerably easier for the American Telephone and Telegraph Company to meet its affirmative action requirements under the consent decree.[6]

Company Image

The concept of company image has several components: overall reputation, student perception, and reputation among working professionals. An early study found that "engineers do have preconceptions about companies . . . and these preconceptions affect their feelings about them as potential employers."[7] Our interviews with recruiters tended to confirm that this is essentially correct.

The factors which contribute to company image and reputation are varied, and unfortunately may be the result of inaccurate or poorly interpreted data. The relationship with the media and the resulting presentation of information can color an individual's opinion. One company felt that its recruitment problems resulted from a lack of consumer familiarity; its name was not a household word because they manufactured only industrial products. Union-management relationships may also create biases. One chemical company men-

---

[6]See Herbert R. Northrup and John A. Larson, *The Impact of the AT&T-EEO Consent Decree*, Labor Relations and Public Policy Series No. 20 (Philadelphia: Industrial Research Unit, The Wharton School, University of Pennsylvania, 1979), particularly pp. 206–11.

[7]Deutsch and Shea, Inc., *Company Image: Its Role in Technical Recruitment* (New York: Industrial Relations News, 1958), p. 7.

tioned that alleged poor relations with both media and unions had once hurt its ability to recruit top-quality individuals.

The information sources which our interviewees declared most important in influencing E/S opinions of firms are those involving personal contact. Personal contact is defined broadly to include conversations with company engineers, discussions with company interviewers, and plant visits. Not surprisingly, E/S seem to prefer to work for firms about which they have a substantial amount of information. Much of this information is formulated through the personal contacts described above, but some is derived indirectly from experience with a company's products or exposure to its literature. Because a company's literature conveys a message, its design obviously requires careful attention. In a real sense, the cost should be considered an investment in the organization's future, for potential employees read it very subjectively. Many companies have found that E/S seeking employment look to company literature for hints as to how the company will contribute to their future growth and development.

Type of Industry

The industry with which a company is associated is a partial determinant of the image which that company projects to E/S. A 1982 employer image survey showed that graduates in various disciplines do in fact favor particular types of firms. Thus, mechanical engineers demonstrated a strong interest in aerospace, energy, automotive, and design/construction firms. Electrical engineers preferred high technology and computing organizations. Civil engineers emphasized design/construction firms, aerospace, and energy-oriented companies. Chemical engineers favored energy-related organizations, major chemical firms, and well-known consumer product companies. Computer scientists and engineers selected large computer companies, as well as major electronics organizations. Interestingly, women generally preferred the same companies as men, but tended to assess the company through personal contacts during interviews while men judged companies by their familiarity with company products and services.[8]

This survey supports the hypothesis that recent graduates consider certain industries more desirable than others. These are generally industries that are growing quickly and characterized by high visibility and publicity. Representatives of less glamorous industries such as basic manufacturing, publishing, utilities, and forest prod-

---

[8]"The Top Employers," *Research Management*, Vol. 25 (May 1982), p. 6.

ucts, affirmed that they experienced difficulties in hiring, especially when they competed for the same skills as the "sexier" industries. A study done by the American Paper Institute, for example, concluded that the pulp and paper industry has a recognition problem: it is relatively obscure, complicating competition with high profile industries for qualified E/S graduates.[9] Again, electrical engineers have concentrated in electronics rather than power, while utilities require individuals with a power orientation. Although publishing has become more high tech, most electronics graduates seem to prefer to pursue opportunities with electronics and computer companies. One publishing company improved its ability to hire electronics engineers by paying special attention to job design. It successfully conveyed the challenging job content to prospective employees. A similar approach is to increase support personnel, such as technicians, clerks, and secretaries, so that the maximum amount of the professional's time can be spent on creative work. Another problem noted by some of the basic manufacturing and design/construction firms was that their "macho" image prevented successful hiring of women.

In cases involving the image of an entire industry, it is not enough for a single employer to increase recruiting budgets and efforts; industry-wide action is warranted instead. Programs must be developed to improve the visibility and reputation of the industry. For example, descriptive brochures discussing the nature of the industry, as well as employment opportunities for professionals, can be printed and distributed in high schools and on college campuses. Industry presence on campuses can be enhanced by offering guest speakers from different companies to discuss professional opportunities. Increased campus visibility improves student education and understanding, and aids in recruiting professional personnel to nonglamorous industries. Cooperative programs and summer internships can be expanded to increase student familiarity with the industry. Field trips to plant facilities can also be encouraged. Those industries which are not fortunate enough to be glamorous but are successful in employing E/S have recognized that they need to work hard to attract high-quality individuals. This can be accomplished through joint industry efforts, as well as by intelligent individual company action.

There is little an industry can do to improve its image when it has instituted mass layoffs and suffered highly publicized declines in profits and employment. The steel industry, especially, but also auto-

---

[9]See the American Paper Institute, *Minority Engineer Recruitment Survey* (New York: American Paper Institute, Employee Relations Department, 1980), pp. 6–7.

mobiles, farm equipment and other heavy machinery industries, have found E/S recruiting very difficult after their 1980s recession experience and will continue to do so.[10]

Location

Facility location can often exacerbate recruitment problems. Corporate representatives cited difficulties with initial recruitment of individuals to certain areas, and also with transferring or relocating existing employees. Regions such as the San Francisco Bay area and Los Angeles valley have become difficult markets primarily because of high real estate costs, but these cities are also considered pleasant places to live and thus have their attractions. New York City, on the other hand, is now often considered a poor location by E/S.

Large firms frequently have manufacturing facilities in a variety of locations, some of which may be remote areas. Companies find that E/S may decline positions they are offered in out of the way places. This is a common problem for forest products companies which must locate near major forests. Several firms also commented on the difficulty of recruiting minorities to areas where there is either a low minority representation in the community, or where the existing minority population is concentrated only in the poorest neighborhoods. Firms experience a similar problem recruiting women to areas where there are few professional women or where social life may be inhibited by remoteness or a small population.

Most companies offer relocation benefits to cover moving costs and often interpret such costs quite liberally. Some offer mortgage relief; others adjust salaries to cost-of-living differentials between areas. One method of attracting E/S to high cost-of-living areas is to award additional incentives, such as "relocation allowances." One engineering construction company employed a consulting firm to study the actual costs associated with residency in particular areas. The firm compared the costs of living in certain locations. An interesting result was that in one particular high cost area, the major expenses incurred were related to the purchase of real estate, but if the employee opted to rent, the area was not unreasonable in cost. In some areas, local or regional recruiting is emphasized and this can reduce both relocation and recruiting costs. One large conglomerate has approached this problem by establishing "satellite" locations in other areas of the country where E/S recruiting is not as difficult or as costly as it is in the prime location.

[10]See Thomas F. O'Boyle, "Brain Drain: U.S. Basic Industries Are Hindered by Loss of Scientific Talent," *Wall Street Journal*, July 27, 1984, pp. 1, 16, for a good account of the problems of these industries in recruiting E/S.

Innovative recruiting strategies may be required to attract individuals to remote locations. Several companies have attempted to match individual life style and the job location. For those who enjoy hunting, fishing, and the outdoors a remote location might be the ideal workplace. A high degree of personal attention is required to find such matches, but this approach seems to have been successful.

Employee relations representatives have developed other recruitment innovations. One oil company experienced trouble recruiting young professionals. The employee relations representative explored the "hot spots" in the area and began distributing information about them to potential recruits to show that the area offered leisure activities of interest to various age groups. An aerospace company started a series of social clubs and activities after it became the major employer in a small town. A forest products company developed a series of career paths to aid the transferred employee in seeing "over the hump." The clear presentation of career progression enables employees to perceive the move in a different perspective, specifically as a necessary step in a successful E/S career. Residency at the "adverse" location then becomes only a temporary stepping stone. This approach was part of a program to develop an attractive long-term employment package which deemphasizes the initial position.

Other experimental and alternative approaches have helped companies recruit qualified E/S, and may prove valuable to firms in less popular locations. Two companies mentioned that they currently have several employees involved in an "expanded workplace" program. Computer terminals have been installed in the homes of these employees. One chemical company instituted a program to allow chemists to elect a part-time schedule, and has found that women particularly choose this alternative.

The increasing number of dual-career families has complicated the process of promotion and relocation for almost every company participating in this study. Most had altered their personnel policies to permit spouses to work in the same location, although rarely in the same department. Employing both spouses is, however, not necessarily the only answer to the dual-career dilemma. Several companies have become informally involved in spouse placement; one company currently pays employment agency expenses for spouses. An equipment manufacturing company gives spouses a formal letter of introduction addressed to prospective new employers. Given the increasing number of women in the workforce, and the increase of technical, professional, and managerial women, it is anticipated that more formal programs will be developed in this area over the next decade. The high cost of relocation has increased both employee and management resistance to movement. This phenomenon, coupled with the increase in dual-career families, is causing some companies to question whether their traditional career path process, which exposes employees to broad work experiences throughout the country, is still the best management development strategy.

MINORITY RECRUITING

The data presented in Chapter II show that women and minorities are generally underrepresented in the science and engineering labor pool. In an effort to comply with civil rights legislation, and to overcome the historically low percentage of "protected classes," companies have developed special recruiting techniques which extend beyond the traditional methods already discussed. One company, for example, has developed internal "stretch" goals which are more ambitious than those presented to the government in their affirmative action plan. Well-publicized programs are also crucial because image is very important in minority recruitment. For example, General Electric's early recruiting efforts at minority colleges now gives it a strong advantage. The early strong push for minority E/S by major aerospace companies similarly aids their recruiting. Such reputations are big assets, especially where the companies continue aggressive programs.

Recruiting Techniques

To recruit experienced minorities, firms generally interact with societies such as the National Society of Black Engineers (NSBE), the National Society of Hispanic Engineers (NSHE), the Society of Women Engineers (SWE), etc. Firms may hold corporate memberships, or encourage employees to become very active in local chapters. Minority organizations also compile directories which help locate skilled minorities and women, and skill banks have been developed at national, regional, and local levels which identify qualified minorities. Some executive search firms also specialize in recruiting minorities and women. Experienced E/S may be reached through advertisements in appropriate minority or women's literature. The military is still another source of experienced minority talent.

Many new minority recruitment programs are targeted particularly to college students. Presentations are made by corporate representatives to minority E/S students for the purpose of promoting their firms as attractive places of employment. Plant tours and cooperative positions are also used as recruiting tools. Several companies involve college faculty in their summer employment programs. One aerospace company employs "minority leaders" on campuses in the hope that through casual social interaction, minority students will become familiar with that company and its working environment. Many companies are active in the secondary school associations such as the National Action Council for Minorities in Engineering (NACME), Mathematics, Engineering, and Science Achievement (MESA), etc.

Most participant companies attempt to recruit a certain percentage of minorities by interviewing students at formerly all-black institutions. Many of these have fine curricula, but the equipment and the teaching faculty are generally considered below the caliber of major universities. It is, therefore, not surprising that a majority of the companies who recruit at minority colleges report that their success in hiring minority E/S is not superior to their experiences at nonminority colleges, and in many cases, it is inferior. In addition, most companies have determined that minorities who are recruited at nonminority schools have had better corporate work records. Corporate representatives attributed this to socialization skills acquired during the university experience.

Some firms have developed innovative internal programs involving minority employees. One chemical company uses a role model program. Newly recruited black E/S are invited to attend conferences with existing minority employees so that the former are able to gain better understanding of corporate life. Such programs can be especially useful in helping recent graduates identify other individuals who have successfully climbed the corporate career ladder. Unless role models are visible and accessible (at least informally), then each minority or female student essentially is in danger of considering himself or herself a pioneer, and can feel quite alone in a corporation. One firm has been experimenting with a series of internal seminars aimed at developing effective black-white relationships within the corporation. The objective of these seminars is to enhance the participants' awareness and effectiveness in dealing with black co-workers, as summarized in Table IV-3.

One electrical equipment manufacturer has developed a special steering committee for minority communications whose functions include communications, community support, and career counseling. Through these activities, the company has increased its visibility both on campus and in the community. Qualified individuals are also invited to attend special seminars to learn about employment opportunities within the company. The seminars for women were discontinued when the percentage of female engineering graduates

TABLE IV-3
Seminar to Develop Effective Black/White Relationships

Objective:	To enhance participants' awareness and effectiveness in dealing with co-workers who are Black.
Intended for:	All levels of management. Especially appropriate for supervisors/managers of Black exempt employees who are recently-hired college graduates.
Supplier:	Consulting firm.
Presented or led by:	Consulting firm and company employee relations department.
Content:	Black realities in corporate life; Black cultural values and corporate norms; negative racial assumptions; effective relationships in the corporate environment.
Presentation method:	Lecture, discussion and case studies.
Number of participants/session:	13–15 White, 1–2 Black.
Time required:	2½ consecutive days.
Location:	Cities convenient to major company facilities.

Source: A chemical company.

exceeded 10 percent. One pharmaceutical company has developed internal programs to heighten the sensitivity of supervisors to the specific problems women may encounter in the workplace and to increase the acceptance of women by their male co-workers.

Pre-Recruiting

Despite the ambitious intent of the programs discussed in the previous section, most companies have found that they have not been successful in meeting hiring goals. In fact, one of the results has been increased competition for the limited number of minority graduates rather than a substantial increase in their representation. Heated competition has inflated salaries and frequently instilled unrealistic expectations in the graduates. One firm commented bitterly that it was difficult to hire minorities if recruiting efforts began as usual during the student's senior year. It found that minority students became affiliated with companies very early in the education process because of paternal programs such as cooperative and summer internships, as well as various financial support arrangements.

Many firms obviously desire to increase the size of the technical labor pool, especially in certain critical skill areas. This interest goes beyond the problem of recruiting "protected classes." Therefore, individual companies offer programs to interest children in science and engineering. Initially, high school students were targeted but experience with attrition has shown that solid mathematics and science foundations must be built prior to adolescence. Thus, some programs are now aimed at elementary school students. These are not expected to increase enrollment in science or engineering immediately. The purpose of sponsoring a series of gradeschool events is rather to cultivate early interest in particular subjects which, at a later date, might encourage the student to explore a technical career.

Pre-recruiting programs which are tailored to children embody the grass roots/role model approach. This approach takes many forms. An aerospace company in Silicon Valley allows children to visit its facilities on field trips. This firm has instituted a discussion group called the California Round Table, which involves children ranging from grades kindergarden through twelve in technical conversations. A computer van which visits local elementary schools is a project funded jointly by several firms in this high-tech area. One member of this team, a computer company, has recently extended its gift program to high schools. One paper company has started a special program to teach children about different occupations. Westinghouse has an extensive science scholarship program through which students compete on a national level for a series of prizes which are awarded for individual scientific projects. This company also sponsors career days at minority high schools to which both students and their parents are invited. One prestigious research laboratory sponsors a special summer science program. Approximately fifty high school students are selected to participate each year in a two-week "technology immersion" during which they are exposed to various scientific concepts and applications.

Several cities throughout the country have magnet high school systems. Often these schools require special entrance examinations. They are alternative public schools which overlay the regional system. Petroleum companies in the Houston area support the local technical high school. New York City also has a magnet school system.

An innovative chemical company has developed a variety of grass roots/role model programs. A group of women scientists from the organization regularly visit high schools to provide career counseling for young women to help them prepare for technical careers. This firm encourages plant visits by local high school students and teachers, and invites them to tour laboratories and visit with scientists and technicians. It also offers a summer technical program in which student groups participate in career exploration. Selected juniors and seniors from local high schools are invited for supplemental mathematics and chemistry training which will prepare them for laboratory work. These classes are given twice per week and extend over a twenty-week period, after which participants are invited to apply for summer jobs.

CRITICAL SKILLS AND ACADEMIA

The recruiting of individuals trained in critical skill areas often requires a disproportionate amount of time and effort. Computer professionals have been referred to as the "nomads of the 1980s." There is a distinct feeling among managements that computer scientists have more loyalty to their profession than to a particular company. They believe that this leads to excessive turnover. It is not surprising, therefore, that many companies experience difficulty recruiting and retaining computer professionals: "Recruitment has become a major issue. No longer just a personnel department concern, it is increasingly a drain on the time and energy of management."[11] Turnover slowed somewhat during the recession, but shortages still existed, and high turnover has resurfaced during the upturn.

Companies have developed several programs in response to this situation. The extension of employee referral programs is common. "Add-a-friend" bonuses and "finder's fees" are offered to current employees. These awards vary and include cash bonuses, vacations, and raffled prizes, among others. An aerospace company employs community college students part time and trains them to work as computer professionals. Another aerospace concern has a full-time recruiter assigned exclusively to software engineers. Internal training programs have been developed which allow current employees to upgrade their skills or alter career paths. The retraining of engineers with obsolescent skills to become software engineers is increasingly common. Detailed career paths and individual career planning sessions may also be offered.

Although innovative solutions in critical skill recruitment procedures may solve the shortage problem, they may produce discontent among employees in other specialties, especially if they perceive that their compensation is inferior or that they receive less consideration than do those in short supply. Therefore, attention must be paid to establishing equity throughout the organization if the mitigation of one problem is not to create others of equal magnitude.

---

[11]J. Daniel Cougar and Robert A. Zawacki, *Motivating and Managing Computer Personnel* (New York: John Wiley & Sons 1980), p. 4.

Interaction with Academia

Companies frequently establish working relationships with certain schools to gain a recruiting edge. These contacts extend beyond the financial and placement offices into specific departments, where relationships with professors are cultivated. These ties allow companies to better explain their needs to the universities, and also permit faculty to learn about developments in the corporations. Corporate representatives thus have an alternate avenue through which to inquire about students as potential employees. Most of these relationships are formed with universities, but they may also extend to high schools and technical institutes.

An electrical equipment manufacturer works with local technical schools to establish programs which are responsive to industries' needs. An aerospace company has a faculty employment program through which professors are offered summer employment. It also offers a technology forum to which professors are invited for two to three days to participate in presentations on new technology. Another company invites high school science teachers to its facilities to educate them about various engineering disciplines so they can, in turn, relate the information to their students.

A new spirit of cooperation seems to be emerging with the current increase of industry-sponsored research at universities. These "business" relationships may provide new recruiting channels as scientists and engineers working on funded research move from university facilities into the laboratories of the very companies which provided the necessary critical resources for their research. The fact that a former professor is employed by a corporation can also be a significant recruiting advantage at the university where the former faculty member once taught. As was pointed out in Chapter III, however, the transfer of key faculty to industry from academia, with its crucial training function, can also reduce the quality and quantity of E/S for the future.

CONCLUSION

Because of the importance of E/S to the continued viability of companies, their recruitment will continue to require the expenditure of considerable resources on the part of companies which are determined to maintain their competitiveness through technological excellence. The most successful recruiters of E/S are companies which project the most attractive image. In some industries this is very difficult because of business conditions, nature of product, location, or other factors. In general, however, a lasting favorable image results from quality products, excellent human resource management, and intelligent public relations and recruitment practices, all linked to an overall business philosophy that reflects both company needs and the aspirations of well-trained, motivated, and highly competent engineers and scientists.

CHAPTER V

Orientation, Training, and Professional Development

Once the recruits are on the job, their education as productive members of the company's workforce commences. Newly employed engineers and scientists (E/S) must be oriented and trained in the company's philosophy and requirements. Since the technical content of engineering and science constantly changes, continuing education and development is essential for the success both of the individual and the employing company. As the employee develops, he or she becomes more valuable to the company and more interested in the prospects for advancement. Therefore, career planning and professional and management development take on added significance. Each step of the development process from recruit to senior employee requires careful management attention if the returns on the company's investment in the individual are to be maximized.

ORIENTATION

New graduates must first make the transition between academia and business. The process is a complex one involving in part the undoing of aspects of the education process and the institution of realistic goals. The ideal outcome of this transition period is goal congruence between the individual and the organization. The expectations of new hires and their employers must be compatible. If they are not, low levels of employee commitment may result from unmet expectations, which in turn can lead to the resignation of the employee and consequent loss of the company's investment before any substantial returns are realized.

Those companies which do recognize the importance of the introductory period have instituted programs to catalyze the initial adjustment process. Ideally, recruiting policies should initiate this process prior to employment. This requires that the recruiters realistically present both the firm and the job, rather than concentrating on "selling" the organization. In practice this is rare; most companies interviewed indicated that it is difficult, in part because recruiters are paid to win recruits, and in part because those recruited often do not have sufficient background to judge jobs and companies realistically. Thus, most adjustment occurs once the individual actually begins working, which is why a well-thought-out orientation program is so important.

One purpose of orientation is to guide the newly recruited engineers and scientists out of college and into the business world. Indeed, one author titled his discussion of the subject: "Undoing the Educational Process..."[1] The usual standard introduction to employee benefits does not constitute adequate orientation. Rather, successful programs among companies interviewed included a review of company history, particularly concerning the role of E/S; a detailed explanation of the organization's human resources policies with emphasis on those especially pertinent to E/S; previews of the types of jobs to which individuals are likely to be assigned during their first few years of employment; and above all, ample opportunity for questions and two-way communication. Well-written, informative company literature, on subjects discussed at orientation meetings and seminars, distributed to newly employed E/S have been found helpful both in answering their questions and in assisting them to retain necessary information.

One petroleum company structures the introductory period so that new engineers are initially assigned a "buddy" to explain general information about the way things work in the organization. The immediate supervisor is responsible for assigning productive work. After about one month, the engineer begins an orientation program. This program explains how each division and operating unit fits into the overall organization, how the individual's department works, and how the particular project of the new E/S fits into the total organization. Then, once a week for four weeks, in two-hour sessions, all new E/S are brought together for additional seminars. The purpose of these seminars is to ease the transition from school to working by discussing differences between the two, such as the fact that reinforcement is less frequent on the job.

One aerospace company responded to new employee complaints of alienation by instituting informal discussions between employees and management. Other companies use various forms of social and business gatherings for this purpose. Peer support often facilitates acclimation. One study of company orientation of recent graduates into industry found that "new organizational members reduced the strain associated with the identity crises they were experiencing by

---

[1]Arthur P. Brief, "Undoing the Educational Process of the Newly-Hired Professional," *Personnel Administrator*, Vol. 27 (September 1982), pp. 55–58.

befriending peers in the same situation."[2] Seminars and social events allow such relationships to be formed.

Once the initial orientation period is over, the new hire is often left alone, unless participating in a formal training program. An aerospace company reviewed internal statistics and learned that, although there were few problems with the initial retention rate, many engineers were leaving the firm after two to three years. It therefore developed a college hire retention program under which the college relations/employee relations personnel "track" new hires for a period of five years in order to ensure that appropriate communications with management occur at timely intervals. Communication is defined broadly to include performance review, merit review, work assignments, reassignments, and career development. The program begins with a formal orientation followed by informal "get togethers" to which new hires, managers, and the prior year's graduates are invited. Two months later, a question-and-answer session is held with the vice-president of engineering. In the third month, the new hire participates in an informal meeting with a college relations administrator. Quarterly discussions with the immediate supervisor are also scheduled. During the second and third year of employment the individual meets with the employee relations staff to discuss career paths, job changes, rotation, etc. Similar tracking patterns continue through the fifth year of employment. Surprisingly, few companies had similar programs which bridge orientation and formal tracking. They might be developed by extending existing orientation seminars, or through interfaces between orientation and subsequent tracking programs, to improve retention over a period of time.

Unlike college recruits, experienced individuals are usually hired for direct placement. Although they have relevant work experience and have already made the transition from academia to industry, a brief orientation is still required. It should give an overview of the organization and familiarize new employees with company policies, procedures, and standards. Formal training may also be beneficial in certain cases.

TRAINING

Training may be informal or formal, on-the-job or off-the-job, or a combination of these. Basically, however, its purpose is to expand

---

[2]*Ibid.*, p. 58.

the knowledge of E/S so that they may in turn increase their contribution to the organization. Training is not necessarily confined to technical matters. It may also involve human or conceptual skills which increase the individual's value to the organization.

Attitudes toward training vary. Several companies interviewed questioned the value of investing in formal training. Utilities which are regulated and are under internal cost pressures, and design and construction companies which are pressured by users to control costs, attempt to keep overhead as low as possible. Several indicated that they have slashed training outlays. Other firms are explicitly antagonistic to formal training. One company spokesman stated:

> We used to have training programs, they created "fair haired boys" and "prima donnas" who thought they were on the fast track and didn't have to work. Others felt they received inequitable treatment and morale deteriorated. We don't have such programs any more.[3]

Comments such as this probably indicate design problems inherent in the program structure, which produced unrealistic expectations. Merely instituting a program is therefore insufficient. To be effective, a training program must be evaluated regularly in relation to objectives, and altered as necessary.

On the other end of the spectrum, there are companies which believe that their long-term performance is dependent upon the continuous development of E/S. These companies integrate human resources planning with strategic planning, and to aid in this process have instituted elaborate training activities.[4] The philosophy of a firm concerning promotion is another determinant of the investment made in training. Firms that follow the promotion-from-within doctrine generally invest heavily in training because their future will be a direct result of the competence and creativity of their existing workforce. Firms that fill upper levels from outside the company, however, often rely strongly upon the training investment made by their competitors.

Regardless of the overall philosophy of a firm, training expenditures are discretionary, and are likely to be reduced during periods of economic adversity. Unless training is continuous and systematic and is undertaken as a continuing planned function, however, it is less likely to succeed in its objectives. Those programs that are conceived as temporary, or are emphasized in good years and scrapped during lean years, are less likely to achieve their objectives.

---

[3]Interview, Midwest, March 1982.
[4]Jonathan S. Monat, "A Perspective on the Evaluation of Training and Development Programs," *Personnel Administrator*, Vol. 26 (July 1981), pp. 47–52.

A related problem is whether E/S should remain in technical disciplines throughout their career. If so, should they specialize or remain technical generalists? An alternative is to offer E/S the opportunity to develop management skills and expand their corporate function. The answer is probably to develop a balanced mix of management and technical abilities. This requires experience in various geographic areas and functional skills because individuals must be groomed through exposure to a variety of jobs and "stretched" through a series of developmental moves. These issues must be addressed before a firm can develop a training policy consistent with its long-term objectives and broad management philosophy. If a company has a clear conception of its philosophy, it can adapt policies consistent therewith and recruit and train E/S accordingly.

Once technical candidates have been evaluated for training, offers will be extended either for a direct placement position or a rotational program. Training in a direct placement situation may be either formal or informal, while rotational programs are generally formal. The training philosophy and resulting exposure may ultimately be similar under both methods.

Direct Placement Training Programs

Engineers and scientists accepting direct placement offers will usually receive on-the-job training. This does not always mean that new hires are thrown into the water either to sink or to swim, although many organizations interviewed seem to like this analogy. There is usually an informal mentor network operating to keep the new hire afloat. If, however, training is left exclusively to veteran employees, bad habits may be passed along. Another danger of the informal approach may be the formation of poor techniques simply because the employee does not have a clear understanding of departmental standards. Inefficiencies then result because the employee requires continual correction and supervisory attention.

The philosophy behind on-the-job training is that most development is, in fact, self-development. Individuals learn and grow only if they expend effort and take advantage of opportunities. Line management is expected to provide these opportunities, consistent with the objectives of the organization and the needs of the individual. Training and developmental opportunities are, at best, planned experiences which take different forms based on varying individual needs. Line managers must maintain continuous association with subordinates. Supervisors at one major chemical company are also expected to use other informal training methods where appropriate, such as performance discussions, coaching, assigning special tasks for broadening experience, etc., including the recommendation and approval of special study.

Such direction is frequently supplemented by more formal on-the-job training aids. One company commences its formal process with classroom instruction and video presentations. The employee is then given a training manual, which outlines the training objectives and basic job requirements. This manual also contains a listing of the tasks which must be performed to department standards in that job description. Continual interaction with management is key.[5]

The relevance of various forms of training is a widely debated subject. For one company, the bulk of technical training is done on the job. It feels strongly that people learn best on a "need to know" basis. Each department is responsible for its own training. For example, the civil and structural departments sponsor workshops twice per year which consider systems planning and design the content of many ongoing projects. The chemical engineering design group has developed slide and tape shows for individuals to use on a "self-help" basis. This is a new approach for the company. Prior to its implementation, the company had a general training program. The predominant feeling among management was that individuals were not receiving maximum benefit from regularly scheduled events. The decision was made to make training more relevant and as directly related to work as possible. One potential problem with this approach is that an individual, not appreciating the "need to know" philosophy, may miss opportunities which would be beneficial in the future. Ideally, after two or three years individuals will begin attending departmental seminars because of both interest and need. This company also offers general courses for technical personnel. A supervisory program for engineers is under development. In sum, the first goal within the overall training framework is developing engineers who perform to company standards. The next step is the development of communication and other management skills.

Not all firms follow the "need to know" philosophy. Many companies supplement on-the-job training with a structured series of seminars which are offered periodically. These are often developed sequentially, going into further depth as the individual grows with the job. They may be structured in either a lecture or video format. Product literature, supplementary reading materials, homework, and tests may be an integral part of these experiences. If several new hires attend and progress through a series of presentations, the

---

[5]John D. Dickey, "Training with a Focus on the Individual," *Personnel Administrator,* Vol. 27 (June 1982), pp. 35–38.

formation of a peer support system, with its consequent benefits, is facilitated.

Rotational Training Programs

Many companies interviewed offered rotational training options for new graduates. One utility had a similar plan for students in cooperative programs. Individuals typically are rotated through a series of projects or assignments which utilize the skills which they have developed in their college major. The amount of time spent in each assignment varies, as does the actual number of assignments. The progression of experiences is usually individually tailored. These programs fulfill a variety of purposes. Initially, they broaden the individual's experience through various selected work assignments. Moreover, working relationships are developed with departments throughout the organization. The choice of a permanent job and department may occur during the progression, but some companies prefer that the entire sequence of experiences be completed before this decision is made. The trainee indicates the available assignment that he prefers. Permanent placement is ultimately a mutual decision based on the individual's input, performance, the firm's current human resource requirements, and other criteria. A chemical company thought that its program was instrumental in improving the retention rate for new graduates.

An aerospace company uses the rotational work assignment to assist graduating engineers in selecting meaningful career paths. The program begins with four weeks of classroom lectures and laboratory demonstrations presented by senior engineers. This segment is designed to introduce the graduate to the organization of the company, the division, customers, and products. The second segment consists of three six-week rotational assignments. Upon completion of both segments the graduate, with the aid of an advisor, selects a permanent assignment.

One manufacturing company interviewed has a more extensive training sequence. The objectives of its program are:
1) To guide the new engineer through the period of adjustment to industry.
2) To provide contacts with experienced engineers through selected work stations.
3) To encourage learning effective approaches to technical problems and the relationships between technical departments.

The fifty-week program is individually tailored to each person's needs before transfer is made to the initial career assignment. During the first ten weeks, trainees are familiarized with the company's engineering, product mechanics, vehicle operation, welding, machine tool operation, computer use, and sales-marketing. The remaining forty weeks involve on-the-job assignments at six stations (four selected by the trainee) in the engineering, research, and technical computing areas. During the program, weekly guest speakers discuss major company departments and the design of products. Field trips include visits to major suppliers, dealers, and various manufacturing facilities.

CONTINUING EDUCATION

Technological developments occur so rapidly in most fields that an engineer or scientist who relies only on a university education will soon become obsolete, to the detriment both of himself and his company.[6] Just as companies have varying philosophies concerning appropriate training techniques, however, they also differ in their support of continuing education. Some firms argue that continuing education is the responsibility of the employee. An individual must assess his personal skills and motivation, identify development needs, set personal goals, seek opportunities, and prepare educational strategies. The organization, however, pursues its goals by appraising individual performance and supporting employee development. Assessment of individual training needs may be linked with performance appraisals and career planning sessions. Support may be informal through coaching and encouragement, formal through increased opportunities for advancement, or monetary through additional compensation. In this section various continuing education options are described. Figure V-1 charts these options.

Vendor Updates

Several companies mentioned that they rely on vendor updates to keep scientists and engineers informed of new developments in equipment and its application. This includes distribution and review of vendor literature, periodic informal vendor sales calls, or formal vendor training sessions.

University Programs

Continuing education programs allow employees to take courses at universities in the evenings. Some universities offer "early bird" programs: classes before work in the morning. Several firms pro-

---

[6]E/S obsolescence is discussed in Chapter IX.

FIGURE V-1
Professional Development/Continuing Education

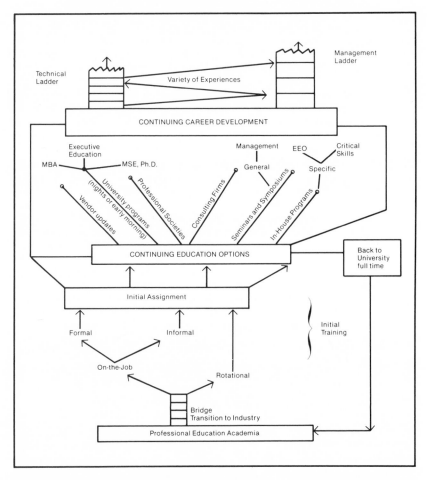

vide more flexible arrangements through the use of closed circuit televisions.

Stanford University pioneered an effective method of continuing education called tutored video instruction (TVI). Unedited copies of video recordings of regular Stanford classes are sent to off-campus locations and played back for small groups of students. The class size typically ranges from three to ten students. The groups are led by a tutor, who need not necessarily be expert in the course material; his main function is:

to foster class discussion by taking advantage of the video playback's unique feature: it can be stopped at any time. Students are encouraged to stop the playback whenever they have a question, and to resolve it through discussion among themselves before resuming. The tutor's job is to make sure that the playback is stopped often enough (every five or ten minutes), and to start a discussion if necessary. The tutor is not there to answer questions, and is specifically instructed to answer them only if the students fail to do so by themselves. Questions that the tutor cannot answer are referred back to the Stanford lecturer by phone, and the proper explanations are then discussed at the next class meeting. All off-campus students registered for credit do the same homework and are required to take the same tests as the on-campus students; homework and tests are all graded by the same teaching assistants.

This methodology has proven to be very effective educationally. Experimental results indicate that TVI students perform at least as well as comparable students that attend the same classes on campus .... They also perform better than students that view the same recordings alone, with or without the help of a tutor....

The TVI methodology offers a simple, economical way of providing instruction to a large number of students scattered at a great many locations. It permits flexible scheduling of classes and does not require special expertise on the part of the local tutors; they only need to be good discussion leaders and have a somewhat better technical preparation than their students. The educational style is more informal and participatory than that of traditional classes, and therefore it is likely to better fit the needs and taste of older engineers.[7]

There are various university programs with more traditional structures. If enough individuals are interested, a firm may sponsor courses on site. In this case university instructors teach at the employer's facility. Occasionally such courses are offered partially on company time. There are, of course, differences in these programs. The courses which are eligible for reimbursement vary, as do reimbursement policies and rates. All firms interviewed had policies permitting employees to take university courses, and individuals frequently take advantage of them. Companies typically reimburse fees upon proof of satisfactory completion of approved courses.

Since continuing education programs are so common, it was postulated that companies might have a preference concerning whether technical professionals should pursue advanced degrees in engineering or in business. The responses indicate that neither degree was consistently favored. Apparently, the choice depends upon an individual's strengths, career goals, current position, and the company's

---

[7]Robert M. Fano et al., *Lifelong Cooperative Education*, Report of the Centennial Study Committee (Cambridge, Mass.: Massachusetts Institute of Technology, Department of Electrical Engineering and Computer Science, 1982), pp. 38–39.

ability to provide opportunities to utilize the new degree. In fact, the attainment of an advanced degree in either field does not, in itself, enhance an individual's opportunity for promotion, but it may. If courses are relevant, performance may improve, which in turn can improve the chances for promotion. Thus, it may only indirectly help an individual to advance.

This was mentioned as a cause for concern by several firms. Employees who pursue advanced degrees often develop unrealistic expectations. One company official cited several scientists who had attained master of business administration (MBA) degrees at night and then felt frustrated because they received no recognition and could not apply their new knowledge. Other firms echoed this response. One chemical company decided to tighten its policy for support of graduate business education and another noted a new policy of advising employees to pursue master's degrees in their technical fields rather than in business.

Not only scientists and engineers attend evening courses. Technicians often attend evening classes in pursuit of bachelor's degrees to upgrade their status. Experience showed one firm that even if the degree recipient received a raise, and was officially upgraded to a professional, his relative status among co-workers remained essentially unchanged. To alter this situation, this company now makes a distinct effort to recognize such achievement by special awards or citations, and occasions such as department luncheons.

One communications company initiated an external program of particular value. In conjunction with another corporation, it helped to develop and to support a master's program in telecommunications at a leading university. This is a key contribution because only a few universities offer such a program. It is also an example of the fruitfulness of industry-university cooperation, which is today increasing.

Professional Societies

Professional society memberships are frequently sponsored by companies. Membership in a society does not in itself guarantee familiarity with current advances in one's field. Since, however, a subscription to a professional journal is usually included in membership dues, exposure to recent developments in the field may be increased. An individual member may attend general meetings, participate in technical subcommittees, and/or become involved in standards setting. Professional societies often sponsor week-long seminars on contemporary topics. Attendance at such seminars exposes technical professionals to state-of-the-art developments both at universities and within other firms.

Consulting Firms

Consulting firms in various fields sponsor update seminars. These firms fill a continuing education niche by condensing information into one or two week sessions and offering practical, hands-on rather than theoretical curricula. They also supply training materials, text books, and workbooks. E/S can absorb the information in a short period of time, return to work, and put it to use.

IN-HOUSE PROGRAMS

Many companies offer various types of in-house training opportunities. These may vary considerably (as noted below) and include general training, technical training, seminars, and numerous variations on the seminar format.

General

The most common in-house programs are general in nature. Course selections are usually monitored by internal training departments. The course selection framework remains relatively constant over time, although individual courses are reviewed and updated. New courses are added where appropriate. Catalogs are published with course listings in various fields: basic management skills, effective presentations, technical material, etc. General in-house continuing education of this kind should be differentiated from courses specifically aimed at reorientation or retraining. Such programs will be discussed in a later chapter.

A review of the courses offered by study participants shows that the primary emphasis of general in-house programs is the development of management skills. This is not surprising given that many of the firms with extensive general programs also follow the promotion-from-within doctrine. As a recent study concludes: "Companies are finding it increasingly necessary that they provide greater attention to the development of their management and executive personnel. One of the more significant trends is the evolution away from reliance largely or wholly on externally-sponsored training and development programs."[8]

Extensive internal training programs are generally designed to fill the gap in continuing education avenues for management development. This gap results from limitations in university-offered exec-

---

[8]Matt M. Starcevich and J. Arnold Sykes, "International Advance Management Programs for Executive Development," *Personnel Administrator,* Vol. 27 (June 1982), p. 27.

utive programs, such as limited enrollment, program generality, length, etc. A survey of companies with recognized programs showed that their in-house efforts resulted from the following needs, which were highlighted also in our interview responses:

1) To provide educational experience as pragmatic as possible while introducing new concepts to participants.
2) To have greater control over course content, curriculum design and faculty selection.
3) To increase understanding of the organization and impart certain beliefs and organizational philosophies to participants.[9]

Strictly technical offerings are noticeably sparse in general catalogs. The implication is that E/S must rely on alternative educational services to upgrade and enhance technical skills. On the other hand, those E/S who choose to advance through management will be able to sharpen their business skills through in-house programs.

Technical

Although general programs are distinctly management oriented, specific programs have frequently been initiated by companies in response to technical needs. Some of the programs were developed and are run exclusively in-house, while others have been developed and are offered in conjunction with universities. The need for supplemental technical programs can be attributed to the following:

1) Inability to fill job openings because of short supply of qualified applicants.
2) Knowledge requirements in interdisciplinary fields. Such programs are not generally available at universities.
3) Advanced study in state of the art of certain fields. The proprietary nature of the topic may require in-house treatment.
4) Training to bridge the gap between theory and practice.

Several petroleum companies have formal courses to train petroleum engineers. These are a direct result of the short supply of individuals with university training in this area. Engineers are hired from other disciplines (i.e. civil) into "post graduate" training. The courses build upon the students' fundamental technical training while presenting new material. Such programs were particularly relevant before the oil glut produced a decline in employment in these firms.

One chemical company has developed a specific sequence of courses for engineers and scientists in decision making and analysis. The purpose of this program is to enhance their technical skills by

---

[9]*Ibid.*, p. 28.

broadening their understanding of business. The intent of this exposure is not primarily management development, but rather to
develop understanding among E/S of the company environment and
to demonstrate how the technical arena relates to other functional
groups. The company believes that an understanding of criteria used
in project funding, planning, and evaluation may lead to increased
innovation in approach, increased cost consciousness, and/or
improved monitoring techniques.

Several paper companies have formal programs in plant operations. Chemical engineers are given training in production, including
product and process technology. They learn the "art" of papermak-
ing, and how to operate the machinery. Engineering theory and
fundamentals acquired in school are enriched by this practical
experience.

Electrical equipment manufacturers and utilities stated that engineers with a concentration in power are difficult to recruit since electrical engineering students tend to study electronics and to pursue
careers with firms in more glamorous industries. Therefore, one utility offers seventy to eighty hours of formal instruction to new graduates to instill a solid power orientation. An electrical equipment
manufacturer donated equipment to a local university, with which
the company cooperates in developing a power program.

Seminars and Symposiums

Many firms offer in-house seminars. This form of continuing education was most frequently cited by companies in the chemical and
pharmaceutical industries, as well as by others with large research
facilities. Presentations by employees and prospective employees of
their research are common. Outside consultants or professors are
also invited to speak. The format of these events varies; they may be
either single occurrences, a developmental sequence of lectures, or a
series of related presentations. Attendance is usually not manda-
tory. A particular lecture, seminar, or symposium is usually offered
only once or twice; new topics are selected for future sessions. This
feature distinguishes the seminar form of continuing education,
since other formal in-house training courses are offered annually.
One aerospace company has a technical training committee whose
mission is to plan relevant offerings. Employees are elected to membership. They select subjects of interest, help choose speakers, and
decide which employee groups shall be invited to attend.

Equal Opportunity

In addition to general management programs and specially developed technical courses, some companies have programs to acclimate and integrate minorities and women into their business environments. These programs may be conceived and implemented in-house, or the services of an outside firm may be used. One chemical company works with an association specializing in integrating minorities into business. Another chemical company invites both women and minorities (separately) to special programs at its headquarters. The topic addressed is decided upon by participants in advance. A third chemical firm uses an outside consultant to show minorities how to advance in the company. The consulting firm offers a variety of sessions, including seminars during evenings and on the weekends. A fourth organization in the chemical industry arranges informal meetings and question-and-answer sessions between existing minority employees and new graduates. A computer company has women's task forces, career forums, and workshops. One firm was experiencing pressure from women employees and complaints about unequal treatment. They began a discussion group composed of executive track women and managers to resolve problems.

In-House Seminar and Training Facilities

Many businesses have their own seminar and training facilities. A pioneer in this respect is General Electric's superb teaching complex in Crotonville, New York, which has very well-appointed sleeping quarters and excellent teaching and seminar rooms, as well as eating facilities. Some such facilities are sparse, others are quite grandiose, but all permit companies to provide isolated facilities with excellent equipment where effective training can be accomplished.[10] Essentially these in-house training facilities permit direct supervision of executive education by the companies, thereby allowing employees to bypass programs at universities. One disadvantage of the isolated location is the absence of other companies' personnel with whom to exchange ideas and experiences. The advantages, however, include a program more directly keyed to the company's needs.

ASSESSING TRAINING

Companies regularly compare projections or specifications to actual results or performance in sales, manufacturing and other functional areas. Evaluation of training programs is not as common.

---

[10]For an account of some of these facilities, see Mary Williams Walsh, "Company-Built Retreats Reflect Firms' Cultures and Personalities," *Wall Street Journal,* August 16, 1984, p. 27.

Two questions which have been identified as generally neglected in the evaluation of training programs are: "1) Did the training program have the intended results? [and] 2) Did the training program achieve its objective at a reasonable cost?"[11]

Programs are developed in response to needs felt within a firm. "Support of training comes about from training's ability to contribute to organizational objectives, not because training is inherently good or will satisfy employees."[12] Expenditures are justified after costs and benefits are analyzed. But justification is often based on quantification of uncertainties. Thus, it is necessary to determine whether the planned benefits are realized and at what actual cost they are accomplished. Intangible costs or benefits may become more apparent or easier to assess with increased experience. As individuals complete programs, changes in job effectiveness may become evident. Allocation and justification decisions may change considerably as these inputs become more accurate. Companies must finally institute systematic evaluation: a process or set of activities to compare results against goals and other established criteria. An analysis of actual evaluation procedures was not covered by this study, but another researcher has concluded that "comprehensive evaluation will use a combination of strategies since different questions and stages of training will require different forms of evaluation techniques."[13] The importance of the evaluation process is often overlooked, with the result that some companies are not certain about their program's effectiveness, or whether they are in need of others. Our interviews did, however, confirm the fact that companies which emphasized training and development seem to be ones that enjoy market and financial success over time.

CAREER PLANNING

The development and pursuit of career paths within an organization are both complex arts. Career paths are built through a series of interactions between individual employees and their employers and based upon the needs of both, as determined by the structure of the enterprise. An individual defines his or her particular career preferences through various exposures and experiences within the work environment. As one company's literature states:

---

[11]Monat, "A Perspective on the Evaluation of Training," p. 47.
[12]*Ibid.*
[13]*Ibid.*

> Personnel development is a highly individualized process. Its success or failure depends on many factors including the motivation, interest and capability of the employee; the skill and interest of the supervisor in assisting subordinates to develop and grow; the general climate for research and engineering; and the availability of developmental assignments.[14]

A corporation must simultaneously identify its strategic thrusts and create internal opportunities to encourage development in desired directions. Although it is important both for individual E/S and corporations to engage in general planning, a plan must be flexible so that unanticipated changes can be absorbed. Flexibility also ensures that opportunities which are not built into formal plans may be seized either by employee or employer as they develop.

Why Companies Engage in Career Planning

The companies participating in the study may be placed along a spectrum of involvement and support of the career planning process. This spectrum ranges from no involvement to a complete interactive planning system. Extensive programs in this area are costly, and demand commitment from management if they are to function effectively. From a short-term perspective, it is easier to leave the responsibility to the individual, but various pressures often encourage the company to develop career planning systems. The depth and breadth of the system designed depends upon the strength of these pressures, the philosophy of the company, and the resources that the company chooses to invest.

There are many conflicting positions concerning the appropriate role of management in employee career planning. Proponents of more active roles suggest establishment of formal career paths, workshops, individual counseling sessions, etc. But career development programs can be risky, because they build the expectations of employees. An ill-conceived or poorly administered program can undercut the organization's philosophy, its credibility, or its commitment to human resources.[15]

Forces which encourage a firm to take an active role in the career planning process are varied. Individuals exert pressure on management by voicing concern about "pigeon-holing" or lack of breadth in job assignment. A firm may develop more precise job descriptions and career path definition because of perceived or demonstrated lack of employee motivation resulting from uncertainty of task.

---

[14]Statement of engineering and research division, major petroleum company.
[15]Karl A. Hickerson and Richard C. Anderson, "Career Development: Whose Responsibility?" *Personnel Administrator,* Vol. 27 (June 1982), p. 41.

Unacceptably high turnover rates may also cause reevaluation of career progression opportunities or attention to personnel development.

A major concern of both E/S and their employers is obsolescence. A professional publication maintains:

> One of the major causes of obsolescence among technical professionals is poor career management. Most engineers and scientists, as well as their managers, freely admit that they had not used any kind of planning to advance their career, but rather arrived at their current positions as a result of events which were usually not in their control. Organizations, as well as individuals, are beginning to realize the importance of career management involving well thought out planning and development approaches to maintain personal growth and technical vitality.[16]

One could argue that although the organization plays a crucial role in stimulating continuing education, it is ultimately the responsibility of the individual to maintain technical vitality. The pressures created by the threats of obsolescence nevertheless exist, as do employee grievances and complaints about lack of specific direction, and management involvement in career planning may ease such pressures.

A firm may also experience external pressures to take an active role in career planning. For example, the threat of unionization may result from employee discontent. Formal plans or documented career pathways can help support a firm's legal testimony in equal employment or other litigation. Programs introduced within a competitor's organization may require internal response or adjustment so that key employees may be retained.

A firm may also decide that the intangible long-term benefits of career planning programs are worth the required investment. For example, individuals may experience increased job satisfaction because career goals are clearer. Career planning may help the development and promotion of protected classes. Formal succession planning may also be improved. The potential for boosting employee morale and productivity through the careful administration of a well designed career planning program is thus promising, but not easily quantifiable.

Career Stages

The major keys to motivation and productivity are the intellectual challenge of the work itself, and the extent to which the individual

---

[16]Harold Kaufman, ed., *Career Management: A Guide to Combating Obsolescence* (New York: IEEE Press, 1975), p. 355.

TABLE V-1
Four Career Stages

	Stage I	Stage II	Stage III	Stage IV
Central activity	Helping Learning Following directions	Independent contributor	Training Interfacing	Shaping the direction of the organization
Primary relationship	Apprentice	Colleagues	Mentor	Sponsor
Major psychological issues	Dependence	Independence	Assuming responsibility for others	Exercising power

Source: Reprinted, by permission of the publisher, from "The Four Stages of Professional Careers" by Gene W. Dalton et al., *Organizational Dynamics*, Summer 1977, p. 23. © AMACOM, a division of American Management Associations, New York. All rights reserved.

perceives the work to be needed and used by the company. As an employee gains experience, the firm should provide opportunities for him to exhibit increased proficiency through assignment of more challenging projects. One firm has described how its job assignments develop individual responsibility:

> As you [the employee] demonstrate capability, the company's objective is to increase responsibility by giving you a larger voice in planning your own work and influencing decisions. For example, you are given an opportunity to plan more and more of your work details, and where practical, you are also given an opportunity to participate in setting project objectives, while objectives are set in terms of end results within budgetary limits. As you demonstrate further competence, you are encouraged to propose projects for future programs. [17]

Implicit in this job assignment progression is the assumption of escalating and expanding levels of competence, responsibility, and authority, as summarized in Table V-1. Of course, not all E/S go through all these stages. Table V-1 illustrates how an individual may progess, and what he must do to move ahead in his work, responsibility and authority. Obviously, therefore, the company must create the environment where this is possible. If a company does not or cannot create the proper environment, it is likely to lose the best of its professionals. This has certainly occurred over the past twenty years to the older mass production industries. [18]

In addition to building an environment which permits progress

---

[17]Note 14, above.

[18]Thomas F. O'Boyle, "Brain Drain: U.S. Basic Industries Are Hindered by Loss of Scientific Talent," *Wall Street Journal*, July 27, 1984, pp. 1, 16.

TABLE V-2

Critical Functions in the Innovation Process

Critical Function	Personal Characteristics	Organizational Activities
Idea Generating	Expert in one or two fields. Enjoys conceptualization; comfortable with abstractions. Enjoys doing innovative work. Usually is an individual contributor. Often will work alone.	Generates new ideas and tests their feasibility. Good at problem solving. Sees new and different ways of doing things. Searches for the breakthroughs.
Entrepreneuring or Championing	Strong application interests. Possesses a wide range of interests. Less propensity to contribute to the basic knowledge of a field. Energetic and determined; puts self on the line.	Sells new ideas to others in the organization. Gets resources. Aggressive in championing his or her "cause." Takes risks.
Project Leading	Focus for decision making, information, and questions. Sensitive to the needs of others. Recognizes how to use the organizational structure to get things done. Interested in a broad range of disciplines and in how they fit together (e.g., marketing, finance).	Provides the team leadership and motivation. Plans and organizes the project. Insures that administrative requirements are met. Provides necessary coordination among team members. Sees that the project moves forward effectively. Balances the project goals with organizational needs.

| Gatekeeping | Possesses a high level of technical competence. Is approachable and personable. Enjoys the face-to-face contact of helping others. | Keeps informed of related developments that occur outside the organization through journals, conferences, colleagues, other companies. Passes information on to others; finds it easy to talk to colleagues. Serves as an information resource for others in the organization (i.e., authority on who to see or on what has been done). Provides informal coordination among personnel. |
| Sponsoring or Coaching | Possesses experience in developing new ideas. Is a good listener and helper. Can be relatively objective. Often is a more senior person who knows the organizational ropes. | Helps develop people's talents. Provides encouragement, guidance, and acts as a sounding board for the project leader and others. Provides access to a power base within the organization—a senior person. Buffers the project team from unnecessary organizational constraints. Helps the project team to get what it needs from the other parts of the organization. Provides legitimacy and organizational confidence in the project. |

Source: Reprinted from "Staffing the Innovative Technology-Based Organization," by Edward B. Roberts and Alan R. Fusfeld, *Sloan Management Review*, Vol. 22 (Spring 1981), p. 25, by permission of the publisher. Copyright © 1981 by the Sloan Management Review Association. All rights reserved.

through career stages, some organizations have recognized and rewarded specific informal but critical behavioral functions which E/S may assume. These functions have been identified by Roberts and Fusfeld. They include "idea generating," "entrepreneuring or championing," "project leading," "gatekeeping" and "sponsoring or coaching."[19] Personal characteristics and organizational activities which describe these functions are summarized in Table V-2.

> Each type [of individual] must be recruited, managed, and supported differently; offered different sets of incentives; and supervised with different types of measures and controls. However, most technical organizations seem not to have grasped this concept. The result is that all technical people tend to be recruited, hired, supervised, monitored, evaluated, and encouraged as if their principal roles were those of creative scientists, or, worse yet, of routine technical problem solvers.[20]

Companies must differentiate and encourage key behavioral functions and recognize their role in effective project conceptualization, development, and execution within a technology-based organization.

Career Path Hurdles

Besides the need to examine E/S individually and to determine career paths which fit their individual abilities and needs, some serious hurdles must be overcome if professional development is to work well for the company and the E/S. The two most obvious are cost and expansion. As one author has noted, it "is not a simple or inexpensive undertaking."[21] Certain industries are limited by the overhead available to invest in training and development. Companies which are downsizing have few advancement opportunities. Several utilities interviewed mentioned careful monitoring of discretionary expenses by regulatory commissions. Companies which rely heavily on government contracts also felt that it was prudent to restrict such expenses. Thus, prior to undertaking a full program, a realistic profile of available resources is required to avoid excessive development commitments.

Table V-3 summarizes other potential barriers to an effective career path system. Although most of the factors are relatively straightforward, our interviews revealed that several companies have experienced problems because of inadequate analysis of potential pitfalls. Some of these problems were attributable to the severe

---

[19]Edward B. Roberts and Alan R. Fusfeld, "Staffing the Innovative Technology-Based Organization," *Sloan Management Review*, Vol. 22 (Spring 1981), p. 22.
[20]*Ibid.*, p. 24.
[21]Hickerson and Anderson, "Career Development," p. 42.

TABLE V-3
Career Path Hurdles

Hurdles	Vaulting Techniques
Resources: cost and time commitment	Perform a realistic evaluation of goals and required resources. Tailor career path planning with availability.
Growth and related opportunities	Build in flexibility to allow for change in the firm's growth rate. Examine internal versus external hire rates.
Determination of openings	Consider *all* employees eligible for promotions. This philosophy can be superimposed over a formal succession plan.
Economy	Flexibility. Design interrelationships and flows to include breadth as well as depth.
Relocation costs	Reevaluate needs for relocation. Relocation packages. Formalize spouse relocation programs.
Time horizons	Develop incentives to encourage long-term human resource planning.
Project orientation	Flexible planning. Design series of experiences to fit with projects as they arise.
Implications and expectations	Define each party's responsibilities early.

recession of the early 1980s which curtailed employment and advancement opportunities, and necessarily disappointed expectations. In general, however, most problems involved staff rotation and employee expectations.

Staff Rotation. Several companies interviewed utilized a project-oriented work structure in which individual E/S typically rotate among projects. This structure is common in aerospace and engineering-construction. At a given time an individual may be working either on a single major contract or on several unrelated projects. There is usually no set pattern for assigning projects or rotating individuals. Questions often arise concerning the optimum time to transfer between projects. For the sake of continuity and familiarity, managers often leave engineers on projects through completion, even through the long life cycles of large defense projects. On the other hand, an individual may resent too much specialization and prefer the challenge of a new project team and situation. At the point of rotation, a related dilemma arises. Should the next experience be similar, or should it require the development of a new set of skills? Often firms do not engage in any staff rotation planning because of uncertainty concerning project lengths and the ultimate outcome of contract proposals. Therefore, short-term considerations are likely to govern. Companies involved have found that flexible guidelines would at least partially accommodate the uncertainty, and have attempted to construct optimum career paths under the circumstances.

Expectations. When career ladders are explicitly identified, individuals tend to form promotion expectations. Employees may infer that management has made a commitment to their growth from the wording of internal publications. Further implied may be "form fit" ladders. Or worse, employees may attempt to climb ladders that they (themselves) create even though no clear skill fit or management promise exists. The question of the ultimate responsibility for career development cannot be avoided, for it defines the firm's position in relation to expectations. If unrealistic expectations are to be prevented, companies must clearly define their position concerning career development during recruiting and early employment stages, and maintain that definition through regular communications.

On the other hand, meaningful developmental planning can help E/S avoid unrealistic expectations. Such planning assumes that all E/S have at least some potential for growth and advancement. In practice, developmental planning may be conceived in either a broad or narrow sense. A manager may informally conceptualize a series of experiences without communicating them to subordinates. The following formally planned series of experiences was recommended by the engineering and research division of one company as a means of overcoming the hurdles created by planning uncertainties arising in a project-oriented work environment:

1) Transition programs—acclimate the individual to the organization.
2) Internal rotational assignments—offer practical training in other areas of company's work.
3) Transfers and loan assignments—to domestic and/or overseas affiliates.
4) Participation in company education programs—for continuing education, upgrading, and/or retraining.
5) Enrollment in courses at educational institutions.
6) Participation in professional and technical societies.[22]

---

[22]Note 14, above.

CAREER PATH TOOLS AND TECHNIQUES

A number of personnel tools and techniques are helpful in constructing and maintaining a sound career path system. These are discussed in terms of their particular contributions to career path success.

Performance Appraisal

Professional development can be enhanced significantly through conscientious attention to performance improvement. Realistic evaluations supply an employee with input which he or she can use to plan future career directions. Through a well-administered performance appraisal process, E/S can identify their strengths and weaknesses. One may choose to broaden his skills by concentrating on overcoming his weaknesses, or he may tailor a growth path following demonstrated and recognized strengths. Thus, effective appraisals supply feedback to employees which allow them to take a creative approach to career development.

Performance appraisal programs are common in industry. A Bureau of National Affairs, Inc. (BNA) survey found that 89 percent of the manufacturing firms interviewed had formal appraisal programs for professional/technical exempt employees.[23] This survey confirmed the results obtained through our interviewing process. Approximately the same small minority percentage of firms interviewed had no formal evaluations of performance.

Although such programs are common, the quality of information recorded and transmitted to employees varies significantly. A properly administered program should present a realistic analysis to the employee which is also preserved in company records. In practice, realistic assessment is not easily achieved, despite its functional importance. Supervisors, like most individuals, find it difficult to criticize people to their face, and too often management does not instruct them how to do so in a constructive manner. "Companies rarely give accurate performance appraisals of their employees . . . and when negative appraisals are given, their results are unlikely to be reflected in the employee's salary. . . . The process is often flawed, subjective or cursory."[24]

There are a variety of problems which a supervisor must overcome

---

[23]*Performance Appraisal Programs,* PPF Survey No. 135 (Washington: Bureau of National Affairs, Inc., 1983), p. 4.

[24]"Compensation Consultants Recommend Close Ties of Pay, Job Performance," *Daily Labor Report,* No. 14, January 20, 1983, p. A-5.

to produce a realistic and unbiased evaluation. The phenomenon of "convergence to the mean" signifies a tendency to rate most individuals average or above average in all categories. Research has shown that in a typical performance appraisal distribution, "98% of employees receive appraisal ratings in the top three categories... while often no one is rated as a 'low' or 'below average' performer."[25] Many supervisors are not comfortable with the fact that they can influence an individual's career progression and so refrain from reporting the negative traits. Only if these traits are recognized and corrected, however, can the individual achieve full potential. The "halo effect" results when a supervisor allows a particular quality to overshadow all categories to be reported; the final appraisal will contain ratings of either all "excellents" or all "poors" rather than presenting a true representation of strengths and weaknesses. The "recency of events" syndrome describes the situation when a supervisor uses only the most recent events in evaluating the employee's performance over the entire period under consideration. The supervisor can counter this tendency by keeping a record of "critical incidents" which occur throughout the evaluation period. Good record keeping is essential for accurate and fair appraisals.

A variety of appraisal methods have been developed to overcome some of these problems. Purely subjective evaluations are no longer common. Most firms interviewed now use a combination of an essay analysis, a behaviorally anchored rating scale, and a management-by-objectives (MBO) program. Occasionally, individuals are asked to evaluate themselves in conjunction with a supervisor's evaluation. This provides excellent preparation for subsequent discussion. In some departments of several companies, particularly in research laboratories, peer reviews are also provided.

The uses for performance appraisals were documented in the BNA study previously cited. The statistical results, shown in Table V-4, are similar to the responses obtained during the field interviewing process. Several uses are directly related to career planning and development within an organization. A majority of firms use appraisal results when evaluating candidates for promotion. Training and development needs are frequently determined through an analysis of these appraisals. Evaluations also contribute to human resource planning. Skills inventories or other employee information systems use information from formal performance appraisals.

Realistic appraisals are also important because they serve as documentation should legal issues (such as discrimination questions)

---

[25]*Ibid.*

TABLE V-4
Purpose of the Appraisal and the Appraisal Form

	Percent of Companies[a] Exempt Professional Technical
Performance appraisals are used for—	(225)[b]
Determining wage/salary adjustments	87
Making promotion decisions	79
Developing communication between supervisors and subordinates	72
Determining training and development needs	72
Human resources planning	40
Developing skills inventories or other employee information systems	20
Determining order of layoff/workforce reductions	14
Other	3

Source: *Performance Appraisal Programs*, PPF Survey No. 135 (Washington, D.C.: Bureau of National Affairs, Inc. 1983), p. 12. Reprinted by permission from *Personnel Policies Forum*, Copyright 1983 by the Bureau of National Affairs, Inc., Washington, D.C.

[a]Percentages are based on the number of companies with a formal appraisal program for each employee group.

[b]Total number of companies responding to the PPF survey.

develop. They can also serve as evidence justifying promotions or layoffs, salary decisions, and other personnel actions, but they must be consistent and objective to be of value in these cases.

Eighty-seven percent of the manufacturing firms participating in the BNA study indicated that performance appraisals are used to determine wage/salary adjustments for professional/technical exempt employees. Although performance data are thus used in salary administration, most firms carry out distinct performance and salary reviews. One utility company performs three separate reviews over an annual period: 1) salary review, 2) performance appraisal, and 3) potential appraisal. The theory behind this is to keep the appraisal process "pure" in order to keep the employee-supervisor interaction during the performance discussion unburdened by compensation anxieties or pressures.

Evaluator training is essential if the appraisal process is to be successful. Ideally, employees should regularly receive indicators regarding the quality of their work. Informal comments and suggestions from peers and supervisors can supply this feedback. In addition, most firms interviewed conducted annual formal performance reviews for engineers and scientists. A substantial number of firms, however, increased the frequency of formal appraisals during the first several years of employment in order to ease the transition from academia, where continual feedback is provided by tests and course grades, to industry where (after the transition period) formal feedback is considerably reduced. For example, one forest products company gives quarterly appraisals to new graduates for three years. Frequent reviews can also reduce the pressures of salary compression by providing a basis for differential adjustment throughout the year.

Administration of performance appraisal is especially challenging in a matrix organization. An individual typically has both functional and project supervisors. Several project-oriented firms mentioned that they have experienced problems in assessing individuals and providing career path guidance. To resolve this difficult situation, some companies involve both supervisors in the appraisal process. The project supervisor evaluates employee performance at critical project point intervals, since skill development needs can be identified best by supervisors observing day to day activities. These evaluations are reviewed and retained by the functional manager. As an employee rotates through a series of projects or experiences, he will develop a track record and sequence of appraisals completed by various project managers. The functional manager is charged with providing continuity and career path guidance through needs analysis. Project assignment can be enhanced through a better understanding of the employee's skills, abilities, and ultimate career goals.

Although a dual appraisal procedure seems time consuming, companies which perform it successfully believe it provides a periodic focus for ongoing informal analyses. When a functional manager uses individual development needs, existing skills, and career aspirations as inputs for project assignment, both the individual and the organization benefit from the increased satisfaction and productivity that result.

Human Resource Data Base Systems

Many companies are now installing human resource data base systems. These systems have exceptional potential in career path planning and development. They can be used to record general personnel data (name, address, job title, etc.), other background information (education, former employers, professional affiliations, etc.), EEO data, and salary information. Confidential information may be shielded or protected using various subschema designs. Human resource data bases may also be used to develop skill inventories, to record career goals, professional activities, performance appraisal results, etc.

One chemical company has developed a sophisticated data base system internally, which is used to track individuals throughout the organization and to identify candidates with specific skills for job openings. An engineering construction company uses its human resource data base for career pathing and project team development. If a particular skill or experience is required for a job, it can perform a query to locate the necessary credentials. These systems are also useful for compiling employment statistics. For example, the number of engineers and/or scientists can be counted and reported in total, by sex, by race, by discipline, by degree, or other attributes.

Succession Planning

Formal career planning and development systems can be extremely beneficial to a company if coordinated with succession planning, which here refers to all professional positions rather than upper management exclusively. Individuals identified as having high potential can be groomed for specific positions. In this way, companies can ensure that they have needed skills when positions become available. One utility company has recently designated a new manpower planning group responsible for replacement planning, which developed a "candidate qualification inventory" by skill description. This allows the company to determine its needs and prepare for them. One paper company has a "management succession" program for women and minorities to ensure that they develop the proper skills through appropriate sets of job experiences within the firm.

Interaction with the External Environment

To provide additional opportunities for employees, several firms use a career broadening approach. Companies share a general goal—to enhance employees' knowledge and stimulate creativity through interaction with the external environment—although the specific activities advocated by each firm vary. Sabbatical leave is frequently encouraged for scientists. Some firms require that employees on sabbatical continue to pursue a scientific field, perhaps in academia, while others place no restrictions on their employees' activities. A multinational oil company sponsors an exchange program for American scientists with their foreign affiliates. A computer company encourages engineers to participate in seminars which allow them to interact with users and customers. In addition, they may spend time working at a customer location to get a firsthand appreciation of actual problems, experiences, and applications. This market-oriented approach is increasingly popular. Many product and/or process innovations result from customer interactions.

Communication

Extensive communication of career opportunities is essential.

> The communication of job availability information (e.g. through job posting) and career counseling, whether through one's supervisor or from a counselor as such, are basic features of most career planning systems. The conduct of these activities brings along with them policy considerations which serve to clear the way for interdepartment or interunit transfers, avoid the blockage of promotion paths and outwardly support career reinforcing activities. But the success of these two activities is also vitally dependent on descriptive information, job-progression ladders, and individual career-pathing procedures if the internal organization mechanism of career planning and development is to work. Viewed jointly, therefore, an interdependency exists between various career planning activities that severely limits the effectiveness of counseling or the communication of job availability information unless other components of the systems have been fitted into place.[26]

There are several communication techniques which, if used effectively, can contribute to the smooth fit of the underlying subsystems.

Job posting is one method. Through this technique employees periodically are informed of actual opportunities within the organization. Job posting usually means that job descriptions and required candidate qualifications are literally "posted" on bulletin boards throughout the organization, but other methods are also utilized. For example, one petroleum company announces job openings in their house organ.

Detailed information on jobs should generally be available within the firm. Job analysis and descriptions permit counselors to understand the behaviors, performances, and skills needed for job success. Individuals involved in career path planning can then develop "professional progression" documents. Formal published literature can be made available to employees describing possible career paths. Pathways should be both logical and flexible.

Group planning tools such as workshops and seminars were mentioned by several companies. One chemical company has a career assessment center where individuals may discuss potential paths. A pharmaceutical company sponsors a series of career planning sessions. Another firm has career review programs for individuals every two to three years. Career information programs can help clarify the responsibilities of both employer and employee. Expectations

---

[26]Elmer H. Burack and Nicholas Mathys, "Career Ladders, Pathing and Planning: Some Neglected Basics," *Human Resource Management*, Vol. 18 (Summer 1979), p. 2.

are likely to become more realistic through participation in well designed group sessions.

At another chemical company, employees are encouraged, through participation in day-and-one-half career planning workshops, to assess their talents and interests, and to evaluate their options within the three corporate professional career paths in engineering, administrative, and general practice, and in technical specialization. The workshop message is clear: an employee must realistically look at future goals, where he wants to go, and what he wants to be. To be effective, this self-analysis must be performed with individual strengths and weaknesses in mind. The employee is made to understand that he holds the primary responsibility for making a career "happen." Supervisors are, however, given special training in listening to employees, in helping them establish realistic, attainable career goals, and in developing specific action plans to attain those goals.

A manufacturing firm has also decided that the responsibility for development rests primarily with the individual. It perceives the company's role in career counseling to be providing supportive information. Employer-sponsored career counseling sessions address the two major subjects of career planning and the selection process. The delivery mode varies, and includes lectures and team activities. Participants also consider the nature of competition, promotion requirements, and sources of opportunity. Information provided at the sessions is supplemented by printed brochures containing job descriptions. Although this program does not create opportunities, it enables individuals to develop realistic goals within the firm's realm of opportunities, and encourages them to take an active role in their own career planning.

Publication of career information need not be limited to brochures distributed by personnel. Opportunities, case histories, and changes in existing programs may reach a wider audience in general house organs. Videotapes provide another medium of communication which is increasingly being utilized.

Attitude Surveys

Attitude surveys measure the general organizational climate and allow better understanding of employee feelings about their future opportunities. Through careful analysis of survey results, career programs can be modified or communication improved so that programs become more responsive to actual employee needs. One chemical company performed a climate study at its research and development laboratory following a change in management in order to

identify attitudinal and motivational problems. The study ultimately served as a tool for organizational restructuring and personnel policy development.

Career Ladders

One of the most widespread organizational results of company
efforts to enhance professional growth opportunities for E/S has
been the development of multiple career ladders. The multiladder
approach was introduced specifically to allow E/S to fulfill individual goals rather than be forced to progress along a predetermined
and inflexible path. In practice there are two types of multiladders,
dual and triple, but the underlying concept in both is to encourage
technical excellence by providing equal prestige and competitive
compensation for individuals who choose technical specialization. In
most organizations that have not developed a separate path for
those dedicated strictly to science or engineering, E/S pursue the
management track because it is the only existing career path.

Advancement alternatives to the management pathway were pioneered by Exxon, General Electric, and other well-managed companies which have had career ladders for scientists, engineers, and
other "individual contributors" at least since World War II. A variety of arguments support the establishment of parallel ladders in an
organization:

> Many engineers who are employed by private or public organizations
> aspire to join managerial and executive ranks.... One important rea-
> son for this trend is that advancement pay scales for managers are
> higher than those for engineers or other professionals employed by
> organizations.... However, a shift into management is often undesir-
> able, both for the employing organization and for the engineers them-
> selves. From the organization's point of view, it loses a qualified and
> experienced engineer; in exchange it may get a mediocre manager
> because an excellent engineer doesn't necessarily make an excellent
> or even a good manager. From the engineers' point of view, frustra-
> tion may result from the fact that, as managers, they will have to deal
> with situations and problems for which they haven't been trained....
> In addition, increasing involvement in managerial duties will proba-
> bly leave the engineer little time for updating professional knowledge.
> Combined with the fast pace of changes in many engineering fields,
> this may accelerate the process of professional obsolescence by which
> the engineer loses his or her vitality as a professional. All these condi-
> tions account, in part, for stresses faced by midcareer engineers who
> are managers or who aspire to become managers.[27]

---

[27]Reprinted, by permission of the publisher, from "Needed: Excellent Engineers,
Not Mediocre Managers," by Moshe Krausz and Shaul Fox, *Personnel*, January–
February 1981, pp. 50–51. © 1981 AMACOM, a division of American Management
Associations, New York. All rights reserved.

With the baby boom generation approaching management age, companies may find it necessary to strengthen the multiladder systems by reinforcing opportunities in the technical progression to prevent job frustration.

Although many firms claim to have multiladder paths, the effectiveness of these programs varies. The first criteria for a well functioning multiladder system is the full support of top management. Without it the technical ladder is destined to end after several rungs. This, in fact, was a problem alluded to frequently during our interviews.

Companies have encountered numerous pitfalls in the administration of parallel ladder systems. They have found it advisable to encourage lateral as well as upward movement in order to maximize development. They recognize that titles should be examined to ensure that they are meaningful, and that position descriptions for the various technical levels should be thorough and discriminating. Companies have also learned that individuals recognized as having high potential should be encouraged on all ladders, or the technical path will be considered a second class alternative. The availability of career counseling on all ladders should be equivalent. Compensation potential, benefits, and perquisites such as office space should also be similar. Under the most successful systems, senior technical employees are encouraged to participate in both decision-making and the setting of strategic priorities.

Several firms have taken specific actions to remedy unbalanced ladders. For example, one petroleum company has recently assigned a task force to determine whether its existing program should shift its emphasis, since management orientation is the current focus. One utility company has undertaken the design of a completely new progression series. Another petroleum company is in the process of developing a program to increase movement between their two existing ladders. During its annual "Scientific Achievement Award" presentation, the chairman of a chemical company introduced a second career ladder alternative for scientists. He stated that the purpose of this addition, the level descriptions of which are found in Table V-5, was:

> To provide more personal growth for scientists who are truly outstanding in their fields. It demands that the individuals' contributions are significant and useful in the areas of discovery, application or analytical technique—and that they have a pronounced or measurable impact on the company's commercial activities.[28]

---

[28]Chemical company materials.

TABLE V-5
Chemical Company
Scientific Career Path Positions

Associate Research Fellow: Is recognized as the division's foremost authority in a specific area or field. His or her own work is relevant primarily to the division.

Research Fellow: Is recognized as the company's leading authority in a specific field or area. The impact of the Research Fellow's work is felt primarily within the company and often transcends functional or divisional lines.

Senior Research Fellow: Has received national industry-wide recognition, and the individual often serves as an advisor to others, both within the company and outside.

Distinguished Research Fellow: Is internationally known as an expert and is responsible for scientific achievements regarded as major advances in a field or technology.

Source: Chemical company.

CASE ILLUSTRATIONS: MULTILADDER PROGRAMS

Several firms have particularly noteworthy multiladder programs. Two of them will be described at length.

Case 1

At the research and engineering company of a leading petroleum firm there are three paths of advancement open to employees: technical, staff, and administrative.

It is intended that through this system individuals will have the opportunity to advance to their highest potential regardless of the choice of career path. This may be done by remaining on one career path or by combining two or three. All advancement depends on relative performance and experience. In addition, administrative advancement depends on the availability of suitable administrative openings. The important features of each path are discussed below.

Technical Recognition Advancement. In 1946, the company started building its Technical Recognition Program, and established the first technical senior associate title. Since that time the program has been developed and refined. Today, the Technical Recognition Program includes the following titles, listed in ascending order:

1) Scientist or Engineer
2) Research/Project Scientist or Engineer
3) Senior Scientist or Engineer
4) Staff Scientist or Engineer
5) Senior Staff Scientist or Engineer
6) Research or Engineering Associate

7) Senior Research or Senior Engineering or Senior Project Associate
8) Scientific or Engineering Advisor
9) Senior Scientific or Senior Engineering Advisor

Technical titles reflect professional growth and increasing value to the company. A technical title is recognition for individual contribution, but does not define the duties or limit responsibilities to the execution of purely scientific and/or engineering work. For example, one may be expected to participate in the planning and development of the careers of colleagues and to accept administrative duties appropriate to one's areas of endeavor. This means that an individual may in some cases act as a project leader or manager, in other cases as a member of a project team, and in still other situations as an individual scientist or engineer.

An employee's initial title is based on educational preparation and experience. For technical advancement, certain criteria based on relative job performance and experience must be satisfied, and recognizable, significant technical contributions must be made. Some of the more important criteria are:

1) Technical contributions which yield or may yield a profitable return on the company's investments.
2) Significant contributions to scientific or technical knowledge in areas of company interest.
3) Proven expertise in a given field of company interest, recognized as such by affiliates, company scientists and engineers, and others in industrial, academic, and/or government institutions.
4) Demonstrated continuing awareness, sensitivity, and responsiveness in contributing to solutions of important technical company problems.
5) A wide breadth of knowledge exhibited in a variety of technical fields; or conversely, deep knowledge in a specialized field.
6) Technical leadership and stimulation of colleagues. This may occur while serving as a project leader or manager, or on an informal basis during day-to-day contacts.[29]

Staff Recognition Advancement. There is also a series of titles for employees who have staff assignments in which analysis, coordination, and/or planning are major responsibilities. At present, the following titles are used:

1) Analyst/Representative
2) Specialist
3) Staff Analyst/Representative
4) Staff Specialist

---

[29]Information from the company involved.

5) Senior Staff Analyst/Representative
6) Senior Staff Specialist
7) Staff Advisor
8) Senior Staff Advisor

These titles are often preceded by an adjective which identifies the functions performed (e.g., financial analyst). Factors important in determining advancement in staff assignments are ability, experience, contributions, and recognition among peers. Staff assignments at all levels reflect a need for a specified job, similar in many ways to an administrative assignment.

There are also paths of advancement in other professional fields, for example, computer technology and law.

Administrative Advancement. An administrative title pertains to a specific position which is based on job content and administrative responsibilities. These responsibilites include the allocation of resources (personnel and finances), the setting of goals, and personnel administration. The degree of authority and accountability increase with each position level.

A staff chemist or engineer may be involved in administrative work at the group head level. The first formal level of administration, however, commences at administrator, section head, or laboratory director, depending on the organization and tasks of the particular department, division, or laboratory.

Among the qualifications for administrative positions are strong technical ability, knowledge, and judgment. Other factors include leadership, planning, organizational skills, and effective communications, both written and oral.

Relationship of Career Paths. Technical advancement recognizes professional growth and increasing value of various types of assignments important to the company. It does not require a specific job opening, as does administrative advancement. The number of technical titles has been increased so that accomplishment can be recognized on a more timely basis, while the number of administrative and staff levels has varied according to organizational needs. As a consequence, there is no direct equivalency between a given administrative or staff title and a given technical title.

The status of each technical title is related to other steps on the technical ladder. Broadly speaking, under this approach various levels of technical achievement merit their own recognition, rewards, and prerogatives. The salary, recognition, and other rewards of leading technical personnel may be, and often are, comparable with those of directors or managers of major company units. Furthermore, the recognition and rewards available to those holding technical titles are based upon individual achievements and competitive practices in rewarding E/S. Technical rewards are not limited by any level of administrative staff rewards.

Case 2

A major chemical company also offers three professional career paths in engineering, which are displayed in Figure V-2. the administrative ladder needs no elaboration. The general practice engineering path also is straightforward.

> The third ladder is for technical specialists in the field of engineering. This path was established to provide professional opportunities for exceptionally talented individuals who choose science and engineering as their life work. The program seeks to encourage originality and innovation in the technical community and to enhance the impact of the company's scientists and engineers on the future of the company. Participants in the program are expected to be active in research or engineering projects and to serve as corporate-wide consultants in key areas of technology. They are also expected to provide strategic and technical leadership to the corporation and to identify and recommend new approaches in wholly new technologies of potential importance to the company's future. Members of this program usually have significant freedom to select and carry out their projects.[30]

The program, established in the late 1940s, is dynamic, and has changed throughout the years to enhance its effectiveness. Since 1980, individuals have been eligible early in their careers for nomination to the newly created position of associate fellow. The firm also removed the compensation "cap" on the ladder, to provide advancement prospects comparable to those in general management. Rigid guidelines for nomination, orientation, review, and promotion of program participants have been developed.

MULTILADDER PROGRAMS: FINAL COMMENT

The multiladder system is a unique approach to career path planning developed for engineers, scientists, and other "individual contributors." Specifically, its intent is to allow and, more importantly, to encourage individuals with outstanding technical capabilities to remain in technical pursuits. Developing management talent and commitment is vital, and many E/S may find administration challenging. Nevertheless, the positive experience of those companies with well-functioning multiladder programs proves their worth.

---

[30]Information from the company involved.

FIGURE V-2
Chemical Company Career Ladder

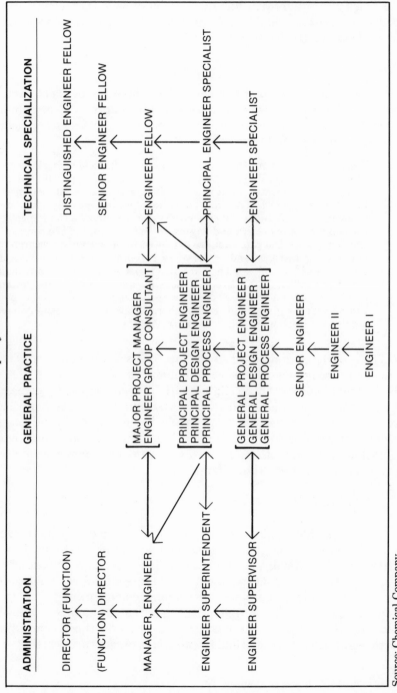

Source: Chemical Company

OTHER CAREER PATH ISSUES

There are other issues and problems involved in career path planning. Care must be taken, for example, to avoid discrimination, apparent or actual. Many companies, therefore, give special attention to developing paths for minorities and women. Career counseling by the personnel department or by line management is important if employees are to make considered decisions in regard to which career path to choose.

Motivation

Several companies expressed concern about motivation problems resulting from the development of formal succession plans and career paths. If individuals feel that promotions are automatic, will they be motivated to perform? The answer seems to be determined by the manner in which such announcements are presented. If the ultimate responsibility for career development is placed on the individual, management can identify potential opportunities without making a simultaneous commitment to automatic progression. To solve this problem, several companies interviewed now design succession and career paths with planned depth and intentional redundance so that competition provides a motivating force. The lack of visible career or succession paths, however, is likely to present motivational problems because future progress seems clouded.

Motivational problems also result from project longevity. A particularly long project may cause a decrease in creativity. In a matrix organization both the timing of transfers among projects and the sequence of project experiences require balance in order to maintain maximum challenge, motivation, and commitment for the employee while the company still receives the benefit of existing skills and design expertise.

Features unique to research laboratories also complicate the development of internal career progressions for E/S. These are discussed in Chapter XI. Here it is sufficient to note that multiladder career paths are also pertinent to research laboratories, because some research scholars become interested in careers in line or staff management. One pharmaceutical firm expects its personnel staff to identify employees who may feel frustrated in research. Through career counseling, such employees might transfer into human resources, general administration, or other functional areas. There are nevertheless many researchers who, having reached their level of competence, choose not to transfer out of research. They may feel comfortable in the creative environment associated with research.

For these people, the pharmaceutical company tries to provide a creative and stimulating work environment.

"The Cream Rises to the Top"

Companies that do not become involved in career planning often claim that "the cream rises to the top," therefore management need not get involved. Such concerns often argue that training programs and career path planning seminars create "prima donnas" or "fair haired boys." Occasionally, firms with such a philosophy have some manner of programs, but only for the "cream." Frequently, companies with general career progressions also have additional elite or fast-track programs. It seems appropriate to question how the elite are selected. If selection is based on demonstrated performance and contribution, these programs may be beneficial to the firm. But if selection is political and perceived as such by other employees, such programs are likely to create internal tension. One paper company interviewed has a professional intern program for the top 10 percent of its engineers. Through this intensive training, future mill managers are groomed. One telecommunications company is currently organizing an engineering associates program, which is designed to be high risk and offer high reward. Successful participants will progress along a fast track. One utility company has a rotational fast-track program especially designed for women and minorities. The intent of this program is to increase the speed of their progression through the advancement structure and thus increase their representation among management ranks.

Location and Rotation

Promotion often means movement to other locations. In certain industries, lateral movement requires a change in location as well. As noted in the previous chapters, some locations are clearly considered superior to others. This can complicate career paths, particularly if the company does not provide offsetting benefits or assistance, and if company policies and communications do not emphasize the transitory and developmental nature of such moves within a total career path. In many firms individuals are also encouraged, through the career planning process, to continually broaden their exposures. The alternative to rotation may be pigeonholing and, ultimately, obsolescence. Although it may seem desirable to develop "experts," many firms interviewed commented that the individuals who were most valuable to their organizations were those who had become well rounded through participation in a variety of experiences and had been challenged by a sequence of different responsibilities throughout their careers. For example, one petroleum firm encourages broad rotation spanning its ten operating companies. Another such company encourages movement between the research divisions and other areas to prevent the former from becoming an "ivory tower." Project rotation also creates management challenges concerning optimal experience time spans and transferability of skills between work assignments.

CONCLUSION

From orientation through professional development and ultimate career pathways, a company's engineers and scientists must have training opportunities if they are to continue to make maximum contributions to the company and to progress in terms of professional accomplishment. Not all E/S, however, either desire to or should remain in their technical profession. Many turn to line or staff management. Those who remain in their profession and continue to contribute must also be rewarded properly. Multiladder career paths have been developed for this purpose, and are found in most of the research-oriented companies interviewed.

CHAPTER VI

Productivity and Utilization

Because industry spends millions of dollars on research and development (R&D), there is much emphasis upon effective utilization of engineers and scientists (E/S). Most E/S employed by companies are performing useful work; but the more important question both for a company and its E/S employees is whether the E/S are engaged in work which requires their full skills and training. If this is not the case, then the company might profit by employing more technicians, laboratory assistants, or other general help, and reassigning its E/S so that they perform less work supplementary to their scientific and professional tasks. Greater E/S productivity would probably result.

More effective utilization has advantages beyond productivity gains. Recruiting and training costs can be reduced by better utilization which lessens the need for additional E/S personnel. Turnover may also be decreased because the number of E/S who feel that the job is not challenging can be diminished. Thus, better utilization can improve morale and job satisfaction as well as productivity.

All the companies interviewed for this study pointed out that it is not possible to maintain a constant level of maximum utilization of E/S because of fluctuating workloads and varying project requirements. Companies do not lay off professional personnel lightly, particularly if additional work is expected within a reasonable period of time. Moreover, scheduling may be in control of the customer rather than of the employer. This is true not only for companies that deal with the government, such as those in the aerospace industry, but also for those that construct, manufacture, or design large and/or complex items that are made specifically for the purchaser.

Despite their attention to the problem of constant maximum utilization, most companies also readily agreed that substantial improvement in utilization was at least theoretically possible within their company and within others of which they were aware. Most also agreed that the ability to improve utilization hinged on two factors: the difficulty of measuring E/S productivity, and the effectiveness of E/S management.

MEASURING E/S PRODUCTIVITY

Measuring the output of E/S is a difficult task. End results are not as easily definable as units of output manufactured. Moreover, years of E/S work may enhance the products and profits of one company, or they may turn out to be wasted time, sometimes despite excellent and efficient work by the E/S involved. Interrelationships between departments of a corporation may result, for example, in a productivity gain in manufacturing but a productivity decline in engineering, both caused by the addition of professional personnel to complete a design which allowed manufacturing to produce more with less personnel and/or capital investment. Thus, project effects can ripple through an organization. The productivity of the organization must both be considered as a whole and broken down by functions and departments for a clear understanding and evaluation of the process.[1]

In all services, it is difficult to link output to input. Moreover, adjustments must be made for varying quality of output. Creative, abstract, and nonrepetitive tasks of E/S are usually subject only to qualitative assessment. Care must be taken to measure results, not activities. Companies must understand that precision is often not possible in measuring E/S productivity.

Several methods of measuring productivity of E/S are currently being utilized, and others are being attempted on a trial basis. Some techniques isolate the individual, others attempt to measure group effort, while still others evaluate entire systems.

The American Productivity Center[2] has developed a system for measuring all white-collar productivity through the following basic equation:

$$\text{Productivity} = \frac{\text{output}}{\text{inputs}} = \frac{\text{output quantities} \times \text{prices}}{\text{input quantities} \times \text{costs}}$$

---

[1]We are here considering total factor productivity, not labor productivity, following the noted authority John Kendrick. See, e.g., his *Productivity in the United States: Trends and Cycles* (Baltimore: Johns Hopkins University Press, 1980). For an analysis of general problems in measuring productivity even in manufacturing, see Gordon F. Bloom and Herbert R. Northrup, *Economics of Labor Relations*, ninth edition (Homewood, Ill.: Richard D. Irwin, Inc., 1981), Chapter 12; and for service industries, Jerome A. Mark, "Measuring Productivity in Service Industries," *Monthly Labor Review*, Vol. 105 (June 1982), pp. 3–8.

[2]A good summary of the American Productivity Center System is found in William A. Ruch, "White Collar Productivity: In Order to Improve It, You Must First Measure It," *World of Work Report*, Vol. 6 (December 1981), p. 89.

The true productivity part of the equation is the ratio of output quantities to input quantities; the ratio of prices to costs is called the price recovery ratio and measures how well the firm is staying ahead of—or contributing to—inflation. Profitability for the firm must be accounted for by relative changes in either the productivity ratio, the price recovery ratio, or both."[3]

This system could help solve many measurement problems, but there are drawbacks:

... because of the nature of white-collar work, one could question whether the input in the current period should be measured against the firm's output in the current or in subsequent periods. Second, knowing that a given group of white-collar workers are becoming less productive by this measure may give few, if any, clues as to how to improve performance.[4]

It is also important to distinguish between intermediate and final sources and products. The measurement of inputs and outputs is nebulous. Data gaps may exist, and time lags may be significant.

From the general definition above, industry-specific or company-specific indicators may be developed. One approach is to develop specific ratios and subsequently to monitor ratio trends.[5] This approach recognizes that absolute measurement of any specific ratio is imperfect but that trend analysis is a valid comparative tool. Ratios at extremes can be studied to determine why they differ from the norm, and conclusions may point to particular problem areas requiring attention.

One computer company interviewed measured the productivity of its programmers by counting the number of kilosteps programmed per person. This technique was also mentioned by an electronics company. This method seems to encourage computer scientists to write inefficient rather than concise programs. Developing efficient flows takes time and thought. Employees are likely to strive to attain excellence in the objectives which are emphasized, however, and if "steps programmed" is considered more important than brevity, programs generated are likely to be long-winded. Imperfect measurement techniques such as this may well be used for lack of better methods, but they convey to the professional that bulk is valued over quality. The resulting inefficiency could contribute to deterioration of the company's product and reputation.

Another company interviewed utilized a time accumulator to record the period that individuals are logged on to the computer. The

---

[3]*Ibid.*.

[4]*Ibid.*.

[5]Robert M. Newburn, "Measuring Productivity in Organizations With Unquantifiable End-Products," *Personnel Journal*, Vol. 51 (September 1972), pp. 655–57.

purpose is to monitor the amount of time that individuals spend working. The possibility exists for a programmer to log on to a terminal and then leave to do other work, or to pursue a problem productively without logging on. In this case, the extra log-in time encouraged by the measurement system may end up costing the company money. Imperfect measurement techniques can thus be foiled, and essentially rendered meaningless. An article on problems of software design summed up the situation in this manner:

> One problem—perhaps unsolvable—is how to measure worker productivity for software, where the degree of difficulty can vary widely among projects. Managers ... say they don't have the answer but that it's worth trying to come up with productivity measures anyway; even the attempt ... will help them understand a little more about manufacturing software.[6]

Given the difficulties, it is also true that there are some predominantly quantitative productivity indicators.[7] Some of these, applying more perhaps to engineers and technicians than to scientists, are listed in Table VI-1. These indicators apply both to organizations and individuals. The listings in Table VI-1 emphasize, by their incompleteness, that any attempts to quantify the work of E/S are necessarily partial measurements and should be utilized with care. There are many quantification methods, but "there are no currently used systems for measuring the productivity of scientific and engineering groups without substantial flaws."[8] E/S productivity must, therefore, be measured by many qualitative productivity indicators as well. Table VI-2 contains a list of qualitative indicators which may usefully be applied, but measurement of such factors is obviously both subjective and difficult.

INCREASING E/S PRODUCTIVITY

Companies interviewed described a variety of productivity improvement methods. These may be divided into three groups: 1) those which increase utilization of technology and capital investment; 2) those which seek better management, organization, and motivation of E/S; and 3) those which attempt to improve the utiliza-

---

[6]James A. White, "Western Electric Is Making Development of Software Less an Art, More a Science," *Wall Street Journal,* December 23, 1982, p. 30.

[7]David J. Sumanth, "Productivity Indicators Used by Major U.S. Manufacturing Companies: The Results of a Survey," *Industrial Engineering,* Vol. 13 (May 1981), pp. 70–73.

[8]Alfred H. Schainblatt, "How Companies Measure the Productivity of Engineers and Scientists," *Research Management,* Vol. 25 (May 1982), p. 10. This article contains an excellent bibliography on E/S productivity.

TABLE VI-1
Examples of Predominantly Quantitative
Productivity Indicators
(Identified by study participants)[a]

Organizational Indicators
• Sales per employee.
• Sales per payroll dollar.
• Profit per employee.
• Profit per payroll dollar.
• Dollar volume of production generated per R&D dollar spent.
• Profits generated per R&D dollar spent.
• Percent of proposals won.
• Dollar value of proposals won versus dollars spent on bidding expense, marketing, travel, etc., to secure those sales.
• Overhead performance—the overhead burden on direct charge labor.
• Measure of earned value—a periodic comparison of actual work completed and cost incurred versus work scheduled to be completed and cost budgeted. (Although such comparison is listed as quantitative, the time-phased program plan on which the budgets are based depends substantially on judgment.)
• Hours of engineering design effort per hundred active circuit elements. (This ratio varies substantially and must be applied with judgment.)
• Drafting time per average drawing. (This ratio varies greatly with product line and type/complexity of drawing.)
• Drawing error rate measurement, e.g., the number of errors detected per square foot of drawing.
• Time per document for processing drawings through an engineering drawing release activity.
• Drawing change rate statistics, e.g., the number of changes per drawing per year. (An excessive drawing change rate on a program may signal broader problems.)
• Hours per standard test.
• Test equipment calibration time, e.g., time per calibration for each type of instrument.
• Computer savings versus investment.
• Ratio of titled personnel to total population. (Monitor ratios for both line and staff functions.)
• Ratio of staff personnel to line personnel.
• Ratio of service and support personnel to total personnel.
• The performance of service and support functions, on the basis of operating statistics unique to each function.
• Secretarial support ratios, e.g., the ratio of secretaries to the managerial, scientific, and engineering population.
• Recruiting performance, e.g., percent of offers accepted, hiring costs per new employee, new hires per recruiter per year, and time required to process job applications and new hires.
• Absentee rate.
• Employee voluntary turnover rate.

TABLE VI-1 (continued)

Individual Indicators
* Computer instructions programmed per programmer per day.
* Engineering drawing releases per clerk per day.
* Microfilm frames filmed and mounted per operator per day.
* Blueprints issued per clerk per day.
* Documents/drawings filed per clerk per day.
* Purchase orders, invoices, etc., processed per person per day.
* Stock requisitions filled per clerk per day.

Source: Reprinted from *R&D Productivity*, pp. 44–45, Copyright © 1974, 1978
Robert M. Ranftl, P.O. Box 49892, Los Angeles, California 90049. All rights
reserved.
[a]Refers to participants in Hughes Aircraft Company study.

tion of E/S. These approaches are not mutually exclusive. Most companies interviewed utilized all three in varying proportions. The first two are discussed below. Improved utilization is a fundamental management imperative, and merits a separate detailed discussion.

Improved Technology

The greatest productivity improvements in our society are the results of new or superior technology and equipment. Potential productivity improvement for E/S is directly related to the increasingly complex technology which has emerged during the 1970s and 1980s. This technology includes a variety of equipment and technological aids, systems-operational aids, and the development of computer aided design and computer aided manufacturing (CAD/CAM).

Equipment/Technological Aids. Many companies described a plethora of tools now available for improving various aspects of engineering productivity. These include, of course, computers, which facilitate complex analyses, simplify performance of repetitive tasks, and afford increased accuracy. New applications for computers are literally being discovered daily. The introduction of the computer increased the complexity and volume of work that could be processed in a given period of time. The number of computers entering the workplace is accelerating as more power becomes available in smaller machines. Computerized equipment allows simplified design and drafting. Depending on the degree of integration with production, a relatively paperless workflow can be created from design conception through product reality. Other significant equipment improves E/S productivity, including word processors, programmable electronic calculators, and microfilm and microfiche machines.

TABLE VI-2
Examples of Predominantly Qualitative
Productivity Indicators
(Identified by study participants)[a]

Organizational Indicators
- The ability to win competitive proposals.
- The degree to which an R&D organization meets its ongoing commitments and performs to requirements.
- The ease, smoothness, and enthusiasm with which specific technical performance, cost, and schedule milestones are met.
- The ability to produce simple, reliable, readily maintainable designs that meet customer requirements.
- The relative ease with which equipment designed by an R&D activity can be put into production.
- Product performance throughout its life cycle.
- The organization's image in the eyes of the customer.
- The tone of the organization—employee motivation, attitude, and morale.
- The degree of professionalism in getting work done.
- The quality and usefulness of ideas generated.
- Progress in acquiring and applying valuable advanced knowledge and skills—the ability to maintain and advance the state of the art.
- Accuracy, completeness, and quality of work.
- The ability to respond to peak demands and emergencies.
- The complexity and backlog of unresolved problems (taking into account task difficulty.)
- Delinquencies, deficiencies, and errors generated.
- Repeat requests support activities get for their services.

Individual Indicators
- Performance relative to job requirements.
- Performance compared with others doing similar work.
- Ultimate impact of work.
- The ability to establish personal goals that complement the goals of the organization.
- Work habits.
- Techniques used to get the job done.
- The degree of application of current and new technology to the job.
- Assignments completed on time.
- Errors and problems created.
- Time/difficulty in learning new routines.
- Interface with immediate supervisor.
- Subjective evaluation by superiors.
- The extent to which the individual's services are requested by others.
- Feedback received from other organizations that have utilized an employee's capabilities and services.
- The respect shown the employee by superiors, colleagues, and subordinates.

[a]Refers to participants in Hughes Aircraft Company study.

One aerospace company interviewed has a corporate investment program to encourage individual engineers to purchase desktop computers. It lends them the required funds interest free and automatically deducts payments through the payroll system. The company then provides software which allows the personal computers to interface with the corporate system. Engineers may take these computers home in the evening for personal use or to dial into the corporate system, essentially extending the boundaries of their workplace. Many other companies have similar programs. For example, a computer equipment manufacturer has invested heavily in small desktop computers, so that for most managers this technology will be almost as commonplace as a telephone in the near future. A telecommunications company tries to increase its programming efficiency by maximizing the number of terminals available. Thus, if a computer scientist wants to access the computer, he waits a minimal amount of time to log in.

Systems-Operational Aids. Computer systems can be used to manage broader engineering functions by improving the communication flow in the company. Computers can aid technology transfer and information retrieval and can enhance coordination between operating units such as research and development, sales, engineering, and production, thereby utilizing the time of E/S more productively.

Both a computer company and a petroleum firm noted that computers have improved information handling and retrieval within the engineering group. For example, the research division of one electrical equipment manufacturer has a database of articles from various technical journals. Through a simple subject query, an engineer or scientist can discover articles pertinent to his area of research. Numerous systems are now available for computerized bibliography services, library information, and data searches.

New devices called intelligent analytical instruments can be used to facilitate experimentation in research and development laboratories. These units

> perform a host of sequential methods-development experiments, predict the outcome of each step, and refine their approach if they're slightly off the mark or start over again if they're on a totally wrong track. Furthermore, when confronted with a task similar to one it has handled before, the computer usually takes less time to solve it— evidence that it has learned from experience.... Today, the average analytical chemist spends more time developing analytical methods than he does performing analyses.[9]

_____
[9]"Instruments That Think Find New Jobs in Labs," *Chemical Week*, March 17, 1982, p. 42.

Microprocessors have outstanding potential for enhancing productivity in the laboratory.

Technology has also entered human resource management. Many companies are developing and installing human resource data base systems which aid in the monitoring of professional development. Salary and performance data can be integrated to improve career planning capabilities. Such data bases can also be used to construct project teams with specific attributes of background, experience, education, etc., and thus provide potential improvement in resource utilization and productivity.

CAD/CAM. The use of the computer in integrated design and manufacturing probably involves the greatest potential for increased E/S productivity. A schematic of a fully integrated CAD/CAM system is presented in Figure VI-1. The development of advanced software, graphics, and computational systems permit highly integrated systems which have spread from manufacturing into other fields.

From the responses of our interviewees, it is apparent that CAD has increased E/S productivity dramatically. Most companies reported that this improvement did not produce a significant reduction of their E/S human resource numbers. In part, this is probably attributable to the fact that CAD/CAM systems have developed slowly during the 1970s and 1980s in most companies, and that this evolutionary growth permits corresponding personnel adjustments, if any, to occur very slowly. More important, however, is that for most firms interviewed, the magnitude, diversity, and complexity of their products expanded during these decades, so that in the absence of CAD, their E/S personnel requirements would have grown.

Of major importance for E/S utilization is that CAD relieves E/S of much routine and repetitive work. Thus, if technology as a whole were to remain at a constant level and CAD systems alone were to improve, one might expect that the demand for E/S would decline. This is unlikely, however, because CAD is a tool which allows a faster rate of technology growth and E/S creativity is vital to this growth process. The CAD life cycle has been compared to the introduction of the computer in the late 1950s and early 1960s—an evolutionary process which allows more growth than it inhibits. Over the next decade, CAD applications are likely to expand dramatically, particularly as CAD/CAM interfaces are improved and other automation links are introduced to manufacturing locations.

Better Management

Improved management, organization, and motivation of E/S

FIGURE VI-1

Schematic for a Fully Integrated CAD/CAM System

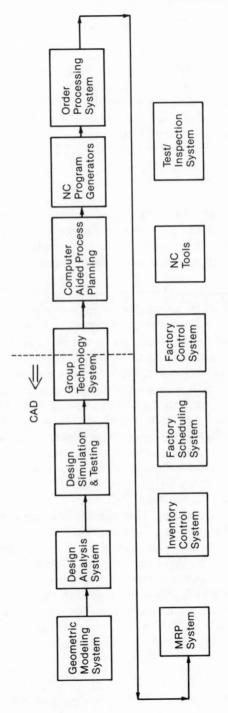

Source: Modified version of a schematic by Paul Kinnucan, "Computer-Aided Manufacturing Aims for Integration," *High Technology*, Vol. 2, (May–June 1982), pp. 52–53.

includes, of course, the technological advances already discussed. Here we explore nontechnical programs designed to interest E/S managers and personnel in order to improve productivity and to obtain better results through organizational routes.

Consciousness Raising. One electronics company interviewed has a series of internally developed seminars which are attended by all levels of management. In these seminars the concept of productivity is introduced. Session attendees are given role playing situations and group problems to solve. The goal is to increase management's awareness and to demonstrate how some common, daily problems can be approached from a productivity viewpoint. The company tries to extend awareness throughout the organization, and encourages employees to internalize the concept so that it becomes a natural, spontaneous consideration both in design and operations.

Another method of increasing productivity awareness is by formal recognition of the problem at the corporate level. One aerospace firm has recently appointed a director of productivity and an electrical equipment manufacturer appointed a vice president in charge of productivity in 1980. The latter also centralized its productivity "push" by establishing a corporate productivity and quality center. Such actions underscore the serious intent of the companies to do all they can to improve productivity.

Centralization, or changes in location, of E/S personnel were also mentioned as tangible indicators of a firm's commitment. Reorganization to improve interaction between research and development and engineering, production and engineering, sales and engineering, etc., can also stimulate E/S productivity.

Improved Organization. A number of companies interviewed indicated that morale and productivity had been enhanced by organizational changes. Over the years, some companies had permitted their E/S staff to grow without corresponding attention to the efficient management of a diverse and highly technical workforce. As a result, E/S were being managed by persons who were not as familiar with new techniques as they should have been or were otherwise lacking in qualifications. These problems were handled by reorganizations, retirements, and other such methods, with consequent productivity improvements.

Introduction of a management by objectives (MBO) system following management training can both increase managerial accountability and increase E/S awareness of productivity needs. An MBO system can both include productivity objectives and specify them as measurement criteria in performance evaluation. Since these two areas are of direct concern both to E/S and to management, MBO can be an important means of integrating the goals of the organization. If introduced correctly, this system can significantly improve management of E/S. Many companies, however, admit that their MBO and performance appraisal systems could stand improvement.[10]

Since the introduction of productivity measures within faulty management systems was often found to be an exercise in frustration, some companies have pursued management programs designed specifically with productivity improvement in mind. One paper company interviewed has developed a "performance management system" for productivity improvement. Through this system, it attempts to measure productivity quantitatively using goal orientation and successful goal development.

Hercules, Inc. has a performance effectiveness program through which a carefully selected and trained group of employees visit the numerous plant sites to conduct "productivity audits." For many years this firm used outside consultants whose expertise helped improve production methods and personnel utilization. The management of the firm decided, however, that individuals within the firm were the true experts on the actual corporate structure as well as on product and process details. This realization prompted the operations division and personnel department to develop an internal consulting team. A consortium of ten plants participate in the program. Each plant lent personnel to the performance team for two years as "resourcers." These employees spent eight of every forty working days on the performance program and the remaining thirty-two at their own jobs. When the performance team goes to a plant, its first task is a seven-day survey of the facility, followed by an analysis of the data collected. Fourteen resourcers are involved in this audit. On the eighth day the proposal for cost effectiveness is presented to the plant's resident manager. Following the initial analysis, the resourcers rotate between their home plant responsibilities and the program. Usually, two resourcers and either a project supervisor or the product manager are on staff. At most plants there can be five people working on the performance program each week. Through this program, plant management has been charged with the responsibility of developing an environment in which each employee can perform in the most effective manner. The general concentration of the performance effectiveness program is on the firm's human

---

[10]William A. Fischer and Curtis P. McLaughlin, "MBO and R&D Productivity: Revisiting the System's Dynamics," *IEEE Transactions on Engineering Management*, Vol. EM-27 (November 1980), pp. 103–8.

resources, and its goal is to improve effectiveness through improved systems and supervisory techniques. Considerable savings have already been realized and the firm is interested in extending the concept to other divisions.[11]

Participation and Enrichment. Various programs for job enrichment, participation, and enhanced quality of work were reported in our survey. The underlying assumption is that involvement and enrichment programs are effective because employees desire increased participation in decisionmaking, job structure, and design. Through group participation, attention to work quality is expected to be instilled in the workforce. The results of these programs were mixed, and the verdict remains to be determined concerning the relationship between E/S participation and increased E/S productivity.

An example of a structured group program is team action management (TAM). It is designed to promote group morale by fostering a spirit of cooperation. Rather than having unstructured discussion groups and vague goals, this approach specifies rules and procedures for the team leader to follow.

> The raw data for the discussions are planning forms, which may be submitted anonymously, each containing a single suggestion. A group of managers responsible for implementing decisions classifies the suggestions and outlines strategies for achieving the desired goals. To eliminate feelings that experts must defend their positions, the managers are assigned to work with topics they do not deal with on a day to day basis.[12]

Many companies have instituted quality circles. One electrical equipment manufacturer has an extensive program of quality circles, several of which have been organized in engineering groups. A defense electronics company has "analysis action teams" which select problems to attack and work at solving them. A pharmaceutical company has a similar "work involvement program" which originated in production and has spread throughout the organization, but has not yet been introduced among the scientific professionals. In fact, an executive of this company commented that the engineers may feel ignored and possibly hostile since they have not been formally included in this program. Some of the production problems tackled by quality circles necessarily involve suggestions to, or solutions from, the engineering department. Alienation is a potential problem if engineering suggestions are not accepted.

---

[11]"Meeting the Challenge of Change," *Hercules Mixer,* No. 1 (1981), pp. 9–14.

[12]"Improved Productivity with T.A.M.," *The Bent of Tau Beta Pi,* Vol. 72 (Summer 1982), p. 4.

A spokesperson at one firm questioned whether quality circles are in fact effective tools for engineers. He felt that the engineers are naturally independent, and therefore may not benefit as much from the quality circle process which requires group activity. He suggested that special courses or seminars which attempt to build quality into design are superior to quality circles for improving engineering productivity. This raises an interesting point: the nature of the individuals who will be involved in potential programs must be considered. Effectiveness or acceptance of a particular program may vary among professional groups.

Quality circles can be effective techniques for improving productivity, but successful work involvement programs require management commitment and training. The mere appointment of a quality group does not guarantee any improvement. On the contrary, hostility and tension may be the result of a floundering or poorly organized circle. Consequently the introduction and supervision of quality circles merits special management consideration. Frequently, facilitators are trained who, in turn, introduce the circle members to group dynamics and problem solving techniques. This training must be structured, interactive, and participative to be successful. The company must be willing to invest in training, and management must be receptive to the ideas and suggestions generated by the employees involved and sensitive to potential problems in the pace and structure of program implementation.

A broader but similar concept to the work involvement team is participative management. One electrical equipment manufacturer has a program called "partners in productivity," which introduces participative management techniques to the workforce.

Other Programs. Many other methods of improving productivity were found during our interviews. One computer company has a "bug" list: a list of problems inhibiting or retarding the progress of its projects. It pays a one-time bonus for elimination of a "bug." This could lead, however, to a disproportionate amount of time being spent on these problems in hopes of qualifying for this additional compensation.

Two other computer companies have developed extensive programs to enhance productivity in systems development by identifying chronological functions and key steps. One firm "is attempting to boost software production by applying the proven manufacturing techniques it uses for hardware. Those techniques rely heavily on setting standards for how software is designed, for how long it takes to be designed and for how well it performs compared to its original specifications."[13] The emphasis is on measuring and documenting progress in a stepwise manner in order to detect problems early, when they are easiest to correct. By requiring increased documentation and creating a more disciplined design process, the company hopes to transform software developments from an unstructured art to a disciplined science.[14]

IMPROVING E/S UTILIZATION

There are many ways in which E/S can be poorly utilized. A company may fail to take advantage of their talents, or individuals may hold back or otherwise fail to give their efforts. In such cases, the professionals are underutilized. In other situations, the E/S may be spending time on work that a nonprofessional could just as easily accomplish. They may be having too many meetings, doing too much paper or administrative work, or otherwise being distracted. In these circumstances, E/S are being misutilized.[15] Our interviews indicate that both underutilization and misutilization are too common and can occur for considerable periods if engineering, scientific, and research departments are not carefully managed. For example, one electrical equipment manufacturer claims that it is not overly concerned about alleged engineering shortages or crises because in practice a good deal of misutilization exists. This company asks: "Why does a technical person get involved in customer order entry? The selection of components can be standardized. The work is then transferred to an order clerk and the engineer is freed for scientific work."[16]

In the discussion which follows, the emphasis will be on the practical approach of "pushing down" certain kinds of work traditionally done by E/S to the technical and less skilled hierarchy below. In our interviews, this was stressed as the most practical way to improve E/S utilization and productivity. The more that routine tasks can be removed from E/S functions and performed by individuals with specific skills, the greater is the availability of E/S for the professional endeavors for which they were trained.

Educational Tiers and Alternate Sources of Supplementary Talent

Figure VI-2 is a schematic of skill hierarchies in engineering and science. Each tier represents the labor pool for a particular constella-

---

[13]White, "Western Electric Is Making Developing of Software Less an Art," p. 30.
[14]*Ibid.*.
[15]R. Richard Ritti, *The Engineer in the Industrial Corporation* (New York: Columbia University Press, 1971), Chapter 5.
[16]Interview, electrical equipment company.

FIGURE VI-2
Technical Employees: Skill Hierarchy

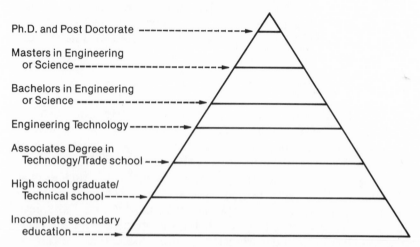

Ph.D. and Post Doctorate

Masters in Engineering
  or Science

Bachelors in Engineering
  or Science

Engineering Technology

Associates Degree in
  Technology/Trade school

High school graduate/
  Technical school

Incomplete secondary
  education

tion of jobs. The highest tier, for which a Ph.D. is the minimum qualification, is occupied by the fewest individuals. As required skill levels become progressively simpler and less conceptual, the size of the
potential labor supply expands.

Typical E/S positions are filled either by masters or bachelors
level engineers or scientists, but individuals holding Ph.D.'s are also
frequently involved in research. Technicians are hired from any of
the lower tiers, depending on company training and philosophy. The
distinction between the job of an engineer or scientist and that of a
technician is often hazy at best. Many technicians have skills that
would enable them to perform jobs for which a degree is traditionally either required or strongly desired. Increasing utilization means
allowing these skilled individuals to perform jobs for which they are
capable, unless specific licensing requirements prove prohibitive. In
addition, it may require enhancing the skills of the technician
through developmental training and encouraging upward mobility.

In a study of unemployment and reemployment pertaining to the
early 1960s, respondents without degrees composed approximately
25 percent of the total population of engineers and scientists
employed by the defense industry. Of these, approximately 46 percent who had attained engineering positions (before they were laid
off) had begun their engineering or scientific careers as technicians.
Fourteen percent began as technical assistants, 8.4 percent as
administrative assistants, and the remainder had worked in other
areas. Relatively more electrical and mechanical engineers began

their careers as technicians, and a majority of chemists and chemical engineers commenced their work as technical assistants.[17]

Most of our interviewees agreed that overhiring of E/S has occurred more since 1982 than in the past. There was general agreement that it has become increasingly difficult for technicians, technical assistants, or administrative assistants to work their way up into E/S positions. Upgrading is more common in engineering than in scientific disciplines, but a profile of the defense industry today would probably indicate a significantly lower percentage of individuals without degrees working in engineering positions. A 1978 survey by the National Science Foundation showed that only 4 to 5 percent of the engineering labor force at that time had less than a bachelor's degree.[18] This survey included all engineering disciplines and was not restricted to the defense industry. Another differentiating factor was that the respondents to the 1978 study were currently working, while those participating in the earlier study had been laid off.

Union restrictions make upgrading more difficult. For example, major engineering unions in the aerospace industry have separate technical and professional bargaining units. The requirements for membership in the professional units have become stricter over the past several decades to make a clearer distinction between the two levels. All new members of the professional unit in one major union must have either an engineering degree or a professional license. Although some of the older members do not have degrees, they worked their way up through the organization at an earlier time when a technician had more upward mobility. Such membership restrictions could inhibit upward mobility, or the upgrading of technicians to engineering positions, and could hinder progress towards maximum utilization of the employees' aggregate skills if the unions become stronger among the professionals.

A question about job segregation or separation was posed to the unions interviewed: "Does the contract strictly define the engineer's job?" This inquiry was based upon the fact that blue-collar unions or skilled craftsmen typically have rigid work rules and territories. Any imposition or infringement by other workers (initiated either by management or another union) on their well-defined jobs quickly sets the grievance machinery rolling. The question attempted to

---

[17]R. P. Loomba, *A Study of the Re-employment and Unemployment Experiences of Scientists and Engineers Laid Off from 62 Aerospace and Electronics Firms in the San Francisco Bay Area During 1963–65* (San Jose, California: Manpower Research Group, San Jose State College, 1967), pp. 31–32.

[18]*U.S. Scientists and Engineers 1978*, NSF 80–304 (Washington, D.C.: National Science Foundation, 1980) Table B-4, pp. 23–24.

determine whether this concept was borrowed by the engineering unions. On the contrary, the engineering unions now seem to recognize the existence of grey areas, and apparently do not generally attempt to restrict professional judgment on skill utilization, perhaps because they do not have the bargaining power to do so. Apparently, technicians may perform higher level tasks when capability exists, but recognition through promotion remains unlikely.

If barriers preventing upgrading can be diminished, alternate sources of talent and support even beyond the hierarchy illustrated in Figure VI-2 are available which enlarge the technical labor pool. For example, many people with military training have had exposure to technology. Individuals may transfer skills from the scientific or mathematical fields. Retraining programs capitalize upon this potential. Engineering students may also be hired for part-time work. A 1951 study by the National Society of Professional Engineers offered the following auxiliary sources of engineering talent:

1. Engineering consulting firms
   a. job shop: to perform a complete engineering job
   b. service company: to work closely with the firm's existing engineers
2. Drafting contract firms
3. Retired engineers on a reduced or flexible schedule
4. Foreign citizens (depending on the current immigration laws)
5. Research organizations
6. Former employees who had been laid off due to lack of work
7. Cooperative students.[19]

It should also be recognized that not all the work performed by engineers or scientists requires technical support. Secretaries and clerical workers can perform many tasks. Computers or other hardware can eliminate repetitive tasks. Alternate labor sources for expanding the technical labor pool and performing nonprofessional functions are diagrammed in Figure VI-3.

Type of Work That Can Be Delegated

Determination of what specific functions currently being performed by degree-holding E/S could be handled by technical support staff is difficult. Categories vary by both industry and company. Careful job analysis is required and employee input is especially important.

---

[19]National Society of Professional Engineers, *How to Improve the Utilization of Engineering Manpower*, Executive Research Survey No. 2 (Washington, D.C.: National Society of Professional Engineers, 1954), pp. 34–36.

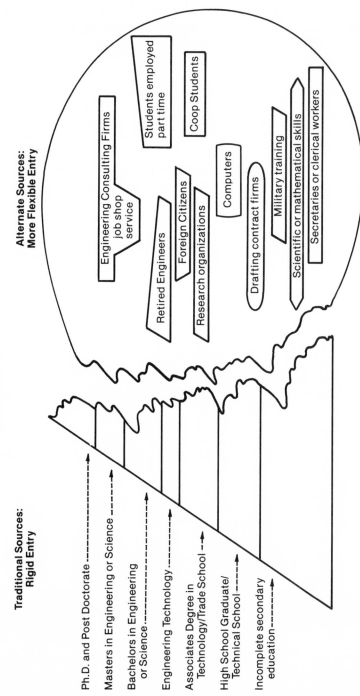

Figure VI-3
Expanded Labor Pool Concept

Traditional Sources:
Rigid Entry

Alternate Sources:
More Flexible Entry

Ph.D. and Post Doctorate

Masters in Engineering or Science

Bachelors in Engineering or Science

Engineering Technology

Associates Degree in Technology/Trade School

High School Graduate/ Technical School

Incomplete secondary education

Engineering Consulting Firms job shop service

Students employed part time

Coop Students

Retired Engineers

Foreign Citizens

Research organizations

Computers

Drafting contract firms

Military training

Scientific or mathematical skills

Secretaries or clerical workers

The National Society of Professional Engineers' suggestions of thirty years ago are still valid concerning the functions that can easily be delegated: drafting, design, changes in drawings, collection and collation of data, calculations, computations, simple layout, expediting, market research, etc.[20] An engineering construction company endorsed these suggestions by revealing that 30 percent of its design employees did not have degrees. An aerospace company made a similar comment about its design group.

If a company is attempting to improve utilization, work simplification and increased standardization should be considered. This allows tasks to be pushed downward through the hierarchy by broadening the base of individuals with skills to perform them, particularly when a computerized data base is developed both for large schematic diagrams and single part descriptions and dimensions.

Several companies described programs to train individuals without technical degrees for technical work. One chemical company with a large research and development laboratory hires high school graduates and trains them as technicians. Most of the individuals working in the network switching department of a communications company are called operating engineers but do not have degrees. They have typically worked their way up through operations or field service. This firm has extensive internal training programs and several training centers. It has developed a set of stringent criteria including aptitude tests, interviews, and performance reviews, to identify employees with potential for upgrading on this program. One industrial equipment company makes extensive use of an in-house, four-year apprentice program as a source of engineers. In addition, it has developed more salary levels below engineers so that individuals can be hired into technical support positions. These programs aim to improve utilization through a reduction in the quantity of the engineer's required paperwork.

Indicators and Measurement Techniques

How can management measure the degree of malutilization in a company? Organization of seminars with the purpose of involving engineers in "work redesign" is an effective technique. Quality circles have been utilized in this effort. Attitude surveys are another method of exposing problems. An individual is, however, likely to give a biased response to a direct question about his job because confessing to monotonous work is not effective self-promotion. E/S are also likely to complain about too much red tape and paperwork

---

[20]*Ibid.*, p. 28.

regardless of the degree to which these are present, but such claims should certainly be explored. Bias does not necessarily render a complaint invalid, it may only be an exaggeration of the truth. Formal recognition of achievement may alleviate dissatisfactions which distort responses on attitude surveys.

Several companies have done studies on optimal engineering/technician ratios, and have experimented with different ratios. One chemical company decided that its optimal ratio of engineers to technicians is one to one. Another company developed optimal ratios by function: manufacturing, design, research and development, etc. The numbers are less significant in this case than the theory. It is possible to monitor ratios over time to determine effective utilization rates. This is very similar to monitoring productivity ratios, as described previously. Such studies can suggest optimal ratios which can be used as a general tool for human resource planning, such as comparison between various operations, developing staffing needs for new divisions, projections under various scenarios of growth, etc.

Reasons for Malutilization

The material presented thus far stresses increasing utilization as a technique for improving productivity and adjusting to shortages. With the expanded labor pool concept, availability is not a critical problem if work is assigned efficiently. Yet many companies still have a tendency to overhire. This practice is recognized as a waste of scientific and engineering talent. There are several reasons why it continues to occur.

At the onset of a project, the depth and breadth of required skills may be estimated, but certainly not predicted with precision. It is literally impossible to synchronize available skills with activities, especially if E/S personnel have become overspecialized.

In addition, small companies may not have the resources to support their scientific professionals. Thus the E/S are responsible for all facets of the job. More specifically, the problem of "providing competitive salary and benefits" was cited as a major concern by 69 percent of the firms surveyed by a National Science Foundation study.[21] The difficulty in compensating key line personnel leads to the conclusion that secondary or support staff are often missing or sparse in these organizations.

---

[21]William L. Stewart and Norman W. Friedman, *Problems of Small High Technology Firms*, NSF 81–305 (Washington, D.C.: National Science Foundation, 1981), p. 4.

The phenomenon of "goldplating" was mentioned repeatedly by engineering construction firms. Engineering construction is basically a service industry, selling design expertise, reputation, and capability. Goldplating occurs because potential clients evaluate proposals submitted by a variety of firms. Judgements are made about individuals composing the project teams based upon their education and experience. The client tends to prefer degree-holding or licensed engineers on the team, even though non-degree personnel might be quite competent for certain jobs.

One petroleum company stated that the explicit company policy is to overhire E/S. It prefers not to use technicians. Its major objection to employing non-degree or technical support personnel to perform some of the more routine tasks typically done by E/S was lack of promotional opportunities if further education is not attained. The company has a carefully developed dual career ladder for E/S. It has found that non-degree or technical support personnel bump up on a barrier and end up as discontented personnel in dead-end jobs, as diagrammed in Figure VI-4. It also has found that some of these personnel are minorities and that equal employment opportunity problems result even from what the company believes are very legitimate professional standards for upward mobility.

A similar attitude was expressed by a paper company, which felt that such a barrier created frustration among technical support personnel, increasing their susceptibility to unionization. The frustration may be even greater in the environment of a research laboratory. The upgrading opportunities that were so common several decades ago have been reduced significantly. Although this might be a product of management bias, it seems most likely that increasing complexity of technology and the fast pace of technological change necessitates higher levels of education for all positions.

To overcome such barriers and to efficiently utilize non-degree technicians, one major conglomerate has recently developed a separate technical administration/general business administration career ladder which does not require in-depth understanding of advanced engineering or scientific theories. This ladder complements the traditional dual ladder, enhancing the promotional opportunities of technicians.

One paper company recognized that few technical support personnel had the background or skills to move up through engineering or scientific disciplines. It therefore established special awards and incentives specifically for technicians to give increased opportunity for professional recognition.

Another career-related problem is the fate of technicians or techni-

FIGURE VI-4
Technical Support Ladder

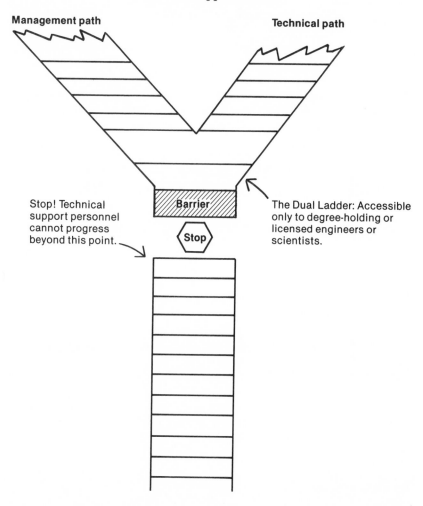

cal assistants who get bachelors degrees in an engineering or scientific discipline at night school. If the company does not consciously attempt to recognize this achievement, the individual will likely not experience a change in status or receive increased recognition through promotion. One company included funds in its budget to ensure that the individual received peer and management recognition through a sponsored event such as a party or luncheon.

If one adopts the expanded labor pool concept, flexible deployment of the technical workforce is enhanced. Flexibility is important in today's environment because the mix of skills required for engineering and technical support have been changing, and will continue to change as automation permeates the workplace. Formal retraining, as described in previous chapters, is becoming more common. Retraining involves engineers, scientists, and technicians. Effective human resources planning demands a critical analysis of the actual skills required to perform particular tasks. When these skills have been determined, consideration must be made of all individuals with the ability to perform these tasks regardless of formal training (unless a license is required for legal reasons).

CONCLUSION

Effective utilization and improved productivity of E/S is a problem that companies continue to address, yet never fully solve. The policies and procedures described herein are examples of attempts to meet a persistent problem with a variety of responses. Clearly, the principle of increasing utilization cannot be applied to every situation, but there are many areas where it is appropriate. Promotional opportunities and related management issues must be analyzed to ensure that logical upward flows are possible. Perhaps new avenues must be designed to allow nontraditional sources of technical talent to filter into and upwards in the organization. Companies that meet this challenge maximize their returns on their capital investment in E/S.

CHAPTER VII

Salaries, Benefits, and Recognition

In order to recruit and to retain a corps of engineers and scientists (E/S), companies must pay salaries and benefits that at least meet market standards. The evidence presented below indicates that, on average, E/S are well compensated, but that there are some problems relating to salary relationship.

Companies have also found it helpful to offer special tangible and intangible rewards to engineers and scientists as recognition for their efforts. Policies of companies in regard to such matters are discussed in the second part of this chapter.

SALARIES AND BENEFITS

Figures VII-1 and VII-2 show the starting salaries of chemists and engineers by degree levels for the years 1966–1982, and 1972–1982, respectively. The upward trend in these starting salaries reflects both inflation and demand. The dip in the upward movement for engineers, 1970–71, is probably attributable to the precipitous decline in the demand for E/S by the aerospace industry during this period. The data in Figures VII-1 and VII-2 show that the return on investment of an engineering master's degree is relatively small in comparison to that of a bachelor's degree, but that the Ph.D. has a very substantial payoff over both lower degrees.

Within the engineering profession, the relative starting salaries clearly reflect demand-supply conditions. Thus in 1980, before the increase in energy supplies thwarted the oil cartel's ability to maintain monopoly prices, petroleum engineers received the highest starting salaries of engineering bachelor's degree recipients.[1] By July 1983, this was still the case[2] despite the oil glut, perhaps because the supply for the major petroleum companies remained small. The starting salaries of computer and electrical engineers for employees of all degree levels have been very high throughout the 1970s and into the 1980s, but the increase in the number of students

[1]Eleanor L. Babco, *Salaries of Scientists, Engineers, and Technicians,* Tenth Edition (Washington, D.C.: Scientific Manpower Commission, 1981), Table 21, p. 16.

[2]Eleanor L. Babco, *Salaries of Scientists, Engineers, and Technicians,* Eleventh Edition (Washington, D.C.: Scientific Manpower Commission, 1983), Table 2, p. 6.

FIGURE VII-1
*Trends in Starting Salaries to Engineering
and Technology Graduates by Degree, 1966–1982*

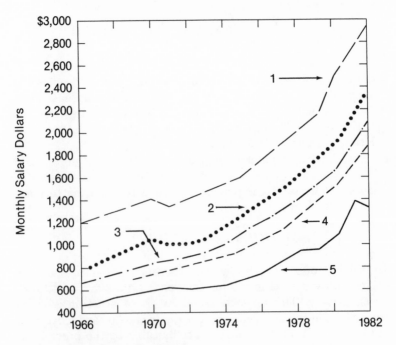

1—Ph.D. Engineering Graduates
2—M.S. Engineering Graduates
3—B.S. Engineering Graduates
4—B.S. Technology Graduates
5—2-Year Technology Graduates

Source: Engineering Manpower Commission, "Placement Highlights, 1982: A Changing National Picture," *Engineering Manpower Bulletin,* No. 63 (November
1982); reproduced by permission from Eleanor L. Babco, *Salaries of Scientists, Engineers and Technicians,* Eleventh Edition (Washington, D.C.: Scientific Manpower Commission, 1983), p. 28.

pursuing computer engineering degrees could dampen the salaries of
this group in the future.[3] Table VII-1 lists the starting salaries of
engineering graduates by curriculum and degree level in July 1982.
Table VII-2 lists the starting salaries for E/S by field of degree,
degree level, and type of employer, for 1982. The data in these tables

---

[3]Bob Davis, "Big Demand for Computer Courses Exceeds Many Colleges'
Resources," *Wall Street Journal,* October 16, 1984, p. 31.

FIGURE VII-2
*Trends in Annual Median Starting Salaries
of Inexperienced Chemists
by Degree Level, 1972–82*

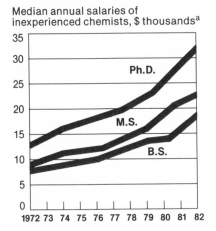

Median annual salaries of
inexperienced chemists, $ thousands[a]

[a]Chemists with 12 months or less of professional
experience; data as of about June of each year.

Source: *Chemical and Engineering News,* October 18, 1982; reproduced by permission
from Eleanor L. Babco, *Salaries of Scientists, Engineers and Technicians,*
Eleventh Edition (Washington, D.C.: Scientific Manpower Commission,
1983), p. 18.

further emphasize that a degree in engineering or science usually
leads to a well-paying starting position.

The salaries of E/S continue to improve throughout the term of
their employment. Table VII-3 shows the number and mean monthly
salaries of nonsupervisory scientists and engineers by degree level,
type of establishment, and selected years since first degree, for
1982. It is interesting to note not only the salary progression as
experience increases, but also the fact that the federal government
pays more for both relatively inexperienced and very experienced
bachelor candidates. The salaries in contract research centers and
industry are higher for those with master's or doctoral degrees, with
industry jobs the best paid at all levels for advanced degree recipients. The salaries of E/S at educational institutions are comparatively low for all degree levels as the data in Table VII-3 shows.
Although many E/S educators have opportunities to supplement
their incomes, the data in Table VII-3 clearly illustrate why the lure
of industry is so strong.

TABLE VII-1
Monthly Starting Salaries of Engineering Graduates by
Curriculum and Degree Level, 1982

Curriculum	Degree Level		
	B.S.	M.S.	Ph.D.
Aerospace	$1,864	$2,231	$3,300
Agricultural	1,922		
Architectural	1,783		
Ceramic	2,137		
Chemical	2,215	2,332	3,006
Civil	1,914	2,183	2,645
Computer	1,968	2,367	3,190
Electrical and electronic	2,058	2,369	2,991
Mechanical	2,097	2,302	2,885
Metallurgical	2,092	2,445	2,756
Mining and geological	2,197	2,463	2,945
Marine	1,988	2,000	
Nuclear	2,106	2,335	2,769
Petroleum	2,578	2,655	3,208
Overall	2,077	2,335	2,941

Source: Engineering Manpower Commission, *The Placement of Engineering and Technology Graduates 1982;* reproduced by permission from Eleanor L. Babco, *Salaries of Scientists, Engineers and Technicians,* Eleventh Edition (Washington, D.C.: Scientific Manpower Commission, 1983), p. 27.

Benefits

Most major companies have complete, and often elaborate, benefit programs which cover E/S. Such plans include pensions; health, life, and accident insurance; and sick leave and disability programs. The 1983 salary and fringe benefit survey of the Institute of Electrical and Electronics Engineers, Inc. (IEEE) found that 88 percent of the respondents who were neither self-employed nor unemployed had employer-provided pension plans; a smaller, but substantial portion of IEEE member employers—62 percent—provided profit-sharing, savings, or other such programs; "very few respondents" reported that their employers did not provide health insurance that included major medical coverage, and almost two-thirds of the respondents reported that their employers paid for the full cost of these plans; 80 percent of the employers provided dental insurance, and 65 percent of those receiving this coverage reported that their employer paid the full cost; and 94 percent of the respondents reported that their employer provided life insurance coverage, 57 percent of those reporting that the employer paid full cost.[4]

---

[4]*IEEE U.S. Membership Salary & Fringe Benefit Survey 1983* (New York: Institute of Electrical and Electronics Engineers, Inc., 1983), UHO 152-9, p. 24.

TABLE VII-2
Starting Salaries of Scientists by Field, Type of Employer and Highest Degree Attained, 1981

Field	Estimated Number Employed in 1980	Type of Employer					
		1981 Private Industry			1981 Federal Government		
		B.S.	M.S.	Ph.D.	B.S.	M.S.	Ph.D.
Engineers	1,200,000	$22,900	$25,500	$32,800	$15,947–19,747	$22,925	$24,763
Mathematicians[a]	40,000	17,700	20,200	26,400	12,266–15,193	18,585–22,486	22,486–26,951
Statisticians[a]	26,500				12,266–15,193	18,585–22,486	22,486–26,951
Agricultural	35,000	15,400			12,266–15,193	15,193–18,585	22,486–26,951
Biological	90,000	15,200			12,266–15,193	15,193–18,585	22,486–26,951
Foresters	30,000		15,200[b]		12,266	15,193	18,585–22,486
Geologists	34,000	22,150	25,320		12,300–15,200	15,200–18,600	22,500–27,000
Geophysicists	12,000	22,150	25,320		12,300–15,200	15,200–18,600	22,500–27,000
Meteorologists	4,000				12,300–15,200	15,200–18,600	22,500–27,000
Chemists	113,000	19,600	23,600	29,800	12,266–15,193	18,585	22,486–26,951
Physicists	37,000	21,840	23,760	30,540	12,266–15,193	15,193–18,585	22,486–26,951

Source: U.S. Department of Labor, *Occupational Outlook Handbook*, 82–83 Edition; reproduced by permission from Eleanor L. Babco, *Salaries of Scientists, Engineers and Technicians*, Eleventh Edition (Washington, D.C.: Scientific Manpower Commission, 1983), p. 29.
[a]Federal salaries are for 1980.
[b]Average salary all levels.

Although these data apply only to members of one engineering society, there is no substantial reason for believing that they are not typical of all E/S working in major industries. Our own interviews also included questions on benefit packages of this nature; in reply to which, the respondents usually provided us with the company's benefit booklet. We found none that did not include the basic benefit package described above, although savings plans were more common (about 85 percent of the companies interviewed had them for E/S and other managerial employees) than profit-sharing plans (about a 35 percent coverage for E/S) and stock options (available for E/S in about one-third of the companies). On the other hand, the high

TABLE VII-3

Number and Mean Monthly Salaries of Nonsupervisory Scientists and Engineers by Degree Level, Type of Establishment, and Selected Years Since First Degree, 1982

Type of Establishment & Degree Level	Selected Years Since First Degree									
	2	4	7	10	13	15	20–21	24–25	30–31	Total[a]
Bachelor's Degree										
Nonprofit research institutes	(160) $1,726	(139) $1,938	(93) $1,972	(64) $2,381	(57) $2,482	(37) $2,711	(68) $2,826	(53) $2,964	(45) $2,813	(2,034) $2,294
Educational institutions	(115) 1,360	(85) 1,372	(37) 1,522	(26) 1,973	(23) 2,204	(14) 1,907	(15) 2,400	(14) 2,707	(11) 2,800	(1,059) 1,738
Contract research centers	(199) 2,158	(177) 2,303	(85) 2,487	(99) 2,740	(86) 2,981	(72) 3,129	(173) 3,381	(170) 3,509	(191) 3,537	(3,650) 2,964
Federal establishments	(69) 1,904	(60) 2,225	(53) 2,355	(51) 2,506	(38) 2,689	(54) 2,935	(166) 3,270	(147) 3,430	(76) 3,367	(2,021) 2,904
Total industry	(2,877) 2,223	(1,682) 2,393	(907) 2,559	(840) 2,778	(662) 2,946	(561) 3,079	(1,034) 3,290	(1,086) 3,396	(1,091) 3,393	(30,188) 2,738
Master's Degree										
Nonprofit research institutes	(12) 2,100	(53) 2,158	(61) 2,316	(74) 2,482	(45) 2,660	(49) 2,822	(73) 3,110	(59) 3,278	(36) 3,333	(1,356) 2,746
Educational institutions	(3) 1,633	(48) 1,633	(68) 1,606	(46) 1,846	(37) 2,146	(34) 2,141	(19) 2,426	(31) 2,532	(17) 2,735	(910) 2,037
Contract research centers	(43) 2,384	(99) 2,399	(125) 2,566	(149) 2,792	(109) 2,999	(103) 3,241	(203) 3,477	(169) 3,614	(151) 3,758	(3,410) 3,186
Federal establishments	(2) 1,650	(14) 2,029	(15) 2,453	(28) 2,457	(27) 2,715	(19) 2,858	(41) 3,293	(23) 3,343	(17) 3,371	(546) 2,864
Total industry	(183) 2,377	(404) 2,512	(577) 2,688	(489) 2,904	(436) 3,108	(428) 3,230	(659) 3,505	(563) 3,641	(459) 3,597	(11,872) 3,146

Doctorate Degree

Nonprofit research institutes	(3) 1,667	(31) 2,445	(57) 2,554	(67) 2,852	(52) 2,963	(72) 3,188	(41) 3,605	(26) 3,762	(1,078) 3,125
Educational institutions	(9) 1,578	(65) 2,032	(89) 2,098	(89) 2,502	(105) 2,567	(127) 2,905	(87) 3,133	(71) 3,369	(1,983) 2,714
Contract research centers	(1) 2,400	(57) 2,858	(115) 2,884	(140) 3,051	(150) 3,283	(274) 3,631	(144) 3,848	(104) 3,809	(3,088) 3,446
Federal establishments	(1) 2,000 (1) 2,400	(4) 2,575	(18) 2,472	(29) 2,590	(23) 2,822	(34) 3,326	(21) 3,724	(9) 3,544	(409) 3,103
Total industry	(12) 3,050	(145) 2,866	(217) 3,086	(230) 3,291	(225) 3,482	(342) 3,847	(234) 3,921	(166) 4,167	(4,778) 3,573

Source: Battelle Columbus Laboratories, *Report on 1982 National Survey of Compensation Paid Scientists and Engineers Engaged in Research and Development Activities,* December 1982; reproduced by permission from Eleanor L. Babco, *Salaries of Scientists, Engineers and Technicians,* Eleventh Edition (Washington, D.C.: Scientific Manpower Commission, 1984), p. 53.

[a]Total includes all years since first degree.

Note: Numbers in parenthesis are survey respondents.

cost of medical benefits has caused many companies to place more of the cost burden of such benefits on employees, and this will undoubtedly show up in future IEEE surveys.

Holidays, vacations, and other paid time off generally vary according to the industry and region, and also tend to vary with seniority. E/S may receive up to six weeks vacation for long service (20–25 years), but one month is typical.[5] Some companies have a formal sick leave plan; most provide sick leave at least informally.

Perquisites

Perquisites can be considered a special subset of benefits for they are a portion of total compensation, but available only to a specially designated group of employees. Many large companies do not offer any perquisites specifically for E/S. For utilities, creativity or flexibility in offering benefits is reduced by regulation. At the other end of the spectrum, small firms tend to use perquisites quite generously, especially in critical skill areas such as computer science and also in those geographical locations where competition for employees is especially strong, such as in the Silicon Valley.

Perquisites are instituted to recruit and to retain employees, and usually originate in response to environmental pressures. For example, some firms award substantial up-front bonuses to E/S with specific critical skills as a recruiting tool. General perquisites associated with retention include flexible schedules, large offices, a campus environment, and lavish athletic facilities (tennis, swimming, racquetball, etc.). Many small, high technology firms offer stock options, discounts on stock purchases, and profit sharing to lure professionals away from competitors. Perquisites can also be used to spur productivity improvement: "Xerox's Shugart Corp. and Advanced Micro Devices dangle cash bonuses before workers who meet or beat deadlines. Data General awards cash and stock to software programmers."[6]

At the height of the oil shortage, geologists, petroleum engineers, and other earth scientists received many perquisites as recruitment and retention bonuses. Likewise, many perquisites have been given for recruiting and retaining computer scientists. For example, existing employees are offered "add-a-friend" bonuses and are invited to participate in recruiting raffles. Computer scientists are frequently given flexible schedules, rewarded with upfront bonuses, given lib-

---

[5]These findings were corroborated by the IEEE Survey, *ibid.*, p. 27.
[6]"Labor Letter," *Wall Street Journal*, May 3, 1983, p. 1.

eral overtime allowances, and are sometimes assisted in the purchase of personal terminals and minicomputers.

Although perquisites are an attractive method of achieving short-term results, they can cause feelings of inequity if they are created as temporary programs or in response to transitory conditions. Moreover, they can be an expensive mistake if conditions change dramatically. For example, special benefits for earth scientists given during the oil boom proved embarrassingly unproductive and costly a few years, or even months, later when the oil crisis had transformed from a shortage to a glut. Long-term commitments which are more likely to reflect an entire corporate philosophy, such as a campus environment or dedication to physical fitness, and which are extended to all employees rather than a few select groups, are less risky than one-time awards. Thus, perquisites which are most closely linked with general benefits tend to be the most successful in creating goodwill among all employees. Special programs or plans can then become an aspect of a firm's reward and recognition policy.

Salary Administration and Compensation Problems

Most firms interviewed had reasonably formal salary evaluation and administration systems covering E/S. Basically, under such systems, positions are evaluated and graded using various criteria, such as the knowledge and education required, responsibility involved, etc.[7] Evaluation plans for E/S must be consistent with those of other employees so that inequities do not appear when salaries are determined.

Salary evaluation or classification schemes do not set salaries or salary ranges, but rather place jobs in a logical order consistent with upgrading and developmental progressions. Salaries are then established based on market realities. In the overwhelming number of situations found by our interviews, salary ranges are established, rather than individual salary rates, so that individuals can be rewarded financially for good work without necessarily being promoted to a higher grade. Most companies have several grades for E/S.[8]

---

[7]Salary administration has a large literature including numerous textbooks. For an explanation of basic job evaluation or other salary classification systems, see, for example, David W. Belcher, *Compensation Administration* (Englewood Cliffs, N.J.: Prentice-Hall, Inc., 1974), Chapters 4–9; also Richard I. Henderson, *Compensation Management: Rewarding Performance in the Modern Organization* (Reston, VA: Reston Publishing Company, Inc., 1976), Chapters 6–12.

[8]The National Society of Professional Engineers recognizes nine different grades of engineers. See *Professional Engineer Income and Salary Survey, 1984* (Washington, D.C.: National Society of Professional Engineers, 1984), p. 11, and Appendix A, p. 24.

Many firms assign overlapping brackets (or ranges) to salary levels using various relative job ranking schemes. Each level is assigned a minimum, median, and maximum salary. Salary guide curves, frequently called maturity curves, are used to show how average salaries increase with greater experience. The ranges for pay are established by curves rather than defined job levels.

When setting appropriate salary levels, a firm must select a basic compensation strategy: i.e. whether it will offer compensation approximately equal to, greater than, or less than that offered by similar firms in the same industry and geographic area. Once this basic strategy is decided upon, competitive levels can be obtained through participation in, or subscription to, salary comparisons performed by consulting firms, or by salary surveys compiled by professional societies. Most firms interviewed seemed to prefer the data provided by consulting firms. Several firms mentioned that they refer to professional society data for general information but indicated that they felt the data are biased upwards. Salary data for E/S, as indicated by the information presented earlier in this chapter, are abundant.

Once salary ranges have been established, the most basic type of increase awarded is the general increase. The firm will designate a set of funds as available for employee raises. Amounts are then allocated to divisional and departmental levels. Each individual a standard salary increase based on his position within the appropriate unit. This may be expressed as a fixed amount per paycheck, but is usually reported as a percentage of current income. One type of general increase which has been quite controversial in regard to engineers' salaries in the aerospace industry is the cost of living adjustment (COLA). This topic received considerable attention when the inflation rate was high. E/S in many firms compared their increase to those obtained by blue-collar union workers covered by COLA clauses in union contracts and found that the salary differentials between the two groups had declined and that their real salaries were deteriorating. At least one nonunion aerospace company gives COLA increases to all E/S. Another firm provided a capped COLA increase as a portion of the salary adjustment section in its engineer union contract.

One firm granted COLA increases as a direct response to pressures created by an organizing drive among engineers. The unionization attempt was not successful, but the firm continues to pay COLA increases to engineers. In 1981, the Engineers and Scientists Guild (Lockheed) struck for nine weeks over COLA. Nevertheless, this radical action was not successful for no COLA clause was negotiated into their contract.[9] Any future periods of high inflation will undoubtedly result in a rekindling of this issue.

Most firms, however, reserve the bulk of their E/S salary adjustment funds for merit increases based on employee performance. In a bracket system, the salary range is predetermined by the assigned level. An individual may, however, receive a bracket merit increase concurrently with a general salary raise. Sometimes brackets are overlaid with performance criteria to create grids. Increases are then assigned based both upon an individual's performance and his relative position within the bracket salary range. In a maturity curve system, relative rankings are assigned to determine which curve should be used to award increases. Both the brackets and maturity curve salary ranges are updated at least yearly. Salary adjustments which are designated as merit increases can either be linked to the performance appraisal process or based on relative performance rankings, or both. Skill and care in administration are required to effectively link performance increases. Special attention must be paid to developing and maintaining realistic appraisals by careful training and auditing of supervisors.

Despite elaborate evaluation procedures and careful salary administration, companies have encountered a number of perplexing problems in compensating E/S, all of which were exacerbated by inflation during the 1970s and early 1980s. These include the relative role of general and merit increases, salary comparisons, other internal equity problems, and overtime payments and hours.

General vs. Merit Increases. Once positions have been evaluated and rate ranges established, the employees themselves must be evaluated and their salaries determined within the established ranges of their positions. Essentially, the task is to identify on a regular basis the relative differences in employee performance within each classification. Typically, each supervisor ranks each subordinate, and peer supervisors then develop a combined list. The next step is to determine whether a salary increase is justified. A target salary is set which reflects the relative performance of an employee when compared to other employees in the same job level or work group. Based on the current salary compared to the target, a recommendation is made for actual timing and size of the increase. Documentation is required to support actions taken during each step. Human resource departments coordinate the entire operation.

---

[9]See Geoffrey W. Latta, "Union Organization Among Engineers: A Current Assessment," *Industrial and Labor Relations Review,* Vol. 35 (October 1981), pp. 29–42, reproduced in Appendix C, for more information on the unionization of engineers.

Such a system relies wholly on individual merit and promotion for salary increases. General salary increases are not given; salary grades are, however, adjusted to account for cost of living increases, labor market conditions, etc., so that upward movement in salaries is not frozen.

A pharmaceutical firm recently made a transition to such a salary policy that provides increases to all exempt employees solely on the basis of their individual performance. This change was enacted to improve the salary increase opportunity for the best workers, to demonstrate commitment to rewarding individual effort, to emphasize productivity, and to improve the firm's competitive position in the industry. The administration of this policy is relatively simple. An individual's immediate supervisor develops a salary plan based on an annual review of the employee's performance. Senior line management and human resources personnel then audit all salary plans and programs for implementation. Human resources representatives work to maintain equitable control points throughout the organization.

One petroleum company reported having a combined system of salary range curves and levels. When individuals join the firm upon completion of a degree, they are evaluated and placed on a curve. The curves determine salary based on rank: 20 percent on the top curve, 60 percent in the middle, and 20 percent in the low range. The pay in this system is based partially on potential. This firm finds that using curves allows it to be competitive and also to deal more effectively with the problem of salary compression. Increases are given at intervals of six to twelve months. Class ranking determines on which curve the individual is initially placed, but performance evaluation is used once the individual begins working. After four or five years in the operating companies (and up to ten years in research), the E/S is placed into a grade or level. Pay in the grade system is based entirely on performance. Curves permit outstanding employees to receive fair compensation. Thus, although one's initial grade is not restricting, it should be a reflection both of performance and potential. Increases in the grade system occur every nine to fifteen months. General or cost of living adjustments also become part of salary increases as grade levels are adjusted yearly.

The system of one metals manufacturer is to evaluate all jobs and place them in grades. For each grade, there is a salary range. Each individual receives two monthly accruals. One is a general economic increase which includes a portion for COLA. The other is a merit increase. Accruals are aggregated over a period of months. When the total of the two accrual pools for an individual is 8 to 10 percent, a raise is given. Thus, all increases are awarded individually. The time period between increases could be eight to fifteen months depending on both the economy and the individual's performance. A continuum is kept of increases occurring throughout the year. All accrual pools are computerized. The supervisor feeds the appraisal into the system and may change it at any time.

Another firm interviewed has a joint type of evaluation which emphasizes merit in order to increase employee motivation. All division managers have a combined meeting to compose a relative ranking order of individuals. Here, the performance review is also the salary review. It has two parts. First, the position rate is reviewed. An individual cannot be awarded a salary greater than the position rate dictates. Second, a merit bonus may be awarded to those who have superior performance. This amount can be up to 25 percent of the individual's annual salary ($5,000 to $10,000) and is paid once a year. Before this program was established, an individual received only an increased salary level. The lump-sum system was adopted to enhance the individual employee's motivation. It could, however, be argued that a bonus system is not necessary. The unit manager at this firm indicated that people who do outstanding work usually do it anyway, regardless of whether or not they receive a bonus. This is supported by the fact that practically 30 percent of the bonuses awarded are repeats.

At the same firm, career planning is differentiated from performance appraisal. In a "potential" review, career possibilities are discussed with the individual in terms of career pathing within the company. It is recognized that an individual's performance may be satisfactory or even outstanding, but that he may not have the potential to advance in the company. The firm also recognizes that an employee who possesses a high degree of potential does not necessarily perform above average in every position which he occupies. Nevertheless, the nature of this company makes it important for each employee to obtain broad exposure; rotation may, therefore, be encouraged especially to strengthen any areas of weakness an employee might have.

Despite several elaborate systems, none of the firms interviewed expressed complete satisfaction over the methods used to deal with problems caused by double-digit inflation. Those who attempted to rely solely on merit increases found, as discussed below, considerable discontent among their E/S. These E/S felt, usually quite correctly, that merit increases did not compensate them reasonably for inflation and that their incomes were both declining in real terms and failing to keep pace with those of unionized employees covered by agreements containing COLA clauses. The point must be made, however, that merit increases are designed to reward individual performance, not to offset the increased cost of living.

General increases to compensate for increases in the cost of living also give rise to problems. Such increases tend to obscure differences in performance among E/S and thus to reward top and marginal contributors alike. Moreover, particularly when the economy is troubled, general increases tend to soak up salary increase funds and leave less available for merit awards. During periods of high inflation, modest general increases plus a merit system may be the best answer. In such times, real income is likely to drop and, as discussed below, compression with blue-collar workers is best avoided by not agreeing to COLA clauses in union contracts rather than duplicating them for E/S.

Compression. As depicted in Figure VII-3, compression is a two-pronged problem. The first is the annual practice of raising the starting salaries of new E/S graduates without providing comparable increases for experienced E/S. This narrows the gap between the salaries of the two groups, resulting in a highly negative response from experienced E/S. Most anticompression policies are aimed at this problem.

There is, however, another problem which is not as severe today as it was during the high inflation period of the 1970s and early 1980s. It involves the perception that the salary differentials between blue-collar and professional employees has been narrowing. The extent of COLA agreements among unionized workers, and the attempts of E/S management to utilize merit programs to handle the inflation problem, undoubtedly gave credence to this perception.

Practically all companies interviewed for this study agreed that compression had adversely affected their internal salary administration process. Although most firms have developed techniques to minimize the problems or inequities which developed as a result of compression, most also believe that such actions contribute only minimally to resolving the problem, given its magnitude. Two firms do not hire college graduates directly from school. Instead, they recruit experienced professionals by "catching them on their second bounce." This helps shield them from the first of the compression forces. At one computer company, salary reviews are given three times per year. Although increases are smaller, employees receive incremental adjustments which more closely track changing prices. One diversified firm has established a salary improvement fund specifically to deal with compression. Disbursements are concentrated on individuals with one to five years of experience so that at least

FIGURE VII-3
The Problem of Compression is Two Pronged

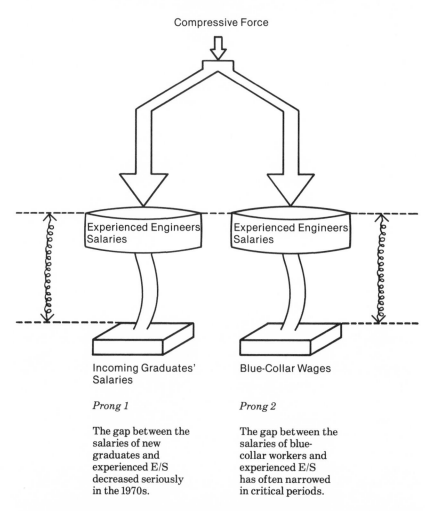

Compressive Force

Experienced Engineers Salaries

Experienced Engineers Salaries

Incoming Graduates'
Salaries

Blue-Collar Wages

Prong 1

Prong 2

The gap between the
salaries of new
graduates and
experienced E/S
decreased seriously
in the 1970s.

The gap between the
salaries of blue-
collar workers and
experienced E/S
has often narrowed
in critical periods.

some differential is maintained with new graduates' salaries. An engineering construction firm has a formal program of scheduled increases for the first two years specifically to deal with compression. A pharmaceutical company has given a few early promotions with no change in job content so salaries could be adjusted accordingly. This, of course, can create other equity problems. Some firms approach the problem by allowing liberal overtime pay to experienced professionals in order to widen this total compensation gap, but as discussed below, that can also create additional problems.

Considerations stemming from the compression problem include the optimal timing of the salary review. Most firms interviewed have annual salary adjustments. New graduates, however, occasionally receive more frequent reviews for two to three years after joining a firm so that effects of compression can be dampened. On the other hand, several firms which suffered from the impact of the most recent recession increased the interval between reviews for experienced engineers from twelve to eighteen months. In fact, those firms most adversely affected by the economy in the early 1980s had resorted to pay freezes as a means of preventing layoffs. Such action, however necessary, can create bad will as well as permanent salary administration problems.

The problem of compression between blue-collar and professional employees relates most specifically to the failure of some companies to treat their nonunion professionals as well as they do their hourly workers. The problem of COLA as a causal factor has already been noted. Overtime payments to hourly employees during a period of extended long hours is another problem, which will be discussed below. Failure to adjust salary schedules as wages rise is a third cause. A fourth cause, very prominent during the recession of the early 1980s, involved wage freezes and "givebacks" from salaried employees without equal sacrifice from unionized hourly workers.

In times of economic crisis, such inequitable approaches are understandable but not laudable. Essentially, they involve treating key, management-oriented employees shabbily. The offending company is likely to lose its key E/S, and/or become susceptible to unionization. Unless the compression between E/S and blue-collar workers is corrected by management, the net result will certainly be a negative one for the company.

Other Internal Inequities. In an endeavor to achieve objectivity, some companies interviewed segregate performance appraisal from salary review; others, however, encourage, or even insist upon, concurrent treatment of the topics. In both cases, the actual salary increase, if awarded at least partially on merit, is supposedly determined by the employee's performance. Several firms claiming to adjust salaries on a merit basis had no formal performance review. Yet lack of documentation exacerbates problems with disgruntled employees. Most firms, however, require formal written evaluations.

Ranking employees may be an alternative to individual appraisals. Rather than completing a specific evaluation on each employee, a supervisor will compare the relative performances of his subordinates. Raises are then administered based on this relative appraisal. Some firms with individual written evaluations also apply the technique of performance ranking for salary administration purposes. Thus both written evaluations and formal ranking serve as input for salary adjustment decisions. This process frequently is monitored by human resources personnel to ensure that uniformity exists across departments and/or divisions, and that aggregate adjustments remain within company guidelines.

Despite apparently heroic attempts by many firms to ensure that merit increases are given where deserved, one compensation consulting firm believes that companies rarely give accurate performance appraisals and that most are biased positively. When negative appraisals are given, however, their results are often not reflected in the employee's salary. This firm finds that rewards provide only minimal differentiation between high and low performers and therefore do not motivate employees to improve their job performance: "There is virtually no penalty at most companies for being a poor performer. More important, there is minimal reward for being a star."[10] When this is the case, the incentive value of compensation in firms is substantially reduced. In fact, this value begins to approach zero and incentive may even decrease if programs which claim to "pay for performance" do so in name instead of dollars.

Despite monitoring by human resources personnel, several firms interviewed mentioned that significant salary differentials existed internally. This may be a result of competitive pressures and/or the structure of the corporate organization. For example, the information systems unit (ISU) of a large petrochemical company found that the computer scientists working in the operating units had a salary scale approximately 10 percent higher than those who worked for their group directly. This was attributed to the generally high compensation in the petroleum industry. When, however, openings in operating units were posted, individuals from the ISU frequently responded. This increased the outflow of computer scientists from the ISU and consequently aggravated this division's recruiting problems.

This experience is typical of what often occurs when critical skill areas develop. Firms then must pay a premium to attract the skill that is in short supply. Frequently, this skews the salary structure, causing inequities and unrest. If the salary structure and salary grades are not adjusted to more closely reflect reality, they can become meaningless under such pressures.

Salary structures must be aligned with upgrading opportunities so that they encourage maximum development of personnel. More-

---

[10]"Compensation Consultants Recommend Closer Ties of Pay, Job Performance," *Daily Labor Report,* No. 14, January 20, 1983, p. A-5.

over, difficulties may arise when this is not the case. At one publishing company the salary differential between the corporate engineering group and manufacturing groups impedes the flow of engineers into the latter. To progress upward in this corporation, however, a broad range of experience is necessary. Thus, this firm's salary structure acts as a barrier to desired employee growth. Clearly, such inequities in salary administration can create tension between employees working in different units (i.e. research vs. manufacturing). For this reason, this firm is secretive about salary ranges for all positions, a policy which can create additional problems.

One petroleum company interviewed found via the exit interview process that the firm's secrecy, about both salary ranges and relative employee positions, was a significant factor in the decision of several E/S to terminate. In response to this, the company formed group sessions to provide salary information to employees with the intent of improving retention. If salary administration is shrouded with secrecy it can be expected that the grapevine will carry highly damaging gossip. On the other hand, the desire of employees for information must be balanced by the firm's need to retain proprietary information.

A final problem revealed through our interviews concerns the relationships between the salaries of management personnel and those who utilize the technical side of the dual ladder. The dual ladder concept, as noted in Chapter V, has been established in no small part to reward E/S who remain in their profession by allowing them to progress within the firm and contribute to its progress. Figure VII-4, based upon the *IEEE U.S. Membership Salary & Fringe Benefit Survey 1982*, provides interesting data on the relationship between management and professional salaries. It shows that the undergraduate engineer who earns a master of business administration (MBA) degree has a smaller income than do those who earned a master's degree in electrical engineering, for the first twenty-four years of working experience; and for those who earn a doctorate in engineering, for the first twenty-eight years of working experience. After these years, however, the MBA recipient moves ahead, and continues his upward movement while the progress of those with advanced engineering degrees either slows or even declines.

It would be questionable to generalize too much from these data since they apply to only one branch of the engineering profession. The data in Figure VII-4 covering master's degrees other than those in business and electrical engineering are probably not representative because most personnel in engineering who are not electrical or electronics engineers would not be IEEE members. On the other

FIGURE VII-4

INCOME VERSUS HIGHEST DEGREE EARNED AND LENGTH OF
EXPERIENCE
(Full-time employed in area of primary technical competence)

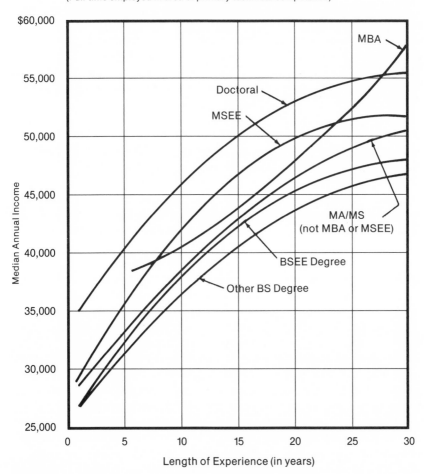

Source: *IEEE U.S. Membership Salary & Fringe Benefit Survey 1983* (New York:
Institute of Electrical and Electronics Engineers, Inc., 1983) UHO 152–9, p.
14. © 1983 IEEE. Reproduced by permission.

hand, the IEEE is the largest of the engineering societies and its
members are very much in demand. Moreover, most of our interviewees who represented companies that have dual ladders conceded
that it was difficult for many E/S to gain top pay comparable to
upper-middle and higher management. In the long run, the IEEE

data would seem to provide strong evidence that, on average, an undergraduate engineering degree plus an MBA provides a greater return than does a doctorate in engineering.

Overtime and Hours. Under the Fair Labor Standards Act (FLSA), certain groups including professionals and managers, as defined by their functional duties, are exempt from the act's coverage. Thus, there is no legal requirement that E/S be paid time and one-half their salary rate computed on an hourly basis for work in addition to forty hours in one week. The same is true in regard to the Public Contracts (Walsh-Healey) Act which requires overtime for covered workers after eight hours in one day where the company has a federal government contract for $10,000 or more. E/S therefore do not generally receive time and one-half for hours worked beyond eight in one day or forty in one week.

Nearly all companies interviewed followed this course and did not provide additional compensation for isolated cases of overtime. Many had no provisions to pay overtime wages to E/S at all. Some firms did, however, have specific pay guidelines for scheduled overtime, while others granted time off to compensate for long periods during which extra hours were required. At least one union has negotiated overtime pay for engineers. One firm used overtime allowances to improve the competitiveness of the total compensation package for its computer scientists. Another firm publicized a bonus award program for E/S to encourage overtime work, but did not inform employees of the amount prior to the award.

The general feeling among respondents was that engineers are professionals, and as such are expected to put in extra hours occasionally. Where extended periods of overtime become necessary, however, a number of firms without paid overtime policies try to show appreciation through a one-time award such as a bonus, a luncheon, the granting of compensatory time off, or some other form of reward or recognition. This serves not only to recognize special efforts, but also to offset compression. In periods in which E/S work extensive overtime, hourly workers may also be working long hours and receiving time and one-half for the extra work. This can put the latter's wages close to the salaries of the E/S (especially when COLA payments are large, as in the 1970s) and bring about dissatisfaction among E/S.

Companies have found, however, that regular payment of overtime to E/S is not wise. In such situations, extra payment is likely to become an accepted part of compensation, and overtime is literally created. Where supervisors who must approve overtime are also compensated, the problem is worsened. Experience with overtime for professionals and/or supervisors in the aerospace industry has led to a rather firm conclusion by most companies that other ways must be found to reward professionals who work long hours, and that the rewards should be neither fixed nor automatic.

Flextime is not widely used by large companies, although some flextime arrangements were found by our interviews in pharmaceutical E/S divisions and in research laboratories. In other laboratories, hours were handled informally, with no one checking on when the E/S arrived, or when or for how long they took lunch breaks. Generally, management reported that successful E/S spent long hours on the job, and that there was little problem in this respect except for a few marginal performers. Hence, they did not perceive any strong demand for a formal flextime policy. Moreover, companies pointed out that to put some employees on flextime and not others had the potential both to disrupt intracompany communications and to cause resentment among those employees who were required to maintain standard hours of work. Other studies have made similar findings.[11]

RECOGNITION

Recognition programs may offer either tangible or intangible incentives, which can be quite important to E/S. One firm, specializing in technical recruitment, found that engineers consider special monetary awards and recognition to be the best incentives to greater productive efforts. Another study, in which over 400 technical professionals were interviewed, concluded that recognition of professional achievement is the most important reward. The same study found the failure of management to recognize individuals for their accomplishments to be the most cited source of dissatisfaction among professionals.[12]

Tangible Rewards

Some firms give tangible rewards such as cash, gift certificates, and nights out on the town. The announcement of such awards are made either publicly or privately. One firm interviewed believes that public announcement serves a dual purpose: it is both a motivating factor, and serves to monitor award distribution. In other words, peer pressure ensures that only deserving individuals receive

---

[11]See, e.g., *Company Experience with Flexible Work Schedules*, Research Bulletin No. 110 (New York: The Conference Board, 1982).

[12]Dolores Frederick, "Motivating Scientists and Engineers," *Industrial Research*, Vol. 9 (March 1967), p. 87.

awards. Other firms argue that special rewards might breed an unhealthy rivalry and discourage the free exchange of ideas among research personnel. A firm must strive to balance cooperation and healthy competitiveness among employees. Free exchange of ideas should be fostered to prevent redundancy and to allow idea piggybacking. The corporate philosophy and the resulting organizational climate are major determinants of whether awards should be made publicly or privately, if at all.

A problem in award administration is the difficulty of articulating performance criteria. Multiple criteria of performance complicate recipient selection. In addition, subjectivity is likely to enter the award designation process and it is sometimes difficult to determine who should be responsible for award administration. In certain cases individual supervisors are in the best position to determine award recipients. Often, however, the number of employees eligible for major awards will extend beyond a single supervisor's control. To overcome this problem, as well as that of an individual supervisor's subjectivity, many firms have formed groups responsible for major award selection. For example, at one pharmaceutical firm a committee in the laboratory reviews job performance and grants bonuses. At another firm, a technical council selects award recipients. One chemical company has assembled an internal panel for technical paper presentation. This panel chooses award recipients and also presents certificates of merit to deserving individuals. The composition of such committees or panels varies. Committee members may be external advisors, such as recognized specialists in particular fields, or they may be representatives of various operating units within the firm. Some firms have established peer review committees, composed of distinguished corporate scientists or engineers.

Monetary awards are usually given for outstanding achievement or accomplishment measured either by the economic value to the firm or contribution to a scientific field. One pharmaceutical firm offers a series of special awards to encourage and recognize any notable ideas or accomplishments of its employees that contribute to the successful conduct of its business. Special awards have been adopted by many firms; but because so few are awarded each year, the actual motivational incentive is low. Thus, monetary rewards are usually also offered for achievement, where achievement is measured by patents, publications, election to a professional society, becoming an officer in a professional society, attainment of a professional license, or other event of significance. Sometimes commemorative plaques or other items are granted instead of cash.

Monetary and nonmonetary awards are also given for achievement or effort above and beyond the normal expectations of the job. One major conglomerate has recently instituted a new corporate program in recognition of engineering talent. Its philosophy is to give tangible awards rather than using salary increases as a proxy for reward because outstanding achievements are often not reflected in salary adjustments. Tangible awards can be issued on a more timely basis. Since they are more direct, this company finds that they serve as better motivators. It attempts to find some method of rewarding all performances where warranted. The cost of a program like this, the corporate representative claims, is relatively insignificant given the aggregate size of the company. He believes that awards can improve morale and enhance loyalty. For example, E/S and their families are sometimes invited to New York City to participate in tours, ceremonies, and symposiums. Spot cash awards are occasionally given. Other forms of recognition include special dinners and tickets to various cultural events.

Some firms choose to recognize achievement by rewarding employees with stock rather than directly with cash. Several oil companies have instituted deferred bonus and "piece-of-the-action" plans. Another tangible method of recognizing contributions as measured by creativity and innovation is to upgrade and/or revitalize the technical ladder. One chemical company has recently uncapped the salary scale on the technical ladder so the potential earnings of distinguished E/S are theoretically boundless. The opportunity for substantial compensation in recognition of achievement is, of course, an important form of recognition.

One manufacturing firm interviewed has recently designed an integrated professional compensation system which was created in recognition of the vital role played by E/S in the progress of the company toward its goal of clear technological and market leadership. The system is based strictly on performance. The firm first established a new career ladder. It then designed a three-stage pay delivery system: (1) a merit plan pays professionals based on job performance; (2) an individual productivity award plan adds a substantial amount (up to 30 percent) to a professional's annual salary; (3) a special awards plan recognizes significant achievement by a superior employee.

This system was developed to motivate and to reward individual contributors. It is basically a performance-based approach. The amount of the individual productivity award is tied to the achievement of productivity goals set in the beginning of the year. Productivity awards can be paid either after completion of major projects or at periodic milestone intervals. Special awards have been established in three categories: originality/creativity, total performance, and professional achievement. A committee has been established to select recipients.

The professional recognition award is designed to encourage professionals who gain recognition for their technical accomplishments, either within the company or in the outside professional community. For example, monetary awards are given for election to an approved professional society, election as an officer in an approved professional society, publication of an article in an approved professional journal, or completion of an advanced degree in the employee's field. Individuals may also be rewarded for technical contributions which directly benefit the company. The inventor's award may be granted to individuals who develop patents or patentable ideas for the corporation, or in conjunction with another professional award if the contribution also directly results in a patent.

In addition to awards based on individual contributions, several firms also recognize significant group accomplishments. Because individual efforts cannot always be isolated as a result of the nature of the development process, or because a number of disciplines must be integrated to arrive at the desired output, group awards are sometimes more appropriate. In addition, this can help reduce tendencies towards secrecy that several corporate representatives feared would develop if only individual contributions were recognized.

Research findings have demonstrated that "R&D effectiveness depends on trust and respect among individuals and on a network of teams that freely share critical information."[13] To encourage the interaction of research teams, one firm sponsors parties or events honoring achievement of particular goals. For example, it may have a party for a contract award, and then, as project milestones are achieved on time, other events or incentives may be offered. If the project is completed on time, a final group incentive may be awarded. Group awards seem most prevalent in the chemical and pharmaceutical industries where a series of individuals frequently become involved in the research and development of a new product or process.

Intangible Rewards

A set of intangible rewards can also be an important motivator.

---

[13]Donald K. Stein and Murray M. Dalziel, *The Organizational Climate in Research-and-Development Organizations: A Synopsis of Research* (Boston: McBer and Company, 1982), p. 9; see also, Jeremy Bernstein, *Three Degrees Above Zero: Bell Labs in the Information Age* (New York: Charles Scribner's Sons, 1984).

TABLE VII-4
Examples of Intangible Rewards

1. Recognition of professional achievements
   a) praise
   b) personal mention in oral and written reports
   c) basing status and salary on technical contribution
2. Work being brought to the attention of top management
3. Recognition of personal achievement by superiors
4. Challenge of projects
5. Variety of work—increases breadth of one's experience and competence as a professional
6. Treatment as a professional
   a) advice sought on technical problems
   b) opportunities to publish
   c) opportunities to participate in professional societies
7. Management's actions towards engineers and scientists—support, genuine interest, etc.
8. Freedom to manage one's own work
9. Acceptance of ideas by management
10. Implementation of ideas by management
11. Opportunity to learn in the field
12. Prospects for promotion
13. Status symbols—title, company name, etc.
14. Regard by associates

Source: Adapted from John W. Riegel, *Administration of Salaries and Intangible Awards for Engineers and Scientists* (Ann Arbor, Mich.: Bureau of Industrial Relations, University of Michigan, 1958), Table VII, p. 32.

Such rewards include a variety of opportunities for recognition, and afford several different methods of attaining prestige both among colleagues and within the overall organization. Examples of intangible rewards are shown in Table VII-4. If intangible rewards cannot be obtained through a job, satisfaction may be low despite the possible presence of an extensive tangible reward program. Most professionals desire to feel that their work is appreciated. Management's attitudes and actions towards E/S certainly also contribute to the amount of job satisfaction which is felt.

"Research shows that scientists feel rewarded primarily by recognition for their research. Effective organizations build systems that allow for individual recognition and that provide challenges that serve as opportunities for individual growth."[14] Professional achievement may be recognized by verbal praise, references in reports, increased visibility to upper management, or other means. Recognition may also be obtained in one's field through publication. Situations in which an individual wants to publish, but the proprietary nature of his work forces the prohibition of exposure through written media, may aggravate the propensity towards professional-

---

[14]Stein and Dalziel, *Organizational Climate in Research-and-Development*, p. 7.

organizational conflict. A firm that discourages publication may well need to develop a strong set of alternative intangible rewards to avoid frustration and resentment over the loss of recognition by the written word.

Another manner of administering intangible rewards is through a creative approach to project assignment. Challenging assignments, variety of work, and opportunity to learn through job rotation have all been cited as motivating factors. Some firms raise the status of E/S in the organization by allowing distinguished "fellows" to participate in corporate decisionmaking, and by requesting input for strategic planning purposes from outstanding personnel. Opportunities for internal recognition can also be created by organizing a series of internal presentations.

Job titles can serve as another source of intangible reward. Often, titles change as one progresses up the technical ladder, with each rung representing a more distinguished or prestigious position. On the other hand, some firms choose generic terms for all technical professionals such as "member of technical staff" regardless of their position on a career profile chart. This intentional omission of title is meant to encourage cooperation and to prevent the formation of caste systems which may hinder research progress. Only the corporate culture or philosophy can determine the optimal practice concerning titles.

Several companies interviewed have established special intangible awards for E/S. One firm designates an "Engineer of the Month" and an "Engineer of the Year" in order to recognize individual contributions. Additional recognition is obtained via the corporate newsletter where recipients are named. Other organizations have established similar modes of recognition. One firm has established a corporate hall of fame for E/S who have received awards for outstanding achievement. Pictures and abbreviated biographies for those honored are displayed in a hall accessible to all employees. In addition to articles in corporate newsletters, some firms issue press releases to local newspapers when special awards are bestowed, or interesting projects are completed. Others purchase advertising space in prestigious publications in which distinguished engineers and scientists are honored.

Other forms of intangible reward include vacation accrual for outstanding service, increased technical support (i.e. technicians), opportunity for sabbatical leave, and large offices. Sometimes authority may be granted for purchasing special equipment. Freedom to choose the subject matter or direction of research is also considered a form of intangible reward. As in the case of tangible rewards, intangible rewards may be given to groups as well. For example, project teams may receive recognition in a corporate newspaper.

As already emphasized, the nature of intangible awards vary by company and individual and among industries because of differences in corporate cultures and competitive forces. The rank order of intangible awards also changes over time and is affected by environmental factors and personal experience. An individual's position in his career cycle also influences the type of rewards desired. Changes in individual priorities do not necessarily complicate the administration of intangible awards, for such awards are most effective if individually tailored. It is wise, therefore, for firms to monitor their organizational climate to ensure that it allows for individual recognition. Because needs patterns change, they must continually be reassessed. The administration of intangible awards must therefore also be continual. Opportunities must exist through which status needs can be met if E/S are to be encouraged to perform most productively.

Patent Policy and Recognition

Recognition for development of patents varies considerably among companies. The already noted IEEE 1983 survey, the results of which are found in Tables VII-5 and VII-6, yielded interesting results. Only 33 percent of those respondents who provided a definite response reported that all patents become the property of their employer. In contrast, our interviews found that this was most always the case. The IEEE survey also found that more than 34 percent of the respondents reported that the patents do not become the property of the employer unless directly associated with the developer's employment. Our interviews indicated that companies take a very dim view of moonlighting if it is associated with the specialty of the E/S, and would likely move energetically to claim patent ownership or use of any company-developed proprietary knowledge, materials, or other company property that were shown to be involved in the patent development. Nearly all companies interviewed had E/S execute a patent assignment contract as a condition of employment. Such contracts typically deal with outside interests, use of company knowledge and property, and company rights in case patents are developed outside of the regular work environment. The large "do not know" IEEE response may account for some of the difference between their findings and ours.

The IEEE survey found that about 80 percent of the respondents received either no compensation for successful patent development,

TABLE VII-5
*Frequency Distribution of Patent Ownership
Among IEEE Members, 1983*

| | Respondents | |
Category	Number	Percent Answering
All patents become property of employer	1,978	33.0
Only those patents directly associated with employment become property of employer	3,242	54.1
Do not become property of employer	769	12.8
Do not know	1,530	—
Total	7,519	100.0

Source: *IEEE U.S. Membership Salary & Fringe Benefit Survey 1983* (New York: Institute of Electrical and Electronics Engineers, Inc., 1983) UHO 152-9, p. 28. © 1983 IEEE.

TABLE VII-6
*Frequency Distribution of Compensation for Patents
Among IEEE Members, 1983*

| | Respondents | | |
Category	Number	Percent	Adjusted Percent
Not applicable to employer	1,763	25.0	—
No monetary compensation paid	2,370	33.6	44.8
Nominal sum paid regardless of patent value	1,811	25.7	34.3
Sum paid based on patent value	539	7.6	10.2
Sum paid based upon number of patents developed by individual	132	1.9	2.5
Compensation based on some other system	435	6.2	8.2
Total	7,050	100.0	100.0

Source: *IEEE U.S. Membership Salary & Fringe Benefit Survey 1983* (New York: Institute of Electrical and Electronics Engineers, Inc., 1983) UHO 152-9, p. 29. © 1983 IEEE.

or only a nominal cash award which was not based on the value of the patent. This comports with our findings. Our interviewees did stress, however, that patent development was certainly a significant factor in merit salary increases and promotions. Moreover, nonmonetary awards were prevalent. The forms of recognition included stories in company papers, press releases, dinners, plaques, special seminars to discuss the use and value of the patented information, etc.

A few companies interviewed do not encourage patent applications, fearing that they reveal proprietary processes which give competitors the keys to developing similar products. Such companies have sometimes found that this policy is counterproductive for E/S morale, but certainly this is not always so. As discussed in Chapter XI, Bell Telephone Laboratories, the premier industrial research laboratory, is not No. 1 in patents received.

CONCLUSION

A basic compensation package alone cannot build a successful organization. It must be supplemented by a judicious use of motivating rewards and recognition if a winning team of E/S is to be developed. The form varies by industry, company, and individual needs. It must, however, be acceptable to the E/S to be successful in its purpose. Moreover, if compensation is considered inadequate by the E/S, other rewards and recognition are unlikely to prove an acceptable substitute.

CHAPTER VIII

Communication

Most employees like to be informed of corporate plans and appreciate opportunities to communicate with their superiors, including those above their immediate supervisor. Engineers and scientists (E/S), by virtue of their education and professional standing, would seem to merit, and also to profit from, something more than an occasional letter from the chief executive or a pat on the back during an annual laboratory tour. Our interviews revealed that communication was very much on the minds of company personnel, engineering, and laboratory executives. When the subject was broached in interviews, executives smiled, nodded, and typically responded with comments such as "We need to improve this area," "We are working on our communications systems," etc. It was often difficult to determine whether communication was integral to a company's philosophy or was merely a corporate "buzz word." Yet despite employee protestations to the contrary, communication does occur in every company. Differences exist in the formality and extent of communication networks, and in the accuracy of transmitted information.

PROGRAMS AND PROBLEMS

A simple approach to communication is to avoid developing formal channels, letting the grapevine operate instead. There is some danger to this technique because although the grapevine may be efficient, it cannot claim a high degree of accuracy. A company that relies on the grapevine subjects itself to the risks of distortion and exaggeration.

Given these risks, why would a company rely primarily on informal channels? One engineering construction company official explained that it is difficult to transmit information to E/S because "you can never supply enough depth." He felt that scientific professionals approach information the same way in which they approach their jobs, that is, by collecting and analyzing all the facts. This habitual hunger for knowledge can become a sensitive issue; sometimes it is in management's interest not to publicize specific reasons surrounding a decision. The problem is further complicated because although an engineer or scientist may be perceptive and well-intentioned, unless he has developed business acumen or become well-versed in specific management skills, the nature or timing of certain business strategies may not be understood. With limited information, an individual could attempt to recreate a situation and arrive at a conclusion contradicting management's judgment. Questions may be raised, faith lost, and conflicts generated. Thus, difficulties in communication may originate both with management and with employees.

It is also difficult for a company to determine the quality, quantity, and nature of the information to be communicated. Will employees view limited or intermittent communication as one-sided propaganda? Will they suspect that employee manipulation is one of the primary motives behind communication? A company must explore these issues when developing a communications strategy. Although it might decide to be honest and open, certain corporate issues are especially sensitive (such as salary levels), or proprietary from a competitive viewpoint (such as a new product or technology). These considerations raise questions concerning how open a well-intentioned company can be. The answer seems to be that there is no substitute for the truth. Those companies with a regular communication policy have more success in gaining E/S understanding on sensitive matters that cannot be made generally known than do those companies which communicate only during crises.

The Flow Problem

Despite these difficulties, most companies have developed multiple avenues of communication. Communication is a two-way process, and ideally these avenues allow traffic to flow in both directions. A corporation which desires an effective and profitable communication flow system must work to ensure that innovative employee ideas reach management levels as readily as corporate directives reach employees.

Many companies were concerned about the effectiveness of their existing programs and expressed an interest in expanding and/or improving their "traffic patterns." Since most of the corporations interviewed had been affected by the 1981–82 recession, they were experiencing significant pressure for efficient financial performance. Several companies had either announced or initiated layoffs of salaried professionals, obviously a major threat to employee security. To mitigate this effect, one company expanded its communication program specifically to deal with the difficult times which they were experiencing. It began inviting employees to executive coffee hours and established a hotline to a public relations group, among other modes of information exchange. Companies have found that the increased communication helped to reduce the anxiety created by uncertain economic situations.

Corporate communication can also assist in other areas, such as familiarizing new employees with the company. Communication can likewise aid in reducing conflicts or dissatisfactions arising from the transition between academia and industry. Similarly, a typical management response to the threat of unionization is to increase communication with employees through a variety of media: newsletters, meetings, presentations, etc.

The difficulty with issuing communications only when there are crises is that employees, including E/S, may tend to question the sincerity of a company management that calls on its employees in such times for understanding or assistance, but that seems to ignore them when no crises exist. Unless companies communicate their viewpoint regularly and directly, employees are likely to learn of events affecting their livelihood only through rumor or via external agencies such as unions. Under such conditions, company actions, proposals, and viewpoints are not likely to be accurately portrayed.

Management must both win an audience among employees and establish its credibility. This requires communicating regularly and accurately over time. When the crisis comes, management can then utilize its functioning communication system to present its views, policies, and programs.

Who Communicates

Successful communication involves much more than a supervisory function, perhaps supplemented by occasional talks, letters, or appearances at meetings by company division heads or top management, although these areas should not be neglected. E/S supervisors are usually professionals who have opted for a management or administrative career ladder, and they can do much to explain the company position if they are properly trained and briefed. Professional employees, however, generally desire to hear from middle and top management, who know more facts and who by the very nature of their positions command more respect. A major effort needs to go into manager letters to the home, "big boss" appearances at meetings, speeches, etc. Effective communication involves use of all available resources, aimed at all the audiences involved, and for E/S particularly, careful consideration of their professional needs, desires, and questions. Some specific communication avenues which can be utilized are discussed below. A general schema of internal and external communication systems and devices is found in Figure VIII-1.

FIGURE VIII-1
*Communication Systems Networks
Internal and External*

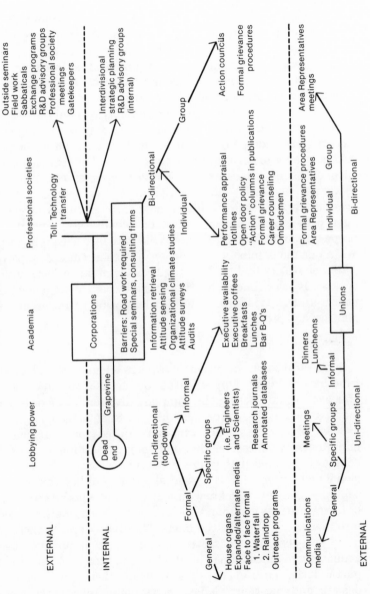

Attitude Surveys

Evaluations of attitude surveys by interviewed companies have been mixed. Some reported little success with this method of ascertaining the feelings of employed E/S; others found surveys quite useful in determining how employees felt about the company and their jobs. Most frequently, an impartial third party such as a consulting firm is called in to perform the survey. Employee anonymity is thereby ensured and results are likely to be more candid. Periodic attitude surveys are one way that organizations can obtain feedback from a large number of people. Problem areas and needed improvements may thus be identified. In particular, several chemical companies found such surveys useful.

One pharmaceutical company interviewed recently changed the management of its research facility and was especially concerned about the organizational climate. The corporate feeling was that "if engineers and scientists have any propensity to unionize in this company, this is where it will happen." The company did not feel that the existing environment was conducive to creative research, and hired a consulting firm to assess this phenomenon. Questionnaires were distributed to the scientists. Responses were scored along six dimensions related to human organizational effectiveness, as summarized below:

1. *Conformity*: Does the company burden employees with unnecessary bureaucratic rules and regulations?
2. *Responsibility*: Do people have enough authority to do the job?
3. *Clarity*: Does the organization have explicit goals? Do individuals know where they fit in?
4. *Standards*: Are challenging goals set? Is there a premium on quality?
5. *Rewards*: Are there both financial and nonfinancial rewards? How are the rewards linked to meritorious performance? Is there a good balance between praise and criticism?
6. *Team Spirit*: How does the organization promote quality human relationships, loyalty, and pride?

The firm found that problems were, in fact, widely present. Scientists felt accountable for their own work, but gained no proprietary satisfaction from individual projects. They felt that they did not participate in decisions affecting their work. They felt isolated within the company, losing track of their work once it left the laboratory. Professional appraisal had been poorly administered over the past few years. The scientists felt that risk-taking was discouraged because there was a tendency to find scapegoats during the performance appraisal process.[1] This research environment was clearly suffering a severe information flow problem. Once problems were identified through formal communication channels, strategies for improvement could be developed.

Feedback Mechanisms/Grievance Procedures

All effective communication systems must have feedback channels which facilitate self-correction and improvement. If communication is only top-down, or if existing feedback channels are routinely jammed or the information rerouted, management will never learn about problems which may inhibit the effective function of the engineering and scientific divisions.

When queried about internal avenues for feedback, many company managers mentioned an informal "open door" policy. This method encourages interaction but may elicit response only from a limited number of E/S, for not all employees are bold enough to walk into a manager's office to offer suggestions or to express discontent. A supplementary avenue is often necessary for those who prefer anonymity.

Most of the engineering unions operate within aerospace or defense electronics companies. Grievance procedures are routinely included in the union contract. Thus, E/S represented by the bargaining unit have formal channels of appeal. Companies have learned, however, that they cannot expect union officials to communicate the company point of view. Union officials have goals and needs of their own, and communicate accordingly. Companies need to communicate regularly and thoroughly with union officials in order to foster and to maintain good relations, but they need to communicate equally directly and thoroughly with employees, to ensure that the company message is received. This is especially important for E/S, whose work is crucial to a company's future and who must remain informed if they are to make maximum contribution.

Several nonunion companies have instituted various forms of feedback mechanisms which bear some resemblance to grievance machinery. For instance, one aerospace company has an employee relations advisory council, established in 1974, which is composed of staff engineers who meet with engineering management to discuss relevant employment issues. The committee publishes minutes of the meetings which are circulated to all engineers. There are two management seats on the council, currently occupied by one line manager and one personnel manager. Guests are invited to attend

---

[1]Report of a consulting firm to a major pharmaceutical company.

depending on the proposed topics of discussion. For example, the vice president of marketing and the vice president of engineering are frequently attendees.

Another aerospace company also has an engineering advisory committee. This group was developed directly in response to a unionization attempt. Its purpose is to investigate and address internal climate problems. Northrop Corporation, which is nonunion, has a grievance system for all employees which terminates in binding arbitration. Few concerns give their unorganized employees such a privilege. One pharmaceutical company has an extensive communications program centering around a personnel representative system. This group has multiple functions: disseminating information, responding to queries, and monitoring feedback and directing it to the appropriate individuals.

Performance appraisal systems provide another channel for communication and feedback. One engineering construction company describes two objectives of its system as follows:

> (1) To foster communications between the employee and his/her immediate supervisor, including setting specific job expectations and providing continual feedback on performance.
> (2) To serve as an information source.[2]

A well-designed system will personalize communication with specific employees.

Technology Transfer Between International or Distant Regional Facilities

The broad concept of communication extends beyond management/employee interaction to include technology transfer and coordination within and between functional divisions.

Many of the companies interviewed were major organizations which have international operations as well as divisions throughout the United States. Although not all facilities perform identical work, some of the technology can be transferred or applied to several locations. Diffusion of developments between divisions is often difficult, especially for new discoveries whose potential applications are not intuitively obvious. A number of companies have developed formal programs to facilitate the process. A chemical company has a seminar exchange program between its eastern and western research locations. A multinational petroleum company has a sabbatical program through which scientists can elect to work for a six-month period in a different location. An American communications com-

---

[2]Information provided by an engineering construction company.

pany, a wholly-owned subsidiary of a Japanese corporation, finds technology transfer difficult, partly because of time and cultural differences between the parent company and the subsidiary.

Efficient transfer of technology is still a challenge for companies even though information management techniques and modes of communication are improving and decreasing in cost. Companies are not only limited by internal constraints, such as what information should be shared, and with which locations, but also experience external pressures. Companies are subject to government security restrictions which may prevent or inhibit intercompany or intercountry technology transfer.

Integration Within and Between Functional Divisions

In a research and development (R&D) laboratory, there may be at any time numerous projects in various stages of completion. The success of some of the projects may be related to the extent to which discussions between scientific personnel occur and are mutually beneficial. If there is no mode supplied by the company to facilitate linkup and interaction, research groups may work in information vacuums.

Communication within R&D has been the subject of extensive management study. Dewhirst, Arvey, and Brown examined the flow related both to cross-functional and internal channels. They attempted "to integrate . . . the communication of scientific and technical information, especially the flow of such information across organization boundaries [and] the flow of internally generated information (goals, plans, and job assignments) flowing down the organizational hierarchy, or the upward communication of proposals, problems, and the results of organizational activities."[3] Their analysis indicates that communication of internal technical information and goal-related information correlate very highly both with job satisfaction and performance. This implies that management, with the aid of employee relations programs, could create a climate in which development engineers want to share technical information rather than hoard it. This is particularly important, because interpersonal (oral) communication with members of one's own organization have been found to be the most frequently used source of useful information.[4] Thus, effective internal communication is very important in R&D.

---

[3]H. Dudley Dewhirst, Richard D. Arvey, and Edward M. Brown, "Satisfaction and Performance in Research and Development Tasks as Related to Information Accessibility," *IEEE Transactions on Engineering Management*, Vol. EM-25 (August 1978), p. 58.

[4]William J. Paisley, "Information Needs and Uses," in Carlos A. Guadra, ed., *Annual Review of Information Science and Technology*, Vol. 3 (Chicago: William Benton, 1968), p. 4.

Gatekeeper Principle

Dewhirst, Arvey, and Brown found also that the accessibility of external information was very significant for research tasks. Among the various roles and activities relating to communication which are assumed by technical personnel in R&D settings, the role of the "technological gatekeeper" is noteworthy:

> A "technological gatekeeper" is an individual who, by virtue of extensive reading of scientific journals and/or by maintaining contacts with colleagues outside his own organization, stays at the forefront of his discipline. The existence of gatekeepers in an organization makes information generated externally much more readily accessible to those organizational members who are not themselves gatekeepers. Thus there is a two-step communication process in which information first flows from outside the organization to the gatekeeper, then from the gatekeeper to the ultimate user.[5]

The concept of a gatekeeper can be applied to the coordination of various internal functional areas. All functional areas of a company must be integrated to ensure goal congruence and efficient resource allocation. This implies that avenues must exist for communication between research and development, sales and marketing, production/manufacturing, service, etc. Technology transfer and support, such as the transition from R&D to operations or manufacturing, is one specific area that can benefit from effective communication patterns. There must also be a correlation between marketing and R&D to ensure that customer feedback (problems, suggestions, etc.) is received.

One petrochemical company interviewed has four major laboratories engaged in applied research and two smaller facilities involved primarily in basic research which collectively service ten operating companies. The laboratories are an integral part of the company's operating structure. The work done in each laboratory crosses organizational subdivisions. Individual laboratories establish work contracts with various operating companies for specific projects. To facilitate the contracting procedure and coordinate the corporate research function, a senior vice president of technology has recently been appointed. He is charged with ensuring that appropriate technology transfer occurs. The company has also established a technology council, comprised of representatives of the ten operating units. The council meets periodically to elect recipients of awards given in recognition of technical contribution.

The concept of gatekeeping pertains originally to the external environment. Research has shown that a high percentage of product

---

[5]Dewhirst, Arvey, and Brown, "Satisfaction and Performance," p. 58.

innovations are originated by users, and then implemented or incorporated into a manufacturer's design. Dewhirst, Arvey, and Brown suggested that R&D managers could be "facilitating the maintenance of contacts with professional peers outside the organization by supporting trips to conferences, symposia, etc. for those who play the gatekeeper role."[6] This interaction with external organizations and personnel can be viewed as an environmental scan. To be most successful, all functional areas should participate in this external sensing to a certain degree rather than relying strictly on sales or marketing.

More structured mechanisms providing for timely exposure to current relevant research are therefore crucial to the maintenance of technical vitality within R&D laboratories. Several companies circulate annotated bibliographies or abstracts which refer to literature on file in the company library. Other companies have abstracts on data bases allowing access to both current and past literature. These policies formalize functions which otherwise would be left to the informal activities of gatekeepers.

An electronics company encourages engineers to spend time in the field to gain intimate knowledge of its customers' operational settings. A chemical company rotates technical personnel into market situations. In these two situations employees, through direct interaction with the market environment, can conceive designs which will best suit actual customer needs.

Other companies mentioned that they organized product or project teams to facilitate external interaction. For example, an applications engineer may be available for customer consultation. This individual then acts in support of the sales personnel, without the pressure of commissions or quotas, or might also handle a reduced product line. As a specialist, this engineer views applications with more depth and can act as a direct liaison to, or even as a representative of, a particular company division. Thus, a direct feedback link is provided from the market to engineering or production.

Another product team might be composed of one representative from R&D, one from marketing, and one from manufacturing. The individual from R&D could work directly with the customer on specific problems, almost in a consulting capacity.

SOCIAL ISSUES

Social or cultural barriers to communication may exist which inhibit the flow of information through even well-designed chan-

---

[6]*Ibid.*, p. 62.

nels. Several companies mentioned problems they experienced in acclimating women and minorities to the corporation. Union/ management tension may also block communication. These particular situations may require special programs to reduce barriers.

One company detected discrimination and tension concerning women in the workplace. It began a series of discussion groups, or "rap sessions," to isolate and solve specific problems. In this way problems were brought into the open and addressed directly, rather than festering beneath the surface and affecting overall employee morale. A defense electronics company replaced its affirmative action committee with a more informal EEO forum for the same purpose.

A pharmaceutical company has developed a particularly vigorous and effective program in response to male difficulties with women in the workplace. It established a series of internal seminars which included participation by supervisors and union leaders, as well as male and female professionals. The educational process involves movies, videos, handouts, etc. The purpose of this extensive program is to modify the internal climate and ultimately increase the acceptance and understanding of female employees. The management has received positive feedback from employees about this seminar series. Another benefit which has accrued through experience with the program is improved communication skills and flows among participants.

One major chemical company has developed an "Effective Black-White Communication" seminar. Its goal, as described in Chapter IV, is to improve working relationships with minorities throughout the company. Another chemical company uses outside consultants to show minorities how to enhance possibilities for promotion in the corporate environment. The consultants offer seminars on weekends and evenings.

One electrical equipment manufacturer has instituted a "steering committee for minority communications." The focus is both internal and external. The major objectives of the group are to: (1) make the firm's interest and involvement in the minority community more visible; (2) encourage young minorities to pursue opportunities in engineering and technical careers; (3) encourage people to become more knowledgeable about energy and technology, and jobs in these fields; (4) stimulate the development of links between local management and the minority community and, through that link, improve their relationship; and (5) provide counsel within the firm on issues related to minority affairs. The committee has interacted with the black community since 1977 and in 1980 began a program to reach Hispanic audiences. It also pioneered a "minority spokesperson" program in which successful engineering professionals travel to cities across the United States to tell minority youths about opportunities in engineering. A variety of media are used including radio, television, and print. Another aspect of this multifaceted external focus is the initiation of career counseling seminars for high school students and their parents. Committee members also cooperate closely with other corporate functions on internal issues. In addition this group interacts with a variety of professional societies.

The existence of an engineering union, or the threat of an organizing effort, may have significant impact on the degree and variety of communications to professional employees. A study of the responses of several companies to organizing attempts indicates a marked increase in the communication effort by management directly to employees. These included: hotlines, sensitivity sessions, meetings, home mailings, newsletters, and development of "advisory" or "action" councils. This increase is especially marked if communication has previously been lax. The major purpose of these efforts is to determine problems, and attempt to mitigate or correct them before the union attains widespread support. Such communications efforts are more successful when the audience has already been developed and credibility established by a regular, noncrisis communication program.

Several engineering unions have extensive communication programs of their own. As has been noted, the corporation then has a choice. It can decrease its communications to engineers and scientists, allowing the union to relay news; it can continue its normal communication mode; or it can attempt to offset union communication. Sometimes simply relaxing union/management tension promotes fruitful communication. One aerospace company has improved union/management relations by inviting professional union members to join the management club, an organization which provides special dining privileges and offers educational opportunities. In general, a balance between regular communication and occasional stepped-up efforts in the face of possibly damaging union interpretations has proved the most practical and successful approach.

METHODS OF CORPORATE COMMUNICATION

The most traditional forms of corporate communication are written materials. Changing technology allows more creativity and variety in communication media, and distribution may be general or specifically tailored to a particular employee segment.

House Organs

House organs are corporate newsletters or newspapers. Most large companies have such a general publication, which may be distributed at work or mailed to the employee's home. A basic problem in the modern workplace is that individual workers are isolated from the end products of their work. They want to know about new or improved company products, as well as fringe benefits, programs, sales information, professional news, etc.[7] General house organs serve these purposes.

Many companies also publish supplemental papers, journals, or magazines, some of which are internal research journals that tend to be quite technical. Other companies publish more general information about scientific and engineering departments, presenting specific product developments or describing projects in progress. These publications may serve not only as communication devices, but also as an avenue for professional recognition, featuring engineers and scientists who have performed interesting tasks, received patents, authored publications, or made outstanding contributions. Peer recognition is an important job attribute. This has been shown in various studies attempting to identify characteristics of engineers and scientists.[8]

Communication, especially publications of the type mentioned above, is a discretionary expense. Therefore, these publications are frequently discontinued when discretionary funds begin to dry up. While the field visits for this study were underway, the United States was experiencing a severe recession. Many companies interviewed had, in fact, recently cut back on their communications, an understandable action but one that fails to recognize that E/S resources are just as important for the company in the long term as operating resources.

Expanded/Alternate Media

The variety of communications media available has increased while the cost effectiveness of alternate modes of information transmittal has decreased. Thus, cable television and video equipment provide alternate channels to reach employees. These programs can often be viewed during lunch, although some companies allow employees to attend formal "viewing sessions" on working time.

---

[7]See e.g., Arnold Deutsch, *The Human Resources Revolution*, (New York: McGraw Hill, 1979), particularly Chs. 6, 8, and 9.

[8]See e.g., Lee E. Danielson, *Characteristics of Engineers and Scientists* (Ann Arbor, Mich.: Bureau of Industrial Relations, University of Michigan, 1960).

Employee hotlines have also been utilized to improve E/S communication with management. Corporate feedback is also possible through the institution of suggestion boxes where responses are made public either in a column of a house organ, or on a simple question and answer sheet posted on a bulletin board.

Other supplemental approaches to communications include bulletin boards, murals, and posters. Gimmicks such as mugs or T-shirts are sometimes developed with catchy phrases printed on them concerning quality or productivity. Several research organizations have developed guidelines distributed in looseleaf binders for new employees. Other companies publish "employee" annual reports which present bottom-line figures and their explanations.

Information Dispersion

Publications are highly impersonal, even when distributed to target groups. Video equipment personalizes the presentation somewhat, but the speaker is still removed from the audience. In an attempt to overcome the distance between management and employees, several corporations have begun face-to-face meetings. These sessions are not restricted to E/S, but are applied to them in a variety of situations.

Personal interaction programs seem to be of two basic types. Type one can be called the "waterfall" effect. At one petrochemical company, top executives prepare flipchart objectives, goals, and strategic plans. This presentation is then given to each of the meeting attendees. The company supplements it with the more specific goals and plans tailored to the particular function or division. This expanded version is then presented by managers to their immediate subordinates.

The entire process cascades through the various management levels in the organization and consequently becomes more focused. As the lower levels in the organization are reached, information relevant to the top corporate segment is gradually reduced or abbreviated so that material is pertinent for meeting attendees at all levels. Each presentation ends with a question and answer period. All messages from the various levels are ultimately transmitted, but they are tailored accordingly as they are passed down so that relevance is ensured. Through this technique employees receive a broad view of the corporation and learn to understand its goals. They develop a better understanding of where their department fits in, and how they can best contribute to its planned direction of growth. This mechanism is quite time consuming but the delivery is personalized, has been well received, and is considered highly successful.

The second approach, which can be called the "raindrop" effect, is a random selection process. The basic unit of this program is a small group of employees who are selected at random and invited to attend a presentation or a discussion group led by a senior executive. This key unit is not homogeneous as in the previous process. Rather, all levels and divisions may be represented via the random selection technique. A pharmaceutical company submits questionnaires to the selected employees prior to the meeting to determine specific interests. The presentation is then structured around the employee input by pooling individual ideas.

One defense electronics company has instituted a similar but more informal program. Employees are selected at random, and ad hoc groups are established to generate discussion among employees and managers. The purpose of these "round table" discussions is to build developmental dialogue. This program also is tailored to specific employee concerns.

At times, more traditional information dispersal channels become clogged, resulting in worker alienation. One large conglomerate received feedback that a few specific units, especially acquisitions, were never fully acclimated to the corporate culture, so it embarked on a special personal interaction program to reach these "fringes" in which large numbers of E/S were involved.

Informal Availability

Often, the most meaningful forms of communication and avenues for feedback are informal. Thus, less structured sessions with executives, including corporate presidents and chief executive officers, have been a recent addition to the diverse communication network. Employees are invited to attend breakfasts, lunches, or executive coffee hours. Typically, there is a random selection process for these meetings. Conversation is spontaneous and questions are encouraged. The new president of a large pharmaceutical company has started this program in an attempt to get to know employees. It has been extremely well received.

The philosophies of top executives seem to have significant influence on both the formality and amount of communication undertaken. Several companies mentioned the relative ease of interacting with key executives based on their accessibility in the company cafeteria, or in hallways.

Career Counseling

Informing employees of their career opportunities is an important avenue of communication, especially as these opportunities are so important to E/S. Verbalizing or indicating potential opportunities is certainly an important form of corporate communication. Most firms have career brochures prepared for distribution to E/S. Since actions speak louder than words, promotions along the published career paths must be visible to the employees who have aspirations to climb these ladders or retention problems will occur. Direct communications are a valuable aspect of all career development programs.

External

Corporate communication extends beyond the internal information which flows from the employees to the external environment. The function of the "gatekeeper" has been discussed, the individual who monitors and interacts with the external environment in a research laboratory. In fact, external communication goes farther

FIGURE VIII-2
Dynamic and Interactive Model of Corporate Communications

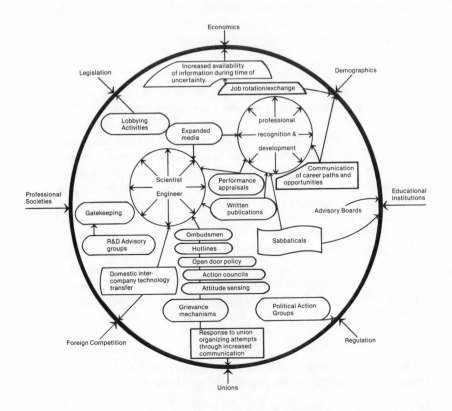

than interindustry or technology transfer issues. In a broader sense, external communication is the way that a company responds to all external forces. A particular example is interaction with various levels of academia. For instance, one electrical equipment manufacturer interacts with local technical trade schools in an advisory capacity. It helps to structure the curriculum by providing insight on industry's needs. One aerospace company has a technology forum to which professors from local universities are invited. Other examples of external interaction with a multitude of organizations are given throughout this book. A successful company program involves external, as well as internal, communications. A schematic of corporate communication is presented in Figure VIII-2.

CONCLUSION

In a real sense, communication is part of every aspect of human resource management. Regular two-way communication between management and professional groups such as E/S may provide the key to proper coordination of R&D activity and long-term corporate goals. Companies employ a variety of informal and formal procedures to establish regular communication pathways, and often develop special mechanisms to handle problems such as technology transfer and the integration of minority groups into the workplace.

CHAPTER IX

Obsolescence and Retraining

Traditionally, obsolescence has been considered to be a problem affecting individuals. Engineers and scientists (E/S) who "fell behind" were in need of "brushing up" or "polishing." They could take courses, or engage in any one of the types of training or retraining described in Chapter V. The E/S who did not keep current fell back, went into other areas, or were dismissed.

Today, the problem is much more severe and may extend to entire groups. Historically, older workers have been most affected by the loss of skills associated with obsolescence, but because of the very rapid rate of technical and scientific progress, the problem has broadened to encompass major disciplinary groups of engineering and scientific employees. E/S may require extensive retraining rather than "brushing up." Such situations can threaten a firm's competitive position, or very existence, as well as the collective security of employees. Clearly obsolescence must be recognized and managed as both a corporate and an individual problem.

NATURE OF OBSOLESCENCE

Obsolescence appears "when an individual uses viewpoints, theories, concepts, or techniques that are less effective in solving problems than others currently available in his field of specialization."[1] It may occur suddenly and dramatically as a result of a new development; more often it develops gradually, perhaps unnoticed until it has become a debilitating constraint on productivity. The more rapid the advances in knowledge, the more widespread obsolescence becomes.

Of course, not all engineering and scientific shortcomings are the result of obsolescence:

> Those who are aware of the best technical solutions to a given problem but fail to apply them because of laziness or a lack of insight into the precise nature of the problems they are facing—these workers should not be regarded as obsolete. Not every instance of ineffectiveness,

---

[1]Theodore N. Ferdinand, "On the Obsolescence of Scientists and Engineers," *American Scientist,* Vol. 54 (March 1966), p. 46.

therefore, can be laid to obsolescence. But, when ineffectiveness does stem basically from lack of awareness of the technical knowledge that is relevant to a given problem area, we are dealing with obsolescence.[2]

Obsolescence may take various forms. It can occur when a professional's technical competence does not include knowledge at the frontiers of his specialty, and worsens as those frontiers become more central to his field. On the other hand, the E/S who becomes a manager and no longer applies the knowledge of his field may become obsolete in a technical sense, but continue to increase his importance to the company through managerial performance.

Motivational obsolescence is another form. It results from the failure of an E/S to work sufficiently hard to maintain a level of work comparable to that of his peers. As the body of knowledge in the field expands, the poorly motivated E/S falls farther behind in knowledge and effort.

As technology changes, entire disciplines may become obsolete. Companies may have E/S working in a technical area which is superceded as a result of the introduction of new products or the application of new concepts by a competitor. The manufacturing mission of a plant may in fact change as a result of new developments in technology. Examples of such major changes include the replacement of vacuum tubes by transistors, or the change from electro-mechanical to solid-state control which has proceeded rapidly in recent years. Discipline obsolescence may have become a greater problem in recent years, again because of the rapidity of scientific and technical progress.

Recognizing Obsolescence and Its Causes

Both individuals and companies can use relatively simple tests to determine if obsolescence is a problem. For example, the following quick test for individuals has been suggested:

1. In solving day-to-day problems, are you less inclined toward rigorous mathematical solutions, and do you find you have forgotten much of what you learned in college?
2. Are papers in your field difficult or impossible to understand, because you are baffled by the math that is used?
3. Does something new, perhaps developed by one of your competitors, make you ask, "Why didn't I think of that?" and lead you to wonder in what direction your field of technology is going?
4. Do new task assignments begin to look preposterous and far too difficult to be "practical"?

---

[2]*Ibid.*, pp. 46–47.

5. Finally, do you realize that your contemporaries no longer seek your advice? Also, do you find yourself asking too often, "What's wrong with the way we are doing it now?[3]

Management also can recognize obsolescence. It is very likely to be present under the following conditions:

1. The main products of a company remain the same over a long period of time.
2. There is an increase in technical errors within an organization.
3. Competition becomes more effective.
4. Technical output in an organization is on the conservative side.
5. Paper work justifying projects is on the increase.
6. Few new ideas are developing.[4]

One chemical company noted that obsolescence may be hidden in its industry until actual process implementation. It then becomes apparent through actual competitive disadvantage, when it is often too late to remedy. In industries in which the products exhibit little change, innovative E/S tend to find the climate inhospitable, and leave. This has certainly been true of steel and, to a somewhat lesser extent, automobiles and heavy machinery during the last decade.[5] Layoffs during the recession of the early 1980s exacerbated this trend. In such situations, it would not be surprising to find considerable obsolescence among E/S remaining with the older industries.

According to Theodore N. Ferdinand, who conducted interviews in the mid-1960s, obsolescence is most likely to occur among E/S when they become settled comfortably in a narrow area that has not been evolving rapidly.

> Their complacency seems to prevent their anticipating or participating in radical developments that may be unfolding in their areas, and their routine involvement in their discipline seems to dull any desire to acquaint themselves with these developments once they have occurred. Thus, considerable obsolescence tends to develop among E/S when their area of specialization has recently experienced accelerated progress after a long period of quiescence.[6]

Obsolescence can also develop when a specialist is given not only primary responsibilities closely related to his technical expertise, but also secondary assignments that distract him from his more crucial tasks.[7] Such misutilization is obviously costly.

---

[3]Suggestions by Alfred Malmros, IBM, presented in "Engineers Talk About Obsolescence," *Machine Design,* June 18, 1964, pp. 148–51.

[4]Derived from Ferdinand, "On the Obsolescence of Scientists and Engineers," pp. 51–56.

[5]Thomas F. O'Boyle, "Brian Drain: U.S. Basic Industries are Hindered by Loss of Scientific Talent," *Wall Street Journal,* July 27, 1984, pp. 1, 16.

[6]Ferdinand, "On the Obsolescence of Scientists and Engineers," p. 51.

[7]*Ibid.,* pp. 54–55.

Companies have also found that obsolescence may be inadvertently caused or furthered by restrictions that E/S believe limit their professional growth. Such restrictions are usually based on sound business rationale but may still have adverse effects. They include such typical policies as:

—restricted travel budgets which limit communications and opportunities to learn what others are doing.
—restricted attendance at professional meetings, which inhibits technical interchange with one's peers.
—security controls which limit technical communication and appear to actively discourage paper writing, and professional society participation.
—reductions in internal education programs, especially when economic pressures are downward and the organization is not adding new talent.
—elimination or reductions in participation in off-site educational updates and short courses.
—restrictions in posting and circulation of professional society meeting notices.
—limited or nonexistent secretarial support for paper writing and editing.[8]

Age and Obsolescence

When interviewees were questioned about the relationship of age and obsolescence, they were nearly unanimous in affirming that obsolescence was very heavily correlated with age, although all agreed that some older E/S (fifty or more years of age) were very productive and up to date, while some younger ones (under thirty-five) have already fallen behind in their specialty. Dalton and Thompson's intensive study of engineers in three aerospace firms and three "technology-based commercial enterprises" found that in "management's evaluations of design and development engineers . . . performance rankings are closely related to age; the average ranking rises with age until the early thirties, drops slightly in the late thirties and falls steadily for each older groups until retirement."[9] Although some other studies take issue with these findings,[10] evidence is strong that obsolescence afflicts older E/S considerably more heavily than it does younger ones. Nevertheless, it is also true that stereotypes can easily affect management evalua-

---

[8]Donald B. Miller, "Changing Job Requirements: A Stimulant for Technical Vitality," in Harold G. Kaufman, ed., *Career Management: A Guide to Combating Obsolescence* (New York: IEEE Press, 1975), p. 70.
[9]Gene W. Dalton and Paul H. Thompson, "Accelerating Obsolescence of Older Engineers," *Harvard Business Review*, Vol. 49 (September-October 1971), pp. 58–59.
[10]See, e.g., Stephen Cole, "Age and Scientific Performance," *American Journal of Sociology*, Vol. 84 (1979), pp. 958–77.

tions, thus hurting those older E/S who have kept up with new developments.[11]

Recent federal legislation concerning old age discrimination prevents blanket dismissal of older E/S who might experience the effects of obsolescence most severely, or whose skills might be considered obsolete by their employer. A number of states, including California and New York, have abolished any upper age limits, and these state laws supersede the federal where they provide more liberal benefits to employees. Moreover, it is not unlikely that Congress will abolish all compulsory retirement in the near future. Companies must now attack obsolescence with far more sophisticated policies than age criteria.

COMBATING OBSOLESCENCE

"There are no secret techniques that provide for the maintenance of vitality in an organization."[12] Given, however, that obsolescence is a corporate as well as an individual problem, companies must have anti-obsolescence programs that help prevent its occurrence as well as offset its impact. Moreover, the techniques utilized should be carefully constructed lest they have an unforeseen negative impact. For example, one company interviewed tries to "accommodate" rather than to reverse the process and retrains employees by giving them progressively simpler job assignments. This technique would seem to accelerate the problem and to reduce, rather than to enhance, personal satisfaction.

Programs for Individuals

Table IX-1 lists a number of techniques that can be utilized to combat obsolescence. Each involves a form of continuing education or retraining aimed at the individual.[13] Although the corporation must formulate policies, no program, however well thought out, can make people learn. The ultimate success of any anti-obsolescence program rests with individual commitment. But the company must provide the climate, the techniques, and the effective communication

---

[11]See Nicholas Di Marco, James A. Breaugh, and Henry Houser, "Worker Motivation: Age Differences in Engineers," *Instrument Society of America (ISA) Conference and Exhibit, Proceedings,* Vol. 34, Pt. 2 (1979), pp. 299–305; and "The Dilemma of Bell Labs Older Professional: Is It 'Age Discrimination'?" Conference of Professional and Technical Personnel, Bell Laboratories, Conference Notes, Vol. 30 (June 1978), pp. 1, 4–6.

[12]C. M. Van Atta, W. D. Decker, and T. Wilson, "Professional Personnel Policies and Practices of R&D Organizations," in Kaufman, ed., *Career Management,* p. 191.

[13]See Chapter V for a discussion of these and similar programs.

TABLE IX-1
Tools for Combating Individual Obsolescence

1. Broad exposure rather than pigeonholing
   a. Rotational training programs
   b. Rotation due to job change
   c. Sabbatical leave
2. Challenging assignments/attention to job content
3. Centralization of technological units
4. Elimination of bureaucratic restrictions on professionalism
5. Continuing education through university courses
6. "Update" courses—developed in-house.
7. Vendor updates
8. Professional societies
9. Centers for professional development

that induces the maximum individual participation and favorable E/S employee attitude.

Job content within a training program is particularly important. Specific attention to job design and task assignment can be effective in maintaining professional vitality. "Natural pressures tend to cause management to leave the person in the area he knows, thus causing a narrowing of knowledge and, in time, a reduction of motivation."[14] Broader exposure can be obtained by any combination of the following:

1. Rotational training programs—a sequence of experiences designed to introduce the employee to a variety of operating areas.
2. Rotation because of job change—this path can be specifically tailored to each individual. Changes may be either lateral, so the employee is exposed to another functional group, or promotional.
3. Sabbatical—a transfer to a different part of the company working with a different technology, an academic leave, or an opportunity to work in a different environment. (One chemical company specified that it allows sabbatical leave to aid in preventing obsolescence.) Sabbatical programs, however, are irregular and individually tailored.

Attention to job content also helps to create and maintain challenging assignments. This involves, first, developing an adequate support staff to absorb some of the more routine tasks, but also much more. One publishing company was concerned about its ability to attract and retain electronics engineers because publishing does not have a high-tech image. The vice president of engineering at this

---

[14]Miller, "Changing Job Requirements," p. 71.

firm concentrates on job content to ensure continuing interest and vitality. A company in the photography business was also concerned about its image. As a result, it attempts to have professionals work on state-of-the-art and high-technology jobs. This approach has a dual purpose: to improve retention, and to prevent obsolescence.

Jobs can be designed to provide motivation for growth and to stimulate development and learning. For example, many aspects of a job can be varied in order to have a constructive development impact:

1. *Breadth*—the task breadth should be broad enough to require learning but not so broad as to confuse the objectives and make for poor relationship to results.
2. *Newness*—the task should require some new behavior and some new knowledge and not just be repetition of past acts.
3. *Reward*—the amount and level of work required to achieve a reward can be varied to emphasize aspects of the task and to provide motivation for further task completion.
4. *Communication*—the requirement for communication with other members of a team can be varied, and increased communications needs are usually associated with an increase in learning.
5. *Research*—the amount of review of prior work and activity necessary to embark upon the task can be varied, with an increase in research requirement usually requiring more learning.
6. *Time Scale*—requirement for response in a short time increases the reliance on what's already known. An increase in time makes possible greater learning and exploration of alternatives.
7. *Documentation*—requiring documentation of results forces clarification of what has been learned through the process of writing.[15]

The motivational aspects of a challenging and stimulating job are widely acknowledged. When researchers asked engineers: "What was the most fruitful learning experience you have had in the past year or two?", the most frequent responses involved on-the-job problem solving. This was further described as "being assigned to interesting tasks," or to "broadening projects," and "writing proposals which force me to dip into the literature and become current on everything connected with the project."[16] It should also be expected that E/S who are not stimulated in this way are more likely to become obsolescent.

The centralization of technical employees who were originally dispersed throughout several facilities can create additional stimulation on the job, and at the same time prevent redundancy. One publishing

---

[15]*Ibid.*, p. 66.
[16]Paul H. Thompson, Gene W. Dalton, and Richard Kopelman, "'But What Have You Done for Me Lately?'—the Boss," *IEEE Spectrum*, Vol. 11 (October 1974), pp. 87–88.

company centralized its engineering group to encourage employee interaction and to build a more stimulating work environment. One pharmaceutical company has a centralized technical unit which must ensure that new equipment meets state-of-the-art standards. Traditionally, the engineers working in this group were scattered in various plants, and there was much duplication of effort in machinery selection. Because of the diversity of company products, engineers were supposed to keep up with technological changes in many fields. Centralization has increased communication and sharing of resources, permitted central strategic planning for new process technology, and improved understanding of new technology on the part of the engineers who were required to investigate the performance and use of new equipment.

Continuing education courses designed to prevent or to offset obsolescence must be carefully constructed. Many engineers and scientists in industry are more interested in doing a good job on their current assignment than in keeping up with technology and science. To hold attention, courses must relate the advances in technology and science to practical goals. Moreover, lower level managers and supervisors are more likely to emphasize current output than future knowledge, and may disparage "theory" learned in advanced courses. Courses must be planned with these considerations in mind, whether developed in-house, at universities, or jointly with other companies.

> It [is] essential that the people running the continuing education program recognize not only what the company's needs for technical knowledge are now but also what they will be in the years immediately ahead. "This means [as one company representative noted] that we must know what new products and new technology will be coming along in the next few years."[17]

A related program utilized by a number of companies to fight obsolescence is to rotate assignments on proposal preparations. In developing proposals, E/S are often required to investigate new areas, techniques, and methods. This is an effective way to learn and to keep current.

Programs for Groups

A broader issue of increasing significance is group obsolescence. When entire disciplines are threatened by order of magnitude changes in technology the problem of obsolescence extends beyond the individual to significant numbers of employees. These groups do

---

[17]Howard J. Sanders, "Continuing Education: The Justified Effort to Keep Up to Date," *Chemical & Engineering News*, May 13, 1974, p. 23.

not need "brushing up" but complete retraining. The update courses mentioned for individuals are of limited value in such instances. Usually, those involved are E/S who, early in their careers, find themselves in administration, plant management, marketing, or confined in a narrow technical specialty. Some are almost entirely obsolete in their professional skills; others may be experts only in a very narrow area. Economic swings or corporate redirection of the company may eliminate their positions. Because of their obsolescence, these individuals are especially vulnerable to layoffs, but because such personnel are often older, there is a potential problem with age discrimination legislation. Many companies interviewed expressed concern because their existing base of engineers is predominately electrical and/or mechanical but their product lines or manufacturing processes increasingly require electronic and computer skills. This problem is compounded by the fact that critical personnel shortages are likely to exist in the emerging technologies. Loss of productivity and profitability may also occur as the company hires new individuals capable of designing or applying the new technology, while at the same time maintaining a substantial workforce with skills in need of upgrading.

Several responses to group obsolescence have been found effective. Structural dimensions of the organization may be changed to permit individuals to channel their resources in new directions. Some companies have also responded to this situation by developing structured retraining programs which can accommodate large groups of people. Such programs may be conceived and implemented in-house, in conjunction with a university, or as part of other outside programs.

Mission Change. Changing the mission of employees is a long-recognized revitalization technique. In such circumstances, E/S are given the opportunity to extend their expertise in a new direction, to apply knowledge within a different framework, or to focus their energy towards a different goal.

> Engineering and scientific teams are assigned work in broad scope by the assignment of missions. Review of development successes and breakthroughs shows they come most often from newly constituted groups or those given a new challenge. In fact, one concept of development management is that breakthroughs do not come from groups heavily committed by the success of their past products. Gaining a new challenge causes reorganization, new learning, and a general stimulation for an organization. Change in the mission of a location, an organization or a group can be used as a deliberate management practice to stimulate further change and growth.[18]

---

[18]Miller, "Changing Job Requirements," p. 68.

Human Resource Strategic Planning. Few companies interviewed had carefully integrated their human resource planning with strategic business planning. As a result, there has been little long-term commitment to offset obsolescence by a strategic approach to human resource development, retraining, and redirection on an overall, rather than ad hoc, basis. As one study noted:

> In most companies, the long-range planning process forces the development of technical, product and other strategies. Notably absent in the past as part of these strategies has been any planning for providing people with proper skills to carry out these strategies. Admittedly it is difficult, but finding a way to make planning for the properly skilled team a part of the strategy can take activities now considered peripheral, like education, broadening of experience, rotation, transfer, and recruiting, and make them mainline committed activities. Management should start asking questions like the following in reviews of strategies:
>
> —What are the technical capabilities of the team today with respect to the technology and the product?
> —What changes in technology,· competence, skills and capabilities will be required over the next five years?
> —Does the schedule allow for the continuing education, broadening experience, etc., necessary to have a more competent team in the future?
> —How has the capability of the team increased over the past year and what were the successful techniques for causing this change?
>
> If management, in establishing a requirement for strategies and plans can require plans for providing the team to do the job, then evidence of the importance of growth and development will be reinforced by the management system.[19]

One chemical company has an organizational development group, which includes among its missions the facilitation of change in the organization. In this company, human resource and strategic planning are well integrated, so that group retraining and mission redirection are coordinated and planned far ahead. The organizational development group is enjoined to avoid E/S obsolescence through careful planning and program development. The firm's top management repeatedly affirms the importance of organizational change as a means of coordinating product development and discipline reorientation, and the concomitant necessity of on-going human resource training and development to prevent obsolescence.

This same company understands the strategic importance of bricks-and-mortar projects in enhancing development and change. The organizational development group participated in the planning of a new technical center, which was designed ergonomically and

---

[19]*Ibid.,* pp. 69–70.

incorporated many features and considerable equipment aimed at stimulating new approaches.

Communication. Communication is an extremely important tool for combating obsolescence. Very often, companies do not sufficiently or explicitly convey to their E/S the nature and extent of new skills that must be acquired. If individual employees are made aware of the strategic orientation of the firm, they are more likely to work actively at upgrading their skills in tandem with corporate objectives and directions. For example, one electrical equipment manufacturer has clearly and thoroughly advised its E/S that its traditional power-oriented product lines, such as motors, transformers, switchgear and related electromechanical products, cannot be expected to expand because of energy conservation and competitive market factors, but that there are great opportunities in its fast-growing, electronics-oriented product lines. Its communications advise E/S in power generation to consider retraining in electronics and related fields, which are the designated areas of expansion under its strategic plans, and it has established the requisite training mechanisms to enable employees to do so. Results include a more satisfied labor force, as well as insurance against excessive obsolescence.

One computer company has a council composed of ten engineering directors whose primary purpose is to combat obsolescence. It also works to develop meaningful career progressions. A second computer company has a professional development group also working to ensure that opportunities for continuing technological progression are available. In both instances, the emphasis is on creating and communicating opportunities for E/S.

Group Retraining. Many firms have developed special in-house courses which are designed to retrain groups of people with obsolete skills. Usually participants receive training to prepare them for jobs in critical skill areas. These are not one-time crisis programs; the firms have made a commitment to the recycling process. Some company courses have had several generations of graduates who have made successful career changes. The overall response to such programs from both managers and participants has been quite positive.

In the aerospace industry, electronic and computer skills are becoming increasingly important. Two companies have instituted software retraining programs. Individuals with basic computer skills in need of sharpening are eligible to enroll in formal classes which are taught on site and on company time. Another computer company follows a policy of on-site retraining at affected locations when "mission transfers" occur. An electrical equipment manufacturer periodically sponsors programs for engineers in need of skill updates. This diverse company works with regionally located universities to develop courses with particular relevance to local employees. Another firm engages university professors to teach at its manufacturing facility. These courses are offered one-half on company time, and one-half on personal time. Thus, some degree of employee commitment must be demonstrated by the individual E/S.

An aircraft equipment manufacturing arm of a conglomerate organization developed a retraining program in response to a particular and severe business need. The engineers who had traditionally been involved in analog design were educated in digital technology, particularly in the design and development of very large scale integration circuits. Two groups of twenty engineers participated. These engineers were not merely "updated." Through an intensive series of courses they acquired an entirely new set of skills. The courses were developed in conjunction with a variety of universities, but were specifically tailored to the business. Considerable company-specific information was incorporated into the course curriculums. The program was initiated in response to a one-time business need, and was discontinued after the desired results were achieved.

Another major aerospace firm foresaw the projected shortage of software engineers as early as 1977 and 1978. The company had great use for software in its weapons systems, electronics, and other areas because electronics is a growing percentage of its work, and was even then projected to reach nearly 30 percent of the costs by 1985. The company had found that the costs of its software engineer recruiting were high and the results unsatisfactory because, as a company personnel executive put it, "you just eat up the seed grain by drawing people away from other companies who then hire them away from you. It is a revolving door." The company, therefore, devised a plan to retrain engineers considered obsolete into software specialists, and won approval from the U.S. Department of Defense to include the retraining cost as a legitimate contract expense on the grounds that the funds were adding to the supply of a very scarce and much needed skill.

The course was taught by a training division of a computer manufacturing company and by the company's own personnel. The oldest persons admitted to the course were in their sixties, the majority were over forty-five years of age, and the youngest had seven years minimum experience. Many engineers who took the course were described as "on the shelf, and off the learning course." They were "riding out their time till retirement." They were capable of rising to a challenge, but were not being challenged; the company, through the training course, challenged the so-called "has beens," who jumped at the opportunity.

The course included an eight-week software programming session, followed by an eight-week advanced systems session. Participants gave their full time to the course. The company calculated that the cost of retraining per individual is $15,000, while it costs $20,000 to recruit a software engineer who may or may not remain with the company. Thus, less money was spent for a proved individual with little likelihood of turnover, and a marginal performance was converted into a highly productive one by dramatic mid-career change.

There have been other benefits. The camaraderie induced by sixteen weeks of study has produced some excellent work teams. Laboratory technicians heard of the program, and were admitted where qualified, resulting in some successful upgrading. The program is now periodically revived as needed, following its termination during the early 1980s recession when course graduates were not in demand and had difficulty with intracompany placement. This program combines combating obsolescence with mitigating a shortage of key E/S personnel, and is among the most successful efforts against obsolescence uncovered in our research.

Another impressive and extensive program has been developed by a chemical company in conjunction with a university. This program provides two options. The basic program is an updating training program for nonpracticing engineering graduates. This option is intended to respond to the needs of selected personnel with long service who decide that career reorientation is appropriate to prolong or to ensure their future with the company. Completion of the program leads to a second career in corporate engineering or manufacturing.

The second option is a process control program which is designed to provide state-of-the-art knowledge and skills for engineers of various disciplines who have been top performers. There is dual incentive to pursue this option. First, no single engineering degree currently provides the broad range of skills necessary for optimum performance in the total control area in the chemical process industry. Second, the company has a significant need for this type of expertise. As shown in Figure IX-1, the majority of the participants were between forty and fifty years of age, received their degrees more than twenty years ago, and have been with the company for at least twenty years.

The program, which takes one full year to complete, is offered at a university. The engineers relocate from their homes to the university location for the duration of the program. The year is divided into trimesters, and each participant takes three courses per trimester.

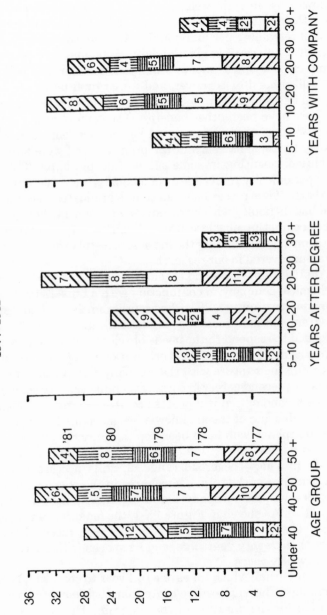

FIGURE IX-1
Profiles of Course Participants
Chemical Company Retraining Program
1977–1981

Source: Information provided by chemical company.

Regular classes meet twice per week in a lecture format and are followed by three hours of supervised problem solving. The courses emphasize fundamental engineering concepts and their application. The material presented has been designed to prepare the "students" for their new jobs, and has a high degree of industry relevance. This can be contrasted with the more theoretical orientation of traditional engineering courses. Of the seventy-three people who participated during the first four years of the program, sixty-eight completed it. Both the sponsoring company and the engineers are enthusiastic about the program and feel that it has helped solve a particularly challenging personnel problem.

FIGURE IX-2
Decision Model
Considerations Costs and Benefits
of Retraining Obsolete Engineers and Scientists

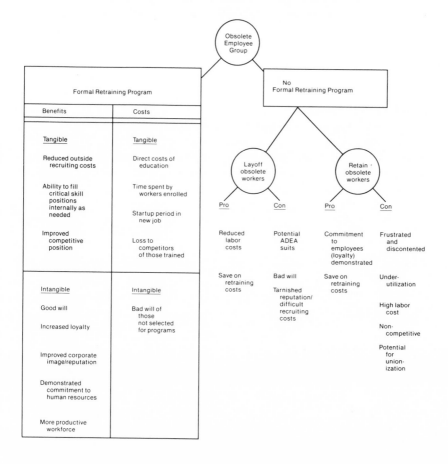

The selection of individuals for rigorous programs such as the two described above is a difficult task. Stringent selection criteria must be developed, because a company must be satisfied that its investment in employee education and retraining is ultimately profitable. Figure IX-2 summarizes the costs and benefits of retraining or not doing so, for an obsolete E/S group. Individual potential and motivation must be carefully evaluated, for again, only those desiring to learn will successfully be retrained.

CONCLUSION

Obsolescence is a serious problem given today's fast-changing technology. The facile equation of age and obsolescence is no longer possible. Technological development may occur so rapidly that any age group can be affected. In addition, not only individuals, but also entire disciplinary groups may become obsolescent. It is important, therefore, for management to take a number of steps to prevent obsolescence, such as focusing attention on job content, encouraging communication, and initiating retraining programs.

Fighting obsolescence, however valuable, is a heavy financial burden. Retraining can be very expensive and many companies will avoid such expenses. Those that can undertake the necessary costs would seem to have the best opportunity of survival and growth in a highly technical world. Moreover, there seems little doubt that keeping obsolescence at bay contributes substantially to a well-motivated, highly productive E/S complement. Thus, the return on the investment in recognizing, preventing, and overcoming obsolescence can be substantial.

CHAPTER X

Retention and Layoffs

The labor market for engineers and scientists (E/S) does not adjust perfectly either at the micro or macro level. Students pursuing a course of study that looked very promising when they entered college may find that job-seekers with their professional training are in surplus by the time they graduate. The sudden downward shift in the demand for geologists following the collapse of oil prices in the early 1980s is a recent, dramatic example of rapid worldwide shifts in the E/S labor market.

Supply and demand inconsistencies often occur at the company or regional level. Even when a company is laying off engineers in one discipline, it may be hiring them in others. While one geographical sector of the country is depressed, and experiencing record levels of professional unemployment, another area may be expanding, enjoying growth and prosperity. Economic adjustment takes time. Technical skills are not immediately transferable, although a solid quantitative base increases the potential for retraining. In addition, most individuals are not immediately mobile. It takes both planning and soul-searching before an individual actually takes concrete steps toward moving to a new location. Changes in the economy affect critical skill disciplines and locations. During an economic upswing some skills are in higher demand than others. The short-term imbalances between supply and demand create challenges for personnel managers and those involved in manpower planning.

It would be ideal if a company could predict its manpower requirements accurately, and simultaneously be assured of personnel availability. In reality such situations do not exist. A firm must attempt to anticipate future demands, and such estimates are surrounded by uncertainties. Some companies are moving towards succession planning and developing skill inventories, as described in previous chapters. Nonetheless, because of fluctuations in the economy which cause peaks and troughs in supply and demand, termination, and the problems associated with it, are unavoidable. Depending upon the firm's situation in an economic cycle, the particular problem may be either attempting to increase retention rates, or conversely, deciding upon appropriate individuals to lay off.

RETENTION

Some turnover is healthy within a corporate organization. Normal attrition causes a firm to search for individuals with skills suitable for above-entry levels, or at least for experienced hires. Attrition also helps create openings which provide increased upward mobility or promotional opportunities for deserving individuals. Moreover, if unsatisfied individuals were forced to remain with a company because of lack of alternate job opportunities, or for other reasons, the resultant discontent would be likely to reduce productivity. On the other hand, high turnover may also hurt performance, reduce continuity in job performance, and create the potential for leakage of proprietary information. For the individual E/S, some mobility is often important to career advancement, but excessive job hopping may both preclude maximum career enhancement and greatly reduce retirement benefits.

Reducing Turnover

All turnover, whether involving laborers or E/S, is likely to be heavily concentrated among new hires. Intelligent, carefully constructed recruiting and orientation programs, as described in Chapter IV, are clearly essential ingredients in retaining E/S. Likewise, training and development programs, which emphasize the unity between the goals of the company and those of the employees, are extremely significant in fostering both high morale and good retention. One paper company found that it could reduce turnover by developing special career paths for new hires. The prospect of moving along a predetermined path seemed to appeal to the E/S in this corporation, and particularly helped to avoid the problem of disillusionment during the first critical months on the job.

How the first assignment is made is very important. A publishing company found that those E/S who were given "a meaty job" right at the beginning, were more likely to be retained than those who were given a peripheral, or seemingly unimportant, assignment "so that they could acclimate."

Finally, communication and community relations were stressed as important factors in the retention of E/S by many companies. Engineers and scientists, like all employees, want to know what is happening in a company, desire a channel of communications, and want a sense of belonging. Communication through written media, supervisors, and peers is an essential ingredient of retention. Assistance in adapting to a community not only helps the E/S integrate into the company, but alleviates family unhappiness that can tip the balance between retention and resignation. Most companies which employ a sizable number of E/S make considerable efforts both to communicate with their E/S personnel, particularly new recruits, and to assist them in adapting to their new environment.

Most companies deplore pirating, yet feel that they must engage in it in order to procure special skills in short supply. An obvious place to seek qualified replacements is among a competitor's personnel. Pirating has a further unethical component, involving the hiring away of personnel who have proprietary information. Increasing litigation has resulted from such actions.[1] As noted in Chapter IV, various other methods for recruiting experienced E/S are utilized, but no matter which avenue is pursued, the end result adds to turnover. For some subgroups in short supply, such as software engineers, the result is an upward spiral of wages and very high mobility. Programs to retrain older workers and professionals in obsolete occupations to become software specialists are an outgrowth of this problem.

The entrepreneurial spirit also stimulates turnover. Silicon Valley is a prime example. Professionals and managers move from one company to another, lured by stock grants and options and by the chance that they might become high technology millionaires. Actually, stock options often turn out to be of little value, either because the once bright prospects of the company did not materialize, or because the potential recipients did not remain with the company long enough to benefit.[2]

Small companies often appeal strongly to E/S personnel, but those who leave large companies for small ones are sometimes disillusioned because they find drawbacks as well as advantages. They discover that the smaller firms may be neither as aggressive nor innovative as they have been portrayed. Often the required institutional and financial support for scientific instruments, or other costly equipment, are not as accessible as they are to major corporations. Working in a small company may also mean the absence of colleagues to discuss problems, and considerably less technical support: "At the independent, you worked alone in your area. No one else

---

[1] A recent example is the movement of key personnel from Commodore Business Machines Inc., to Atari Inc., after Jack Tramiel, past president of the former, purchased the latter company. See Andrea Knox and Reid Kanaley, "Commodore Says 4 Stole Trade Secrets," *Philadelphia Inquirer,* July 12, 1984, pp. 1-A, 10-A; and Reid Kanaley, "4 Ex-Workers to Allow Commodore to Search Personal Effects," *Philadelphia Inquirer,* July 14, 1984, p. 5-B.

[2] The Wharton Industrial Research Unit's forthcoming study of "Personnel Policies of High Technology Companies" discusses this and other features of developments in these concerns.

knew anything about it."[3] The net effect of assessing small company opportunities idealistically instead of realistically is likely to be increased industry-wide turnover, as E/S who move from a large concern to a small one often seek reemployment in a major firm after a relatively short tenure in a small company.

Earth Science Turnaround. In 1981, when this study commenced, earth scientists (geologists and geophysicists) were in high demand and short supply. These individuals were being lured away from major oil companies by small independents with promises of freedom from corporate hierarchies, and with profit sharing, stock options, and other programs. Large companies retaliated by introducing a myriad of special perquisites, including deferred bonuses, cars, and housing allowances. Other creative plans were developed by companies with separate operating subsidiaries in oil exploration, such as phantom stock plans, and limited "piece of the action" plans.

When the oversupply of petroleum products overrode the OPEC cartel's price policies, petroleum prices fell, major companies downsized their exploration activities, and many smaller ones went bankrupt or otherwise ceased operations. The earth science field was suddenly afflicted with oversupply. Many geologists who had left major companies sought to return, having found "that overrides aren't worth much in a slump."[4] Major companies offered bonuses, superior pensions, and other "golden handshakes" to induce exploration personnel to terminate, but some companies continue to pay geologists the perquisites inaugurated during the OPEC's days of control. Other geologists and geophysicists have never regained the status nor income which they so briefly enjoyed.

Computer Professionals. Turnover is very high among computer professionals. Nearly every company has noted the difficulties in retaining such personnel, particularly those expert in software engineering development and utilization. Many companies feel that technical employees can be ranked in order of those whose loyalty is chiefly to their profession rather than their corporate employer: first, computer professionals; second, scientists; and third, engineers. The majority of companies feel that engineers adapt to corporate goals more easily than either scientists or computer personnel. In their book dealing with personnel policies for computer professionals, Cougar and Zawacki identify a variety of personality characteristics of computer personnel. In particular, they conclude that computer personnel exhibit a lower social need and a higher need for

---

[3]Roger Lowenstein, "Geologists Return to Big Oil Firms, Giving Up Hopes of Striking It Rich," *Wall Street Journal,* July 27, 1982, p. 33.
[4]*Ibid.*

self-fulfillment and growth than do other workers.[5] Subtle personality differences of this type have clear implications for job design and worker motivation, and it is worthwhile to consider such factors in the development of retention programs.

The labor market situation of computer professionals, particularly software engineers, is probably more significant than personality traits in stimulating turnover. Computer professionals, like many engineering and scientific specialists, are a multi-industry resource, and therefore have a variety of alternative opportunities. Their jobs are not extremely sensitive to supply and demand forces within particular industries because if one industry is in a slump, computer skills can often be transferred to another one that is prospering. As long as computer professionals are in such short supply, their turnover rate will be high. This means, of course, that industry must work hard to maintain as low a turnover as possible, and internal development of this management capability is an intelligent investment.

One company mentioned that it paid special attention to job content for computer scientists to ensure that they feel challenged by their work and desire to remain. The vice-president of a Silicon Valley company related that a top-notch software engineer told his supervisor that he had recently been curious about employment alternatives, and had interviewed with another company in California. It offered him $10,000 more per year than he was making at his present job. He realized as a result of this interview that he was receiving less than the market rate, but he decided to stay with his original job because he enjoyed it. The company then adjusted his salary to better reflect market conditions, but waited a few months before making the change.[6] One aerospace company has attempted to increase its retention rate of software engineers by establishing a comprehensive professional development program which includes career paths. This company has been noted previously because of its successful software retraining program which reduces the number of computer professionals that it must recruit on the open market.

Because computer scientists are alleged to exhibit different personality traits from other professionals, perhaps special career paths should be developed which will satisfy their specific needs and expectations. A company that is willing to recognize these differences and work with them, rather than trying to fit computer scientists into traditional or established career paths, will undoubtedly

[5]J. Daniel Cougar and Robert A. Zawacki, *Motivating and Managing Computer Personnel* (New York: John Wiley and Sons, 1980), pp. 82–92.
[6]Interviews with company representatives, Silicon Valley, California, May 1982.

have a better retention record. Such career development planning is an investment, but a cost-benefit analysis may show that it is worthwhile because it can offset the costs of hiring and relocation. Increased job satisfaction also would be an intangible benefit accrued from establishing this type of system. On the other hand, it should also be recognized that the labor market is likely to remain the key factor contributing to turnover among software engineers and other professionals when the demand for specialists exceeds the supply. Thus, programs designed to increase a company's supply would seem to be the option that would return the most dividends. Attacking the problem in various nonexclusive ways also makes good business sense.

Problem Industries. The older basic industries are at a particularly serious disadvantage in retaining young E/S because often they cannot provide exciting work. For example, an engineer who designs new and improved equipment may be frustrated because the company will not spend funds to scrap older machines and install the new ones; yet the cost-benefit economic calculations may not justify doing so. Similarly, in some mature industries, innovation moves slowly either for economic reasons or because of cautiousness and lack of interest on the part of management reared in a traditional setting. The president of the Allegheny Ludlum Steel Corporation probably spoke for other industries when he stated: "There isn't any doubt that basic American industry—and steel in particular—has suffered from its inability to hold and attract talented people."[7] The severity of the 1980–1982 recession in the steel, automobile, and other basic metal industries, and the resultant layoffs of managers and professionals, as well as blue-collar and clerical employees,[8] have also induced many of the superior E/S who were not laid off to seek careers elsewhere.

Race and Sex. Turnover rates can also be affected by the race and sex of the E/S employed. A number of companies stated that the shortage of black engineers and scientists made them especially vulnerable to pirating and turnover. Companies located in areas that had few black residents emphasized that they had great difficulty both in recruiting and in retaining black professionals.

Several companies mentioned that although the number of dual-career couples has been increasing, they still found that many women leave when their spouse is transferred. Thus, some compa-

---

[7]Thomas F. O'Boyle, "Brain Drain: U.S. Basic Industries are Hindered by Loss of Scientific Talent," *Wall Street Journal,* July 27, 1984, pp. 1, 16.

[8]U.S. Steel was still laying off managers and professionals in July 1984 when it announced plans to dismiss 500 such personnel associated with two plants.

nies reported that female turnover was higher. In a few cases, companies also noted that they had lost male E/S because their wives had found better jobs in another location.

Location. The location of a facility can greatly affect retention. The movement to the West and to the Sunbelt has drawn engineers and scientists from the Northeast and the Midwest. The concentration of high technology companies in the Silicon Valley area has increased the propensity of E/S in this area to change jobs. On the other hand, the concentration of such companies around Route 128 in the Boston area seems to have resulted in less inducements for intercompany mobility. Whether the difference is the result of the greater maturity of the Route 128 concerns, the more flamboyant life style of California, or a combination of these and other factors, is not clearly understood.[9]

Southern California boasts the largest concentration of aerospace concerns in the nation and, therefore, the largest concentration of E/S in industry. This tends to encourage some job mobility, but the major firms, conscious that pirating can work both ways, attempt to discourage it. As shall be explained below, the practice of "lending" E/S has curtailed job movement in the Southern California aerospace industry.

Companies which are located in isolated areas, such as those in forest products, often find it difficult to both employ and retain E/S, even though some persons enjoy the more isolated, quiet life. Women engineers and scientists in particular have often refused to locate to such areas, possibly fearing a restricted social life.

Exit Interviews and Post-Employment Surveys

Exit interviews are widely utilized by companies to increase their understanding of the reasons for E/S resignations. Assessments of the value of this technique are mixed. Most company personnel executives do not believe that E/S are completely candid in such interviews. It is not uncommon for E/S to reapply for jobs which they have left. Hence, they often apparently hesitate to be completely frank about their reasons for leaving lest such discussions inhibit their opportunity to return. Nevertheless, companies have found that exit interviews are useful in providing at least some clues concerning reasons for resignations and for uncovering major, recurring problems.

---

[9]N.R. Kleinfield, "A Few Clouds Over Route 128," *New York Times*, July 18, 1984, pp. D-1, D-17. These differences were clearly brought out in the interviews in the two areas, both in 1982 for this study and in 1984 for the forthcoming study on "Personnel Policies of High Technology Companies."

One company has instituted a "quick response program" to help combat high turnover. When an individual gives notice of resignation, he is asked not to publicize it. Within twenty-four hours an exit interview is held with a personnel representative. The purpose of this interview is to uncover, and work at eliminating, specific dissatisfactions. Since the employee has not widely disclosed his intent, there is no humiliation if the decision is changed. Through these interviews, this major conglomerate claims that it has eliminated 50 percent of its potential turnover.

A small, high-tech, high-growth company located in the Silicon Valley was experiencing an annual professional turnover of 34 percent. The manager of training and education undertook a study of this turnover.[10] He called professionals after they left the company, and also developed a "forced exit response form." This form includes a multiple choice series of questions on reasons for leaving. The primary findings were that individuals left the firm because they felt 1) that they were underutilized or poorly utilized and had no authority or power to change this; 2) that their abilities were not recognized; or 3) that there was a lack of opportunity, so that they did not advance as expected. They perceived their new positions in other companies as having increased advancement opportunities and/or more challenging assignments. These perceptions may well be optimistic and may prove unfounded after the employee has had experience in the new position, but realistic or not, such expectations add to turnover.

Because of the possible biases and reserved responses elicited by exit interviews, some personnel managers claim that post-employment surveys result in more valid responses to questions on voluntary termination. These surveys are usually mailed to the former employee approximately two months after resignation. In this case as well, however, the belief that successful reapplication might be obviated by frankness could also add a bias to responses. Moreover, the return of such questionnaires is often small, increasing the possibility of biased results. Like exit interviews, post-employment surveys are a helpful tool in uncovering reasons for terminations, but neither can be utilized as the sole basis for policy development.

Reapplication

Even after an engineer or scientist has left a company, it is not unusual for him to reapply after a period of time. Some reasons have

---

[10]Interviews with company representatives, Silicon Valley, California, May 1982.

been mentioned throughout this section: false expectations, lack of technical support, no interaction with other personnel, etc. One company in Florida indicated that 60 percent of its voluntary terminations reapply within eighteen months. Policies concerning rehiring have interesting implications. If a company essentially closes its doors by discouraging reapplication, it limits its potential applicant pool in the future. Given the cyclicality of the economy, it seems unwise to discourage qualified workers from any source. One engineering construction company has a policy that if an individual terminates employment and then decides to return within five years, his benefits are reinstated. Aerospace companies make a practice of rehiring former employees who have had satisfactory records. These companies have found from experience that such E/S often have an advantage by knowing the company, its policies, and its products. Given the expansion and contraction characteristic of their businesses as a result of government procurement decisions or changing commercial needs, these companies have found it wise not to restrict their E/S labor market by excluding former employees.

LAYOFFS

Retention of competent engineers and scientists is a major concern of well-managed companies. Even the best managed companies, however, may find that their economic situation has altered and that a surplus of technical talent results. In such situations, layoffs are necessary. Here the company must act with great care in order to avoid difficulties from various legal constraints, or union rules if applicable, and it must above all act with discretion so as to avoid permanent damage to its reputation which can injure recruiting efforts in the future.

Although E/S, like other employees, are subject to permanent layoffs, temporary furloughs, or downgradings when business declines so dictate, employers are generally reluctant to take such steps. Companies have invested considerable sums in recruiting, developing, and compensating professional employees. To lay them off jeopardizes this investment, particularly since E/S have less difficulty than most employees in finding other jobs. Even during the severe recession of the early 1980s, when general unemployment hovered around 10 percent, the average unemployment for E/S (including social scientists whose unemployment rate was the highest of the various E/S classifications calculated) was only 2 percent for men and 4.2 percent for women.[11] (See Figure X–1.) Engineers' and scientists' unemployment also varied considerably by field and by level of education. The shortage of computer specialists is emphasized by their lower unemployment rates. Those who possess doctorates also have much lower unemployment rates than their fellows in the same field. Obviously, E/S are not lightly dispensed with by their employers.

Nevertheless, unemployment does occur. Many engineers and scientists in the aerospace industry have lost their jobs when the federal government has canceled a contract. In 1977, for example, when President Jimmy Carter stopped the production of B-1 bombers, the contractor, Rockwell International, laid off thousands of E/S.[12] When President Ronald Reagan reestablished the program in 1981, a whole new E/S labor force had to be reassembled, with many new personnel and much valuable experience lost. When layoffs do occur, whether massive or small, companies must have policies to deal with the situation. Such policies must not only conform to the various state and federal laws, but if carefully thought out, must give due regard to long-term corporate requirements as well as to immediate needs.

Historically, layoffs of E/S have been a major problem in two industries, aerospace and construction. Uneven and changing governmental procurement is the basic reason for the aerospace industry's problems; in construction, the unstable and highly cyclical nature of the industry generates layoffs throughout company organizations.[13] During the severe recession of the early 1980s, manufac-

---

[11]The higher unemployment rate for women E/S has persisted for many years. Studies of this subject have indicated that this is because "women are more likely to restrict their job search because of geographic location, family responsibilities, and desire for part-time employment. Evidence shows that if unemployed scientists and engineers of either sex who have job search restrictions are excluded from the computations of unemployment rates, the unemployment rate is virtually identical for male and female scientists and engineers." *Women and Minorities in Science and Engineering* (Washington, D.C.: National Science Foundation, 1984), pp. 18–19.

[12]Rockwell International laid off 2,000 employees immediately and 6,000 more within thirty days. These layoffs included all classes of employees, but professionals and managers were heavily represented. See "End of Bomber Production Spells Unemployment for Several Thousand," *Daily Labor Report* No. 129, July 5, 1977, p. A–10.

[13]The recession of the early 1980s, the oil glut which cut spending on large projects by Arab countries, and overspending on projects in previous years have all greatly reduced construction "megaprojects," forcing cutbacks by the larger construction companies, including the largest: Bechtel. See Victor F. Zonana, "Idle Giants: Builders' Megaprojects Fade with the Dreams of Oil-Rich Countries," *Wall Street Journal*, June 27, 1983, pp. 1, 25; Carrie Dolan and Bill Richards, "Bechtel to Cut Its Work Force About 10% in 1984: Nuclear-Power Plant Woes Cited," *Wall Street Journal*, February 27, 1984, p. 4; and "Bechtel: Fending Off the Recession by Hitting the 'Small Time,'" *Business Week*, March 7, 1983, pp. 54, 58–59.

FIGURE X-1
*Engineer and Scientist Unemployment Rates
by Field and Sex, 1981 and 1982*

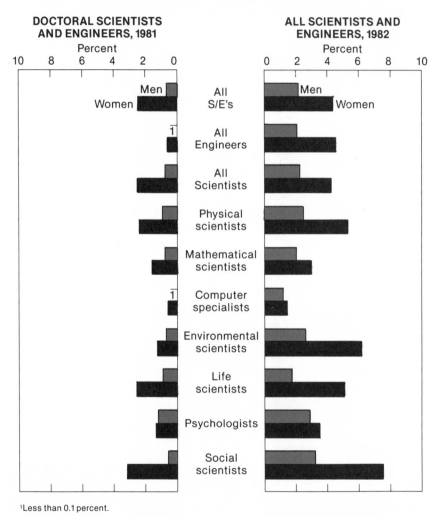

¹Less than 0.1 percent.

Source: *Women and Minorities in Science and Engineering* (Washington, D.C.: National Science Foundation, 1984), p. 18.

turers of steel, automobiles, farm equipment, and other durable goods industries, which suffered major downturns, also laid off a considerable number of E/S. Interestingly, the interviews conducted for this study found that those least vulnerable to the layoffs were the E/S working in research and development. Since research superiority is crucial in maintaining long-range market and competitive positions, firms are understandably reluctant to reduce staff in this area unless economic pressures to do so are overwhelming.

Layoff Criteria

Whether termed reductions in force, downsizing, or layoffs, the effects of such actions are that some employees are dismissed, either permanently or temporarily, and some are downgraded. For blue-collar employees, seniority is the most usual criterion utilized to determine who remains in the company workforce and who is laid off. Since it is in the corporate interest to retain the most competent and productive professionals, such a standard is rarely utilized on a strict basis for E/S even in those situations in which a union represents them. The interviews did affirm, however, that seniority played a role where ability was judged equal. The seniority criterion may also be plausibly invoked when comparative ability is in doubt, or when a supervisor or manager prefers not to make a judgement.

To lay off (or to promote) on the basis of merit requires objective evaluation of both performance and specific skills. Merit selection is undoubtedly a more reasonable and preferable method both from the point of view of management and that of the conscientious professional.[14] It is also more difficult to administer and to defend. Careful documentation is required since layoffs must often be defended against charges of age, sex, or race discrimination. Performance appraisals done by the same supervisors and managers who determine layoff selection may have contradictory evaluations of people selected for layoff. Subjectivity can be the chief weakness of the evaluation process. Moreover, other considerations, such as avoidance of lawsuits and satisfying government-imposed affirmative action requirements, also play a significant role. Merit selection for layoffs is as important as merit selection for employment. In both situations, the future of the enterprise can be seriously affected.

---

[14]In a 1974 survey of attitudes of research and development engineers employed by the federal government, the statement: "The [union] practice of emphasizing seniority for promotions would have a negative impact on the morale in my organization" was agreed to by 66 percent of those surveyed, disagreed to by only 10 percent, with 24 percent uncertain. A follow-up study two years later found these percentages to be 61, 11, and 28, respectively. T. Roger Manley and Charles W. McNichols, "Attitudes of Federal Scientists and Engineers Toward Unions," *Monthly Labor Review*, Vol. 98 (April 1975), p. 59; and Manley and McNichols, "Scientists, Engineers and Unions Revisited," *Monthly Labor Review*, Vol. 100 (November 1977), p. 33. The data for 1974 are reported differently in the two articles. The figures most favorable to unions were used here.

Because of their frequent experience with layoffs, most aerospace companies stress performance appraisal and have instituted elaborate training programs to teach supervisors and managers how to evaluate people for promotion and layoff. Consistency and objectivity in evaluation are the central themes of training, in addition to basic techniques and administrative requirements. Sometimes, of course, a cancelled government contract wipes out a whole division of a company. Even then, however, competent E/S are usually selected for transfers rather than layoffs on the basis of their skills and performance. Determining who should be laid off, who retained, and who transferred or downgraded is a difficult but necessary job. Few managers perform this task perfectly, but the pressures to do so have forced attention to the need for more thorough, objective appraisals throughout the working life of E/S.

Notice and Severance Pay

Both professional societies and unions advocate notice of layoffs and transfers, and detailed explanation of the reasons therefor, usually at least one month before the layoffs or transfers are effective, or longer if the employee has considerable service. In addition, these organizations usually advocate severance pay equal to one week's pay per year of service.[15]

As noted in Chapter III, unions in the industry perform at best a modest function, and most companies do not believe that recommending terms and conditions of employment is a proper function of a professional society. Nevertheless, advance notice and severance payments are both common where practical, with severance pay sometimes more liberal, sometimes less so, than the commonly observed one week per year of service. Unfortunately, the sudden cancellations of contracts by government agencies makes advance notice either difficult or impossible for aerospace companies, although severance pay can frequently be provided.

Outplacement Services

Outplacement service support increased considerably during the 1980–82 recession. Companies frequently offered job-finding assistance in the past, but more recently in many companies these services have become formal policy for E/S and other professionals and managers. Today, most companies offer at least some assistance to employees who have been terminated because of economic adversity,

---

[15]See Appendix B for recommended policies of some professional societies.

or factors other than their own poor performance. Consider the following examples:

A paper company offered secretarial support, and paid for transportation to all interviews within the company. A chemical company coached individuals to prepare them for the ensuing job hunt. A construction firm has a brochure prepared for terminated employees to assist their job search, and contacts other companies to see if they need personnel. A petroleum firm offers help with career orientation and résumé preparation. A pharmaceutical company uses industry contacts to locate other positions, and assists with résumé writing. A machinery manufacturer provides extensive outplacement support, supplying office space and secretarial service, and even employing consultants to help its employees with their job search. Another machinery manufacturer sends letters to other firms informing them that some of their engineers would soon be available, and offering to send résumés if requested. Other companies provide similar outplacement services to varying degrees, including making company facilities available for interviewing, providing secretarial support both for résumé preparation and contact letters, making telephones available to establish contacts and interviews employing consulting firms for reorientation and counseling, providing handsome severance benefits, etc.

Some of the firms that were affected by the recession of the early 1980s have been forced to lay off E/S with many years of service. The difficulties faced by these individuals in entering a depressed job market were augmented by their lack of familiarity with job hunting and interviewing procedures, and companies recognizing their problems developed procedures and policies to assist them. It is likely that such outplacement services will become a permanent feature of many companies' policies for E/S and managers affected by layoffs resulting from factors beyond the individual's control.

Plant Closures

Plant closures dislocate E/S as they do other employees. The policies followed for E/S are similar to other terminations. Transfer opportunities are offered if at all possible; otherwise notice and severance pay is usually provided (except in sudden government contract cancellations), and outplacement services are provided.

Legislation restricting plant closures is strongly advocated by the AFL–CIO, and particularly by the unions in the older mass production industries which have been hard hit by declining employment and layoffs. A few states have enacted such laws, and bills have been introduced into Congress, but to date the impact of such legislation on company policy and economic realities is at best debatable.[16]

EEO Legislation and Layoffs

Companies often attempt to utilize layoffs as a means of ridding the workforce of inefficient employees. Since, as was discussed in Chapter IX, age and obsolescence are often equated for engineers and scientists, it is not surprising that older E/S historically have suffered layoffs most heavily. A study of layoffs among sixty-two aerospace and electronics firms in the San Francisco Bay Area during 1963 and 1965 reached the following conclusions:

> Defense-oriented firms in the San Francisco Bay Area appear to have laid off engineers and scientists primarily on the basis of their age. For example, 33 percent of the laid off engineers and scientists are 45 years of age or older. In view of the estimate that 17 percent of the industry's engineers and scientists are 45 years of age and above, proportionately twice as many engineers and scientists who are in the 45 years plus category were laid off. When educational background, technical publications, patents, membership in professional societies, and number of engineering and scientific courses completed at work are considered, there is no statistically significant difference between laid off and working engineers and scientists.[17]

Older Workers. In 1967, Congress enacted the Age Discrimination in Employment Act (ADEA) which severely restricted the right to concentrate terminations among employees of and between forty and sixty-five years of age. As of January 1, 1984, the law's coverage was extended to persons seventy years of age. Employees cannot be forced to retire before age seventy or be otherwise dismissed or discriminated against without cause. Moreover, several states, including New York and California where the aerospace and electronics industries employ large numbers of engineers and scientists, have abolished compulsory retirement altogether. Where state laws are more liberal in this regard, they prevail, and Congress may well decree the end of compulsory retirement in the near future.

In the early 1970s, the aerospace industry was hit by a severe downturn. Unemployment among engineers, professional and tech-

---

[16]See, for example, Antone Aboud, ed., *Plant Closing Legislation* (Ithaca, N.Y.: ILR Press, New York State School of Industrial and Labor Relations, Cornell University, 1984); and "Plant-Closing Bills: Labor Takes a Beating," *Business Week*, August 20, 1984, p. 40.

[17]R. P. Loomba, *A Study of the Re-Employment and Unemployment Experiences of Scientists and Engineers Laid Off from 62 Aerospace and Electronics Firms in the San Francisco Bay Area During 1963-65* (San Jose, California: Manpower Research Group, San Jose State College, 1967), p. 103.

nical workers rose to 2.9 percent in 1971 at a time when the civilian labor force unemployment rate was 5.9 percent.[18] Table X-1 shows that engineers over age forty-five suffered disproportionately heavy layoffs. According to the U.S. Bureau of Labor Statistics:

> There was an inverse relationship between age and unemployment in the age group of 25 to 39 years, but at 40 the rates began to increase with age. Older engineers may be considered by many potential employers to be less adaptable or too specialized. Also when the layoffs occurred, the younger, less experienced engineers were laid off first. These workers looked for jobs and by the time RIF's (reduction in force) hit the older, more experienced engineers, most of the better engineering positions had already been filled.[19]

Recent unemployment among engineers and scientists hit older E/S much less disproportionately than prior to the passage of the ADEA. Although this law was enacted largely because of alleged discrimination against older blue-collar workers, its main beneficiaries have been managers and professionals. In fact, studies by the former vice-chairman of the Equal Employment Opportunity Commission (EEOC) covering the period 1981–1983 found that plaintiffs in age discrimination cases are typically Caucasion male white-collar workers in their mid-fifties, who are challenging their termination from employment, and who had worked for a company nearly twenty years. Among the plaintiffs in 1982–83 were an engineering manager, several engineers, a communications specialist, a cartographic draftsman, and numerous other executives and professionals.[20] Of course, these data do not include the myriad of settled cases experienced by nearly all companies that have laid off professionals or managers.

Because of the incidence and costs of age discrimination cases, companies have expended considerable effort developing policies to circumvent them. These policies include improvement of appraisal systems, retraining, and "golden handshakes." The first two policies have been fully discussed in relation to obsolescence and general layoff policies. Golden handshakes involve incentives to retire, such as increased termination pay, pension supplements, or other bonuses. To avoid legal proscriptions, such incentives must be voluntary and open to a representative group, not focused upon selected

---

[18]Kathleen Naughton, "Characteristics of Jobless Engineers," *Monthly Labor Review*, Vol. 95 (October 1972), p. 16.

[19]*Ibid.*, p. 19.

[20]See Cathie A. Shattuck, "Cases Filed Under the Age Discrimination in Employment Act," mimeographed (Philadelphia: Industrial Research Unit, The Wharton School, 1982); and Shattuck, "ADEA Litigation Survey—1983," mimeographed (Philadelphia: Industrial Research Unit, the Wharton School, 1984).

TABLE X-1
Unemployment Rates and Percent Distribution Among Engineers by Age Group, June–July 1971

Age group	Unemployment rate	Unemployed EJC survey respondents	EIC survey sample universe
Total	3.0	100	100
24 years and under	5.5	4	2
25 to 29	3.3	12	10
30 to 34	2.2	10	13
35 to 39	2.2	10	13
40 to 44	2.7	14	14
45 to 49	2.8	16	16
50 to 54	3.3	14	12
55 to 59	4.1	11	8
60 to 64	4.2	6	5
65 and over	3.4	2	6
No report	2.4	1	1

Source: Original data from the National Survey of Engineering Employment, 1971 (New York: Engineers Joint Council, 1971). Table reprinted from Kathleen Naughton, "Characteristics of Jobless Engineers," *Monthly Labor Review*, Vol. 95 (October 1972), p. 19.

individuals. Thus, often persons whom the company desires to retain accept such offers, and others at whom the retirement incentives are aimed may decide to remain employed.

Sex and Race. As the data presented in Chapter III clearly demonstrate, minorities and women are underrepresented among engineers and scientists. Nevertheless, the data also demonstrate that these classes have continued to increase their ratios despite the fluctuations in the business cycle. It was clear from our interviews that companies expended much effort to retain minority and female E/S in any layoff. This was especially true for companies such as those in the aerospace industry which, because the government is typically their customer, are under intense pressure to meet "goals" for minorities and women. Other companies endeavor to retain any minority and female E/S whom they have employed because it is so difficult to replace them.

Although retention of minorities and women during layoffs solves affirmative action problems, it can also dilute the process of maintaining the best and most productive professional labor force. Company personnel managers freely admitted that affirmative action had prompted them to retain some professionals who otherwise would have been furloughed or dismissed. Although it was frequently stated that those who were laid off so that minorities could be retained understood that this was both a social cost and a necessary approach for a major supplier to the federal government, it is difficult to believe that such departures from the merit selection process of a company are satisfactory to those who suffer a resultant harm, or that serious morale and productivity problems do not result.

At-Will Employment. In recent years, courts in a number of states, particularly California and Michigan, have read contractual obligations into the wording of employee manuals or other company employment forms and have thus greatly modified, without legislative sanction, the traditional United States law and custom which (absent specific legislation) provides that an employee is hired "at will" and can be terminated, just as he or she can leave employment, for any reason not in violation of existing law. Under the recent judicial rulings, substantial sums have been awarded to employees who have been determined to have suffered loss of jobs in violation of "implied contracts," or without "just cause."[21] These decisions underscore the need for companies to develop and to institute well-thought-out policies that can provide a strong defense against judicial appeals when layoffs or discharges occur.

CONTRACTING OUT PROFESSIONALS

Engineering and scientific firms which do contract work for major companies have existed for many years. Such firms are typically busy and profitable in periods of high employment. Major companies have historically utilized their services in these periods, in part to avoid excessive hiring which could later require large layoffs, in part to make up for a shortage of needed in-house E/S, and in part to meet required completion dates. When sales decline, however, companies tend to decrease the number of subcontracts and, therefore the subcontracting firms' sales and profits often decline sharply. E/S who work for such firms can experience, alternately, considerable overtime and serious job dislocation.

Industry Employee Lending Program

The concentration of aerospace firms in Southern California, with its fluctuating job market as contracts are won or lost, have induced a number of firms to "lend" their engineers and scientists to other firms rather than to lay them off or to terminate them. The lent employees remain on the company's payroll, but work for another

---

[21]See *Daily Labor Report, The Employment-At-Will Issue,* DLR No. 225 (Washington, D.C.: Bureau of National Affairs, Inc., 1982).

company which reimburses the lending company for payroll and other costs. E/S involved in such programs avoid layoffs, continue to accrue pension credits, and maintain salaries and benefits. The lending company does not lose its investment in the employees, and the company to whom E/S are lent gains valuable talent without a permanent investment and fluctuating E/S employment. Similar programs are frequently found within companies, with one division lending to another.

Lockheed has one of the more sophisticated of these programs, known as "Lending Employees for National Development" (LEND). It permits

> temporary placement of employees of the Lockheed Corporation into other companies where an acute need exists for their specialty. LEND, in effect, establishes a bank of engineering and manufacturing talent from which other firms by contract may draw to help them over peak workload periods. Employees who take such assignments continue as Lockheed employees and their regular company benefits and seniority remain intact. . . . The receiving companies gain immediate aid and circumvent the costly recruiting and training process. They eliminate layoffs at the end of the peak period.[22]

According to Lockheed, companies utilizing the LEND program avoid the costs of loss of efficiency, layoffs, training, relocation, hiring, and recruitment. "The LEND program also works in reverse. Lockheed is adding flexibility to its own engineering and manufacturing branches by utilizing professional, fully qualified loanees [sic] from other companies to meet requirements."[23] The full benefits of the LEND program, as seen by Lockheed, for the lending and contracting companies and the individuals lent are summarized in Table X-2. Such "lending" programs were found only in the aerospace industry where government contracting policies and the magnitude of projects make them exceedingly appropriate.

Many companies are reluctant to borrow E/S from competitors or to lend them, because of the fear that proprietary knowledge or practices will be jeopardized. The lack of such exchange among divisions and departments within companies is, however, less comprehensible. Customer-vender "lend" relationships may also prove feasible. Industry lending programs have helped alleviate some difficult problems in the aerospace industry and have contributed to more stable employment for E/S.

---

[22]Printed material from Lockheed Corporation, explaining the "LEND" program.
[23]*Ibid.*

TABLE X-2
Benefits of Lending Engineers and Scientists

For the Loanee [sic]
  Enhanced job security
  Improvement of skills through challenging assignments
  Retention of company benefits
  Better professional approach to employment
  Fuller utilization of talent and experience
  Broadening experience and improved job opportunities

For the Lending Company
  Less reassignment to non-design tasks
  Better utilization of talent
  Better morale and employee security
  Talent remains on tap for own future needs
  Employees return with broader experience
  Improved technical relationships with other companies
  Higher company morale

For the Hiring Company
  A pool of diversified professional and technical skills on tap
  Experienced employees, fully-qualified, requiring no training
  Minimization of hiring contract personnel
  Minimum or no supervision required
  Balanced manpower peak and valley loads
  Minimizes costly recruiting, hiring, training and relocation expenses
  Avoids morale-shattering layoffs
  LEND is more proficient than past hiring practices
  LEND brings a more professional approach to engineering and manufacturing
  Answers engineering and manufacturing build-up needs quickly.

Source: Materials provided by Lockheed Corporation.

Employee Leasing

Employee leasing activities, although apparently similar in nature to the aerospace industry's employee lending programs, appear to be expanding. Here the purpose seems to be to reduce costs, avoid benefit costs, and in effect to subcontract employee relations structures. Permanent leasing of employees seems to find favor among small employers. Such arrangements are intended to be permanent, rather than temporary.[24] Our field efforts did not discover any E/S involved in such arrangements, although temporary use of E/S employed by consulting firms is, as noted, quite common in periods of high employment. Occasionally these contract employees work on the premises of the contracting-out firm, but not usually, and then only temporarily.

---

[24]"Idea of Employee Leasing Gaining Popularity Among Smaller Employers," *Daily Labor Report,* No. 137 (July 17, 1984), pp. A-2-4.

CONCLUSION

Given the generality of their skills and their frequent commitment more to their profession than to a particular job, turnover among E/S seems likely to be high when demand exceeds supply. Thus companies have gone to considerable lengths to retain satisfactory E/S, and to handle them with considerable care when economic conditions require layoffs. Since many E/S who leave companies return at a later date, well-thought-out policies strive to maintain a positive company image despite turnover or layoffs. The failure of E/S to affiliate with unions despite periodic layoffs indicates both that E/S believe that they can handle their own problems in adversity and that company policies have been reasonably successful in allaying serious dissatisfaction.

CHAPTER XI

The Research Laboratory:
A Distinctive Environment

In September 1984, E. I. duPont de Nemours, the country's largest chemical concern, opened a new $85 million research center which now houses 700 scientists and support staff. The center includes a health science building and an addition to DuPont's agricultural research facility. Speaking at the occasion, a retired chairman of DuPont observed that "Research is an extremely risky business . . . because the failures outnumber the successes by a very large margin," but he noted that when research results become well-known, like DuPont's nylon and cellophane, "you realize you've done a good job."[1]

The personnel employed in research laboratories like DuPont's are a precious corporate resource. They may be working on basic research, applied research, or development projects. (See Table XI-1 for definitions.) Their success or failure may be reflected in the corporate profit and loss statement in the long or short term. Since research involves a major financial commitment, any company is certain to want results that provide a satisfactory return on investment.

Researchers may, however, feel quite different about the nature of their work. They may believe that they are contributing to knowledge, and that the economic results should not be the determinant of their value; or that they are making a product more reliable, useful, or long lasting, and that even though this does not necessarily contribute to profit because it is not cost effective, it is a contribution well worth reward. In short, the attitudes of researchers are often academic rather than economic, and this view can often pervade the research laboratory. To the extent that the academic approach contributes to superior research and development, it is profoundly sound; to the extent that it causes laboratory management and researchers to lose sight of the economic needs of the corporation, and therefore, of costs, results, and the profits needed to finance the

---

[1]Quoted in Neill Borowski, "DuPont's New Center to Probe Life Sciences," *Philadelphia Inquirer*, September 15, 1984, p. 7–D.

TABLE XI-1

Definitions of Types of Research

Research and development encompass an extremely broad spectrum of activities, ranging from the search for new knowledge to the development of new technologies. While the boundaries are by no means clear, it is possible to analyze national R&D expenditures in terms of the intended purpose of the scientific activity. Thus, research and development may be distinguished on the basis of advancement of fundamental scientific knowledge (basic research), practical or commercial application (applied research), or generation of new products and processes (development).

The National Science Foundation (NSF) utilizes the following definitions of character of work in its resource surveys.

Basic research. Basic research has as its objective "a fuller knowledge or understanding of the subject under study, rather than a practical application thereof." To take into account industrial goals, NSF modifies this definition for the industry sector to indicate that basic research advances scientific knowledge "not having specific commercial objectives, although such investigations may be in fields of present or potential interest to the reporting company."

Applied research. Applied research is directed toward gaining "knowledge or understanding necessary for determining the means by which a recognized and specific need may be met." In industry, applied research includes investigations directed "to the discovery of new scientific knowledge having specific commercial objectives with respect to products or processes."

Development. Development is the "systematic use of the knowledge or understanding gained from research directed toward the production of useful materials, devices, systems or methods, including design and development of prototypes and processes."

Source: National Science Board, National Science Foundation, *Science Indicators 1982.* Report of the National Science Board 1983, NSB-83-1 (Washington, D.C.: Government Printing Office, 1983), p. 45, and Appendix Table 2-5, p. 237.

laboratory and its personnel, it can be a source of frustration, conflict, and poor performance.

EXTENT AND CHARACTER OF RESEARCH

Figure XI-1 shows the increased expenditures for research since 1974 and the sources of these funds. Table XI-2 shows three measures of the leading company participation in research as of 1983— total dollars, percent of sales, and dollars per employee. Of great interest is that research expenditures rose in constant dollars during the recession of the 1980s as companies sought to improve their competitiveness, and therefore resisted the temptation to reduce this short-term discretionary expense.

It is also noteworthy that the federal government remains committed to support of basic research. Despite reductions in various services by his administration, President Reagan announced a determination in his 1983 State of the Union message "to keeping America the technological leader of the world now and into the 21st

FIGURE XI-1
Research Expenditures and Sources
1974–1984

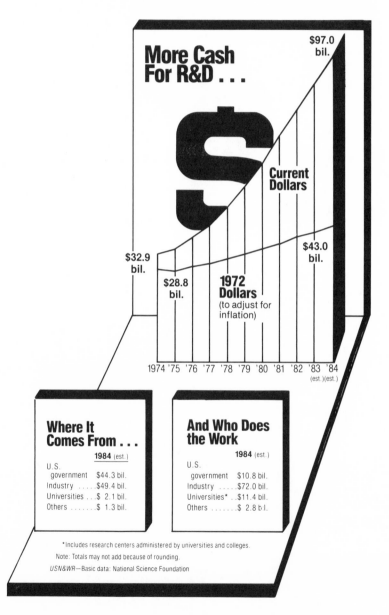

More Cash For R&D . . .

$97.0 bil.

Current Dollars

$32.9 bil.

$43.0 bil.

$28.8 bil.

1972 Dollars (to adjust for inflation)

1974 '75 '76 '77 '78 '79 '80 '81 '82 '83 '84
(est.)(est.)

Where It Comes From . . .
1984 (est.)
U.S.
government $44.3 bil.
Industry . . . . .$49.4 bil.
Universities . . .$ 2.1 bil.
Others . . . .$ 1.3 bil.

And Who Does the Work
1984 (est.)
U.S.
government $10.8 bil.
Industry . . . . .$72.0 bil.
Universities* . .$11.4 bil.
Others . . . .$ 2.8 bil.

*Includes research centers administered by universities and colleges.

Note: Totals may not add because of rounding.

USN&WR—Basic data: National Science Foundation

TABLE XI-2

THREE MEASURES OF THE TOP 15 IN R&D SPENDING

IN TOTAL DOLLARS (millions)	IN PERCENT OF SALES	IN DOLLARS PER EMPLOYEE
1. General Motors ... $2,602	1. TeleSciences ... 31.6%	1. Ultimate ... $37,089
2. IBM ... 2,514	2. Policy Management Systems ... 26.6	2. Fortune Systems ... 19,390
3. AT&T ... 2,491*	3. Fortune Systems ... 22.3	3. TeleSciences ... 18,797
4. Ford Motor ... 1,751	4. Management Science America ... 20.8	4. Convergent Technologies ... 18,721
5. United Technologies ... 971	5. King Radio ... 20.0	5. Activision ... 16,667
6. Du Pont ... 966	6. Dysan ... 19.4	6. Cray Research ... 16,467
7. General Electric ... 919	7. Advanced Micro Devices ... 19.4	7. Management Science America ... 15,563
8. Eastman Kodak ... 746	8. Modular Computer Systems ... 17.6	8. Amdahl ... 15,413
9. Exxon ... 692	9. ISC Systems ... 16.6*	9. Digital Switch ... 15,017
10. Xerox ... 555	10. Computer Consoles ... 16.6	10. Policy Management Systems ... 14,677
11. ITT ... 518	11. LTX ... 16.4	11. Applied Materials ... 14,545
12. Hewlett-Packard ... 493	12. Ramtek ... 15.6	12. Auto-trol Technology ... 14,413
13. Dow Chemical ... 492	13. Applied Materials ... 15.6	13. Computer Consoles ... 13,816
14. Digital Equipment ... 472	14. Auto-trol Technology ... 15.4	14. Network Systems ... 13,292
15. Boeing ... 429	15. Kulicke & Soffa Industries ... 15.3	15. LTX ... 13,229

*Includes $1,599 million spent by Western Electric Co. and other subsidiaries, not reported in AT&T's 10-K

DATA: STANDARD & POOR'S COMPUSTAT SERVICES INC.

Source: Reprinted from the July 9, 1984 issue of *Business Week* by special permission, © 1984 by McGraw-Hill, Inc. Data are for 1983.

TABLE XI-3
Federal Government Funding for the Physical Sciences
1982-1984
(In millions of dollars)

Department or agency	Obligations		
	1982 actual	1983 estimate	1984 estimate
Agencies supporting primarily physical sciences and engineering			
National Science Foundation	916	998	1,181
Energy Related Activities	777	861	1,021
Defense—Military Functions	686	769	867
National Aeronautics and Space Administration	538	605	682
Interior	74	88	89
Commerce	17	18	16
Other agencies	9	7	8
Subtotal	3,017	3,347	3,864
Agencies supporting primarily life and other sciences			
Health and Human Services	1,953	2,184	2,238
(National Institutes of Health)	(1,840)	(2,049)	(2,086)
Agriculture	331	362	381
Smithsonian Institution	55	60	68
Environmental Protection Agency	33	21	17
Veterans Administration	13	15	15
Education	16	16	14
Other agencies	22	22	22
Subtotal	2,422	2,678	2,755
Total	5,439	6,025	6,619

Source: Reprinted from the March 23, 1983 issue of *Chemical Week* by special permission. Copyright 1983 by McGraw-Hill, Inc., New York, New York.

century."[2] This was followed by increased budget allocations for basic research. The funding for the physical sciences in fiscal year 1983 is shown in Table XI-3.

Basic research in the United States accounts for more than one-third of the reported world total.[3] Federal support of research is concentrated on development projects. Universities, of course, are major centers of basic research, accounting for about one-half of the total,[4] but the bulk of their research is funded by government and industry. Overall, about 65 percent of all research expenditures go to develop-

---

[2]Quoted in "An Overdue Infusion for Basic Research," *Chemical Week*, March 23, 1983, p. 44.

[3]"Technologies for the '80s," *Business Week*, July 6, 1981, p. 48.

[4]"An Overdue Infusion for Basic Research," pp. 44–50.

ment, 23 percent to applied research, and 12 percent to basic research.[5]

Industry-University Cooperation

The link between industry and universities has been given particular attention recently because of its importance to the progress of industrial innovation. The new alliances have been strengthened by the needs of both parties. Industry views academia as a source of research talent, ideas, and future employees. The universities turn to industry to ease their difficult financial situations. Most universities are experiencing reduced enrollments as well as cutbacks in federal support to education. As was noted in Chapter III, other aspects of the current university crisis include outdated laboratories, faculty shortages, and consequent difficulties in maintaining a quality engineering education.

Arrangements between the two sectors vary in form. They include the establishment of industry-funded or "generic technology" research centers, and grants or contracts for specific research projects. An agreement between Monsanto and Washington University is among the most extensive and noteworthy of these arrangements. Through the agreement, Monsanto has taken a rather unorthodox approach to expanding its pharmaceutical business. A more traditional move would have been the acquisition of a drug manufacturer, or the declaration of a concerted effort to build its own internal capability.

> Both parties believe that the agreement, which takes steps to preserve academic freedom, may become a model in the current rush by industry to tap academic science. . . . The agreement provides for two-thirds of the research to be devoted to projects for which there is obvious commercial potential; the remaining third will be exploratory research. Research projects will be selected by a committee made up of four Washington University faculty members and four from Monsanto. Scientists funded by Monsanto will be free to publish their findings. Patents will be held by the university, which will grant exclusive licensing rights to Monsanto.[6]

The Monsanto-Washington University agreement is just one of several such partnerships that have been formed in recent years. Such arrangements are not without critics. Some claim that academic freedom is imperiled by them. Others fear that the price of

---

[5]National Science Board, National Science Foundation, *Science Indicators 1982,* Report of the National Science Board 1983, NSB–83–1 (Washington, D.C.: Government Printing Office, 1983), p. 47.

[6]"Monsanto's Academic Route to Growth," *Business Week,* June 21, 1982, p. 45.

business involvement on campus will be a shift away from the fundamental research historically performed at universities toward product-related development. Along the same lines, some educators speculate that the joint effort will turn the nation's universities into trade schools.[7] As will be discussed below, these issues are of interest to R&D personnel working for industry, and not only to academicians, many of whom have long received industry grants, worked in buildings endowed by industry and industrialists, and consulted for industry without losing their freedom. As one professor commented, "the new partnerships illustrate the pragmatic ability of higher education and industry to adapt to changing times."[8]

Industry-Government Relationships

Although most of the R&D in the United States is performed by industry, a significant part of this effort is actually supported by the federal government. Federal support of industrial R&D was at its highest in the early 1960s, reaching almost 60 percent of the total. By 1979, government support had decreased to 34 percent. The largest fraction of this federal investment has always been in such areas as defense, space, and air traffic control. In addition, the federal government has undertaken R&D where there was a perceived need to accelerate the national rate of development of new technologies in the private sector.[9]

Government support has thus been unevenly distributed among various industries. For example, the aircraft and missiles industry and the electrical equipment industry receive most of their R&D support from the government. The government also provides much R&D support to nonmanufacturing industries. This is particularly true of "business services such as R&D laboratories, management and consulting services, and data processing, where the Government provides about 80 percent of all R&D Funds."[10]

During and following World War II, a number of laboratories were created by government. These include Sandia, Argonne, Brookhaven, Oak Ridge, and Lawrence, Berkeley. In recent years, these national laboratories have sought industrial work, particularly as the federal government has finally concluded that these laboratories are "a tremendous resource of both talent and facilities that

---

[7]"Business and Universities: A New Partnership," *Business Week*, December 20, 1982, pp. 58–61.
[8]*Ibid.*, p. 61.
[9]National Science Board, National Science Foundation, *Science Indicators 1980*, Report of the National Science Board 1981, NSB–81–1 (Washington, D.C.: Government Printing Office, 1981), pp. 92–93.
[10]*Ibid.*, p. 99.

aren't being used very effectively to influence our industrial competitiveness."[11] This increased receptivity was stimulated by recent legislation which requires the laboratories to identify research with industrial potential and move it into the marketplace. The laboratories and the Department of Energy are also revising regulations related to proprietary research. For example, companies can now do proprietary work at these laboratories if they pay for the use of the facilities on a cost recovery basis. Patent restraints are also undergoing changes with the intent of increasing the attractiveness of such partnerships. The interaction process is still relatively new, but is expected to increase. Further adjustments will of course be necessary, but according to industry observers, "the struggle will be worth the effort if it provides an added push to U.S. industrial R&D and keeps technology from languishing on the shelves of the labs."[12] For engineers and scientists (E/S) working both in national and industrial laboratories, industry-government cooperation provides additional sources of equipment, access to advanced developments, and opportunities for professional cooperation.

Despite this auspicious government laboratory-industrial laboratory cooperation, there is considerable controversy over it. The debate focuses on the use of supercomputers. Some scientists claim that funds for this use are too heavily concentrated in the government laboratories, which in turn can attract and monopolize the limited personnel capable of handling them. As in all discussion of government-university-industry scientific relationships, fears of government control and concentration of scarce equipment and personnel resources are the source of most objections and doubts.[13]

Industrial Cooperation

Historically, technological and scientific cooperation has been avoided by industrial corporations. The primary reasons have been the unwillingness of executives to share decision making, their concern for proprietary information and fear of antitrust implications, and their failure to perceive the benefits of cooperation.[14] In recent years, however, these barriers are being eroded as corporate executives have realized that an enormous amount of redundant research

---

[11]George A. Keyworth, presidential science adviser, quoted in "Industry Finds a New Ally in the National Labs," *Business Week*, April 18, 1983, p. 44E.

[12]*Ibid.*, p. 44K.

[13]Leon E. Wynter, "Critics Fearful of Federal Influence on U.S. Supercomputer Technology," *Wall Street Journal*, October 3, 1984, p. 33.

[14]William C. Norris, "How to Expand R&D Cooperation," *Business Week*, April 11, 1983, p. 21. Mr. Norris is chairman and chief executive of Control Data Corporation.

is being performed in industrial laboratories throughout the nation. Moreover, some of the potential antitrust restraints have been loosened.

An example of a large-scale industrial cooperative effort is an organization, formed by ten companies in the semiconductor and computer industries, called the Microelectronics & Computer Technology Corporation (MCC). The objective of this organization is to "develop a broad base of fundamental technologies for use by members, each of which will add to the technology and continue to compete with products and services of individual conception and design."[15] The ten corporate participants have initial rights to the technology developed, but eventually it will be licensed to other firms. Such access is important for small companies. Similar industrial alliances will likely soon be formed.[16] Again, the E/S involved will have greater opportunities for career development, for exchanging information, and for testing ideas and concepts.

RESEARCH LABORATORY CLIMATE AND POLICIES

The industries which lead in R&D expenditures and number of research E/S are listed in Figures XI-2 and XI-3, respectively. Since these industries were well represented among the companies included in field visits, considerable attention was given to the organizational climate and personnel problems and policies in their laboratories.

Organizational Climate

Most research laboratories are situated in academic-like settings, with attractive landscaping, well-built and well-equipped buildings, and numerous amenities for the E/S employed. Indeed, the image created is one of an idealized university setting that far exceeds what is found in most universities. Moreover, whether as a cause or effect of the setting—perhaps both—the overall atmosphere is likely to be academic as well.

Academic rank, for example, is extremely important in the industrial research laboratories. Degrees determine the hierarchy. The Ph.D. is essential for top rank; master's degrees place one a decided

---

[15]*Ibid.*

[16]For example, in October 1984, eleven major aerospace and software concerns began exploring a joint effort to develop software for defense applications in order to reduce costs for the U.S. Department of Defense; see David Stipp, "Eleven Concerns That Develop Software for Defense Mull Joint Research Venture," *Wall Street Journal,* October 9, 1984, p. 2.

Figure XI-2
Expenditures by Selected Industries

R&D expenditures by selected industries

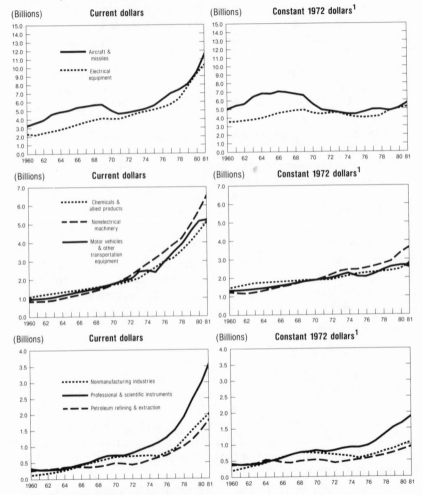

[1]GNP implicit price deflators used to convert current dollars to constant 1972 dollars.
NOTE: Preliminary data are shown for 1981.

Source: National Science Board, National Science Foundation, *Science Indicators 1982,* Report of the National Science Board, 1983, NSB-83-1 (Washington, D.C.: Government Printing Office, 1983), p. 95.

FIGURE XI-3
*Concentration Ratios[1] of Scientists and Engineers
in Selected Manufacturing Industries: 1980*

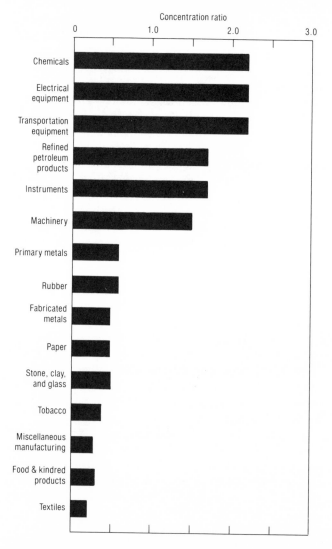

Source: National Science Board, National Science Foundation, *Science Indicators
1982*, Report of the National Science Board, 1983, NSB-83-1 (Washington,
D.C.: Government Printing Office, 1983), p. 91.
[1]A concentration ratio relates each industry's share of science and engineering
employment to its share of total (S/E and non-S/E) employment.

step below; bachelor's degrees rank at a much lower level; non-degree personnel have little status. It is apparent that research E/S in industry have a compelling need to prove to themselves and to the outside world that they are true to their professions and of equal rank with academicians who remain outside the business world and its rather crass pursuit of profit. Yet laboratory E/S, like professors, are also very much concerned about their remuneration, benefits, and working conditions.

Desiring to maintain a satisfactory research climate and staff, companies have created various status titles such as Distinguished Researcher or Scientist, or Company Scientist (modeled on distinguished or university professorship), or other such nomenclature, with commensurate salary. Where a particular scientist or engineer has made substantial contributions, a special section or department may be created for this person, or he or she may be given special privileges, such as those accorded a research professor who no longer is required to teach, or is given a substantially lighter teaching load. Sometimes, however, these status distinctions become too cumbersome. A major petroleum company now has only one classification for its laboratory Ph.D.'s although a broad salary range exists within that classification.

Successful industrial laboratories differ in a significant way from academic settings in that there is less departmental compartmentalization. This spurs interdisciplinary contact and cooperation among scientists that is often missing in a structured academic setting. The small offices and intimate working relationships at Bell Telephone Laboratories apparently make an important contribution to the scientific cooperation that has won this extraordinary organization seven Nobel prizes in physics, numerous useful developments, and a rank at the top of the world's industrial laboratories.[17]

Scientists in the top laboratories have another advantage over their academic counterparts: they are not required to scrounge for grants and funding or to publish papers that please their superiors in order to gain promotion. Thus in many ways, their concentration on their work may be less interrupted and their worklife more serene.

Goal Congruence

The managers of research laboratories have the difficult task of aligning the goals of the participating E/S with those of the corpora-

---

[17]These points are mentioned several times by Bell Laboratory scientists quoted in Jeremy Bernstein, *Three Degrees Above Zero: Bell Labs in the Information Age* (New York: Charles Scribner's Sons, 1984).

tion. Our interviewees emphasized that the majority of individuals working in their corporate R&D laboratories were scientists rather than engineers. Unsatisfactory goal congruence is potentially more significant among scientists than engineers because the nature of their work is usually concentrated on long-term basic research, while engineers are more involved in short-term development projects. The results of an engineer's work are usually much closer to commercial innovation and production, and are thus easier to measure financially. There is considerable research to support the view that the value systems and role expectations of scientists do in fact differ from those held by engineers. Scientists tend to be oriented more toward their profession than toward the goals of the organizations for which they work. In addition, scientists, more so than engineers, view recognition in their profession, rather than advancement within the organization, as a major criterion of success.[18] It is thus probable that scientists are more likely to appreciate the pseudo-academic climate with loose work rules and strict degree hierarchies.

In particular, scientists often desire the opportunity to participate in the selection of their project and direction of their efforts, and are often more effective in gaining results when these responsibilities are granted to them.[19] At one research facility scientists are allowed to devote 15 percent of their time to projects of their own choice. The scientists who receive the highest distinction attainable on the company's technical ladder are given significant freedom in selecting and carrying out their own projects.

The existence of an effective dual ladder, as described in Chapter V, seems fundamental for maintaining satisfied scientific personnel and effective research results. Unless scientists can progress *qua* scientists, the morale and climate of the laboratory seem certain to be less than ideal. On the other hand, scientists must also be given the opportunity to become managers. Most successful laboratories are directed and managed by E/S personnel. Few scientists apparently desire to be managed by nonscientists. The successful manager-scientist has the delicate task of integrating the goals of the corporation with those of the laboratory scientists to the satisfaction of both. The most successful industrial laboratories—e.g., Bell, General Electric, Westinghouse, Merck, DuPont, General

---

[18]See, e.g., M. K. Badawy, "Organizational Designs for Scientists and Engineers: Some Research Findings and Their Implications for Managers," *IEEE Transactions on Engineering Management,* Vol. EM–22 (November 1975), pp. 134–38.

[19]Donald K. Stein and Murray M. Dalziel, *The Organizational Climate in Research-and-Development Organizations: A Synopsis of Research* (Boston: McBer and Company, 1982), p. 4.

Motors—are all managed by scientists or engineers with substantial laboratory research experience.

Integrating Strategic Planning

A company's strategic planning should determine the nature of its research program. In turn, the type of business in which the company operates and the availability of funds for research are major planning determinants. It is important that the managers of research laboratories take part in strategic planning, and that the laboratory E/S be appraised of their role in bringing the plans to fruition. Repeatedly, our interviewees emphasized that if the goals of research scientists and the corporation are to be made congruent, the scientists must have a fundamental understanding and appreciation of the corporate goals and of the strategies designed to meet these goals.

The mission of an industrial research facility may range from a basic research orientation to one which is more focused on development. Most interviewees agreed that linking the research organization with the rest of the corporation is a planning challenge. The broad direction of the corporate R&D activity must be clearly defined. Innovations occurring within the laboratory must be introduced within operating divisions; technology transfer must occur throughout the company, and be made an explicit part of planning and action.

Effective communication is, of course, very important here, but much more is involved in strategic planning of R&D. One approach to developing a systematic technology strategy is for a corporation to establish a technical advisory committee. Often, this group is composed of both outside experts and internal executives from various corporate functions, although membership representation varies by firm. This group usually acts in a general advisory capacity concerning research direction, and also serves a variety of other functions. One petroleum company has recently formed a Science Advisory Council, composed of external advisors who are experts in various fields related to the firm's business and who listen to the presentations by E/S concerning their current research. The council members also provide input as to the overall direction of the R&D thrust. This council's chartered mandate is "to advise the company's scientists and management on emerging and future technologies that might create opportunity and risk for the company and its customers or other publics."[20]

---

[20]Literature provided by the company to the Industrial Research Unit.

In one metals company interviewed, the direction of research and its integration with overall company planning is established by committees on which laboratory, production, marketing, and other functional groups are represented. Thus, a variety of viewpoints contribute to the research direction. These committees also establish research budgets. One chemical company, which has a separate research laboratory for each of its five divisions, has recently established a Research Coordinating Committee to promote interaction between the facilities. This group is designed to foster synergistic relationships, to integrate business and research planning and goals, and to avoid redundant projects.

Two firms interviewed had recently integrated technology planning with their general strategic planning systems. This step was taken to improve the general corporate understanding of the mission of the research laboratory and its potential contribution to the organization, and to improve research funding patterns. Individuals attaining distinction on one firm's technical advancement ladder are expected to be active in research or engineering projects, and to serve as corporate consultants in key areas of technology. They are also expected to provide strategic and technical leadership to the corporation and to identify and evaluate new approaches and new technologies potentially important to the company's future.

One research director noted that a resource conflict existed between the long-term orientation of the research unit and the short-term pressure for financial performance imposed upon the operating divisions. Some firms funded basic research at a corporate level, but individual divisions were required in most cases to fund a large portion of their own developmental projects. The potential for lack of both consistent long-term planning and integration of strategic decisions in such situations is considerable.

Internal committees or groups were also formed by various companies to facilitate the transfer of technology developed in industrial R&D laboratories to various operating groups. One firm conducted a major study which focused on avenues through which technology could flow between research and development, which are two separate functions at this firm. One forest products firm recently realigned its research organization to improve communication with its marketing groups. Rather than remaining within the former horizontal research structure, scientists are now assigned to specific vertical divisions so closer relationships with marketing professionals can develop. The goal is to facilitate the diffusion of stimulating ideas between the marketplace and the research organization.

Another method of transmitting the ideas and concepts developed in an R&D laboratory throughout the organization is to encourage an actual physical employee flow. Engineers and scientists can be transferred between the laboratory and the operating units via a sequence of career steps. Such organizational designs are intended primarily to enhance work environments and improve interfunctional cooperation, but such integration is fundamental if strategic planning is also to include the R&D organization and to take advantage of the contributions of the R&D laboratories. Precisely this kind of cooperation is essential if the R&D scientists are to achieve congruity of their personal and professional goals with those of the organization.

Encouraging Innovation and/or Invention

As has already been noted, fundamental to the success of an R&D facility is the freedom for scientists to spend at least part of their time on projects or ideas which they themselves have developed. Particularly where the "concentration ratios"[21] of E/S are the highest and where the laboratories have been the most successful, this is a considered corporate policy. A key person in the project which led to the development of the transistor at Bell Telephone Laboratories was quoted as follows:

> ... we didn't enlist anyone against his will into the transistor project. Indeed, once or twice we found a man who had been contributing well, whom we wanted to stay on the project, and who said, "No, I want to work on something else." Which he then did.
>
> This sort of freedom is a very important part of preserving a research laboratory's élan ... [22]

Such freedom appears fundamental not only in increasing the commitment of E/S to the organization, but also in encouraging innovative ideas which improve products or reduce their costs, lead to new uses of existing products, or develop entirely new products. To accomplish this purpose not only must the climate in the laboratories be balanced between attention to basic research and to potential industrial applications, but the E/S involved must understand what is technically feasible and economically possible. New developments typically do not involve inventions. Rather, most new commercial products are developed by applying existing basic technology in a new direction within the constraints of an existing or novel product line.

---

[21]"Concentration ratios" relate each industry's share of E/S employment to its share of total employment.

[22]Bernstein, *Three Degrees Above Zero*, pp. 101-2.

Corporations, both large and small, throughout the United States have been recognizing the potential of product development ideas generated within the marketplace. For example, one study participant encourages R&D engineers to spend a period of time up to several months working at customer locations so that they become involved in actual applications. To achieve direct feedback from the market to product designers, another firm sends engineers to visit customers and dealers. Along the same lines, one pharmaceutical company has formed a new market-oriented R&D group responsible for, among other things, market followup and new drug applications. An increasing emphasis on market feedback for innovative ideas is expected in the future.

To supplement their R&D organizations, several companies interviewed have attempted to create special entrepreneurial situations, which might enhance innovation, within their overall corporate structures. For example, one computer firm has a highly decentralized, divisional organization. This corporate structure was selected to encourage entrepreneurial spirit. Managers are essentially given "their own business," so they feel a strong sense of ownership and commitment. A danger with this approach is that, since individuals develop the ability to run a "small business," many have departed to begin their own ventures. Another firm decided to institute a new business internally by creating an "upstart" research environment. It hired experienced research professionals and provided them with a brand new research facility. No stringent interaction requirements with corporate headquarters were imposed. At the time of the interview, this facility's basic product was still in the development phase.

Along similar lines, one chemical company has established an innovation steering committee. Its mission is to ensure that research projects with the greatest potential for impact on earnings are exploited to their fullest. The company's R&D organizations are represented on the committee. Another firm "has rebuilt its product organizations around a series of strategic business units in which small engineering teams compete for the opportunity to take an idea from the concept stage to a feasibility model."[23]

For such tactics to be successful, traditional bureaucratic structures may have to be altered. The "entrepreneurial pocket" must truly be able to operate like an upstart company. Traditional managers may not be able to function in a restricted, frequently disorganized environment. Moreover, the R&D operation must have close liaisons with the entrepreneurial function if development is to be

---

[23]"Big Business Tries to Imitate the Entrepreneurial Spirit," *Business Week,* April 18, 1983, p. 84.

successful. Thus, many such operations have not worked out as hoped. Simulated entrepreneurial operations can be an adjunct to an effectively integrated R&D laboratory, but certainly cannot take its place.

Basically, for stimulating innovation, there are no substitutes for a solid compensation and benefit system that the E/S themselves believe is fair, and a corporate atmosphere that encourages research and development. These must be buttressed by a careful recruiting and personnel development program, with dual development ladders and proper rewards and recognition. Once the atmosphere is set, the rewards vary because they must fit the needs of the E/S and the environment in which they work. Opportunities to utilize their capabilities must be continually available, either as E/S or as managers, if the R&D function is to make an optimum contribution to the corporation.

R&D Productivity

In the final analysis, the R&D operation must contribute to the profitability of the firm, both in the short and long run. Therefore, E/S involved in R&D must "produce." Measuring this productivity has been found to be a serious problem.[24] Where E/S create, develop, or improve a product that enhances the sales and profits of a firm, or supply the engineering or scientific data necessary for production and/or sales, their contribution is relatively easy to recognize. Often, however, such contributions are less obvious, particularly in relation to individuals. Qualitative measures are therefore often essential despite rigorous attempts to apply quantitative ones.

Patents are frequently considered a measure of research output. Since inventions are often patented, patent counts theoretically make it possible to estimate levels of technical invention. Of course, "an invention is not itself an innovation, but is a technical achievement on the way to a possible commercial introduction of an innovation. . . . Patents, therefore, are not the ultimate measure of innovation, but they do represent the level of proprietary technology available for marketable goods and services."[25]

Companies, however, take varying approaches to patents. Many firms interviewed expressed a reluctance to apply for patents on the grounds that patent application, by stimulating copies or alternative developments in closely related areas, actually could endanger the proprietary nature of their work. The General Electric Company's

---

[24]The difficulties of measuring E/S productivity were discussed in Chapter VI.
[25]National Science Board, *Science Indicators 1980,* p. 109.

research facilities, on the other hand, are the leading patent applicants in the country, followed by International Business Machines, Westinghouse Electric Corporation, and DuPont. Bell Telephone Laboratories ranks behind these four.[26] Yet most observers regard Bell as the finest industrial laboratory in the world. Obviously, patents as a reward criterion must be placed in proper perspective.

Publications in technical and professional journals are also considered an indicator of successful research. Some R&D managements encourage this, but others do not; some sponsor their own journals. Here again, the criterion must be evaluated with individual company policies in mind.

CONCLUSION

There are many factors which affect the success or failure of an R&D laboratory. The organizational climate must offer E/S an opportunity to pursue their professional goals while they strive to fulfill the goals of the organization. There may be an inherent conflict between the two sets of goals. Thus, the organization is challenged to develop human resource policies which simultaneously encourage goal congruence, creativity, and risk taking.

Successful R&D facilities begin with sound recruiting. Engineers and scientists involved in R&D desire the admiration of their peers, and according to Dr. Edward Scolnick, head of basic research at Merck: "I wouldn't want to hire anyone who doesn't want to be famous."[27] Many firms have tried to create an atmosphere encouraging and recognizing achievement by instituting multiladder advancement systems. As discussed in Chapter V, such a system is conceptually appealing but difficult to administer. It must be continuously monitored and adjusted in order to properly encourage E/S, both as researchers and managers. Other factors contributing to an ideal research environment include (1) the opportunity to do challenging work; (2) some freedom to select projects; and (3) wise administration of proper tangible and intangible rewards.

Organizational climate can be upset by reorganizations or failures, which can create a depressed atmosphere. Even so successful a company as Hewlett-Packard has found that poorly communicated organizational changes, however justified, can seriously and adversely affect product development and cause the defection of key E/S and

---

[26]Stuart Diamond, "Testing the Formula for a New Du Pont," *New York Times,* October 7, 1984, pp. F1, F12.

[27]Quoted in Shotford P. Sherman, "Eight Big Masters of Innovation," *Fortune,* October 15, 1984, p. 84.

managers. Hewlett-Packard's line of computer aided engineering (CAE) hardware and software was announced for November 1984, but then delayed. Critics blamed a "tumultuous" upheaval resulting from reorganization designed to improve company integration. Upset by the reorganization, and fearful that it would require transfers from California to Colorado, many key E/S and managers left the company, putting the program in jeopardy.[28] Perhaps a less drastic approach to reorganization and one that was better communicated could have accommodated the same overall needs without so adverse an impact on the CAE program and its research and development E/S.

Some, but by no means conclusive, research claims that despite the resources expended to create stimulating R&D environments, the research arms of large organizations may not be as productive as those of small firms. Thus, an alternative method of creating an innovative environment, one adopted by some firms, was explored through an analysis of the factors pertaining to the success of a high technology upstart. Its single-minded focus, intensity of task, opportunity for financial gain, challenging work, project orientation and lack of bureaucracy, all seem to contribute to successful innovation. It is not likely, however, that small entrepreneurial divisions and large corporate organizations can easily mix, despite a decentralized structure. Such attempts have not generally been adequate substitutes for a well-functioning R&D laboratory. The record of the great industrial laboratories in the United States, and their success in attracting E/S, are clear indicators that their human resource policies are both carefully thought out and well received by the E/S involved.

---

[28]"Delays and Defections at Hewlett-Packard," *Fortune*, October 9, 1984, p. 62.

CHAPTER XII

Distinctions Among Industries

In the previous chapters, the discussion of personnel policies for engineers and scientists (E/S) has distilled the policies of the approximately 100 companies interviewed for the study, as well as those of many more which were obtained through the extensive secondary sources that treat this subject. Before expressing some general conclusions in the following chapter, it is appropriate to set forth some key industry distinctions and trends.

Structural differences among industries create significantly distinct approaches to personnel policies. To be successful, the personnel policy of a company in a particular industry must give due weight to the environmental and institutional constraints under which it operates. Thus, a paper company may fully appreciate the aversion of many E/S toward locating in rural towns of the South or Northwest, but it is unable to alter its basic locations which must be where the timber is found. Hence, its policies attempt to overcome this recruiting and retention difficulty. Nevertheless, to compete head-on with, for example, the attractive campus location of an electronics company is virtually impossible.

Similarly, an automobile company must find E/S who are willing to work on its products, rather than on a related product, such as space vehicles, which may seem more exciting and therefore attract E/S more easily. A company may have great reluctance to lay off E/S but if a contract is cancelled, or lost, as often occurs in the aerospace industry, the company may have no choice unless it can contract out the services of these employees. Each industry and company reacts to problems that must be accommodated; the successful ones develop policies that mitigate structural constraints. Key industrial illustrations follow.

AEROSPACE INDUSTRY

Including its significant electronics component, the aerospace industry employs nearly 20 percent of all research and development (R&D) E/S. A considerable force affecting personnel policy development in the aerospace industry is the cyclical nature of the business. Cycles result both from fluctuations in government spending and the contract award procedure. Sinuated employment patterns are characteristic of individual firms, as well as the industry as a whole. Alternating periods of mass layoffs and acute shortages are common. This instability of employment has contributed to an atmosphere in which engineering unions have been more successful than in other industries. Even aerospace companies that have no E/S unions are influenced by union pressure because of the threat of organization. For example, one firm awarded COLA increases to its engineers to thwart a unionization attempt. In 1981, the Engineers and Scientists Guild struck in a vain attempt to win a COLA clause in its contract with Lockheed.

Many firms in the aerospace industry are concentrated in California. Although this remains a preferred location for E/S, housing prices are now so high in this area that many E/S are reluctant to relocate from other parts of the country. Consequently, recruiting has become a problem. Some firms have established subsidiaries or satellites in alternate locations to obtain needed personnel.

The aerospace industry is in transition as electronics has become increasingly important in product development and manufacture. As a result, both for commercial and defense-oriented work, the demand for computer scientists and electrical engineers with training in electronics has surged.

Computer aided design (CAD) has a variety of applications in the aerospace industry. Individuals trained on CAD equipment are currently valuable; but as applications increase, software becomes more sophisticated, and more equipment is put in place, the demand for designers and draftsmen may begin to wane. This decrease in demand would be accelerated if a decrease in defense funding occurred.

Because of the project-oriented nature of the aerospace industry, career pathing and development cannot be standardized. The optimal timing for transfers between projects is difficult to identify. Ideally, rotation between projects would expose an engineer to several types of experiences and he would thus develop a variety of skills. More often, no planned pathing occurs, and individuals can become pigeonholed. Although supervisors should develop a planned set of experiences for each of their subordinates to facilitate the reassignment process upon project completion, this is often not done or is even not possible. Career development is often limited because the funds available for human resource development tend to be restricted. A high reliance on government contracts effectively limits the amount of overhead available for training and organizational development.

As a result of fluctuating human resource requirements, termination is an important issue in this industry. Unions have bargained for the inclusion of retention criteria in their contracts in order to provide a more objective approach to layoffs and to reduce the anxiety of individual employees during downswing periods. Firms in this industry have also pioneered such concepts as intra- and intercompany lending as well as extensive outplacement networks. Because job changes are common, some E/S may never accumulate enough service with any one company to obtain a vested pension, despite the fact that they may work continuously in the industry throughout their careers.

In monetary terms, the aircraft and missiles industry performs the most industrial R&D. This industry is also the most dependent on federal R&D funding. In addition, the aircraft and missiles industry is one of the leaders in R&D as measured by the personnel effort which they allocate to that activity.

Because aerospace companies employ so many E/S, they are faced with specific problems caused by a mass employment situation. Often, E/S work in "bullpens"; an environment that can rarely satisfy the professional's needs for recognition and status. Some firms have developed intangible rewards for outstanding achievement such as the designation "engineer of the month." Others publicize the names of their most distinguished technical employees. In general, however, bullpens create a situation in which engineers feel that their individuality is submerged. This is another reason why aerospace has more E/S unions than any other industry.

ELECTRONICS, COMMUNICATIONS, AND COMPUTER INDUSTRIES

The electronics, communications, and computer (ECC) industries have experienced high growth and rapid technological change over the past decade. The boundaries between these industries have become blurred because products of one are components in the products of another. Similar technical skills are often needed by all three groups. Strategic growth and diversification have also caused these industries to overlap. All three industries also overlap the electronics segments of the aerospace industry, and vie with aerospace as the largest employers of E/S.

Although these industries offer high salaries, benefits, and attractive working environments, they have suffered from shortages of engineers. Recruiting engineers with state-of-the-art knowledge is difficult because the supply of individuals with necessary skills does not match the demand. Firms frequently offer sign-on bonuses for new employees and some have instituted add-a-friend bonuses. Special attention is often paid to the working environment; large offices and facilities similar to those of a college campus are used to attract engineers. Small companies frequently sweeten the compensation package by offering stock options or discount purchase plans to lure engineers from larger corporations.

Human resource planning is another challenge in this field. The intense demand for electronics engineers and computer specialists has led to high turnover rates and caused related retention problems in the ECC industries. Lack of availability of technical talent has inhibited the growth of several electronics companies. The American Electronics Association (AEA) recently published a supply and demand study which predicts that shortages will worsen over the next five years.

Companies dependent upon computer scientists and electrical engineers have found it necessary to create flexible and innovative human resource policies. At large firms, career pathing is well developed and many opportunities for continuing education exist. E/S are encouraged to participate in professional societies and to keep up with the latest developments in their field. Special attention has been paid to improving the productivity of software development. Design productivity has been improved through the utilization of CAD systems. Where work is project oriented, E/S are frequently rotated through a variety of projects to increase their practical experience. Both shortages of E/S and obsolescence caused by accelerating technological change have caused upgrading and retraining to become important features in organizational development programs. Some firms have begun in-house courses which concentrate on critical skill areas, while others have established similar programs in conjunction with universities. Other program participants include long-service employees whose skills require upgrading. A number of the participants in our study have also become active in grass roots programs aimed at encouraging pre-college students to pursue career opportunities in mathematics and science, and several have assumed an active role by working with universities to resolve the crisis in engineering education. For example, employees may be encouraged to work as faculty members, equipment may be donated or funds granted, etc. Other methods are also used to improve the quality of an engineering education, and to increase the capacity of engineering schools.

In spite of the fact that recruiting E/S is a challenge for firms in the ECC industries, corporations in other industries that require electronic and computer skills have found it even more difficult to recruit personnel. In particular, many firms attribute this to the fact that they cannot offer salaries competitive with the ECC industries. In addition, the ECC industries are popular because they offer excitement and have glamorous images. Industry image in general, and company image in particular, are important determinants of recruiting success. Because these fields are comparatively young and still emerging, women seem to enjoy a relatively equitable status in the E/S areas although their representation rates are still low. In general, the EEO problems experienced by other sectors do not seem as prevalent in these industries, undoubtedly because of the wealth of opportunities.

Despite the high demand for E/S and the mobility of the technical workforce, engineering unions have been established in a few firms in this industry. This may be partially attributable to the fact that defense electronics firms are closely related to the missiles and aerospace industry and experience similar fluctuations in funding. Some larger communications and electronics companies also have working environments quite similar to those in aerospace: bullpen arrangements. Also, jobs are frequently team and/or project oriented so an E/S may be confronted with the conflicts associated with being trained as a professional but working in a mass employment situation. If job mobility were restricted (that is, if supply catches up with or exceeds demand), E/S would lose the opportunity to change employers as a means to resolve dissatisfaction, and organization could become an attractive alternative. Several unions have identified high technology employees, including white-collar workers, as organizational targets. It is possible that organizational activity among firms in the ECC industries may increase in the near future, but thus far unionization attempts have been conspicuous only by their failure to enroll E/S.

Research is extremely important in the ECC industries because of the rapid pace of technological change. In addition, foreign competition has become particularly threatening to many firms in these industries. Continued research and innovation has been advocated as one method of improving the technological position of the United States. As a result, many firms have tried to create environments which foster innovation. Upstart firms are also common in the ECC industries. These small firms have been described as incredible engines of development; and the efforts of E/S in these firms become extremely concentrated. Productivity in small companies is often extraordinarily high. Many large firms have tried to capture some of this energy by trying to develop internal environments which mimic those of an upstart. Increased attention is being paid to capturing and encouraging the entrepreneurial spirit among E/S.

The ECC industries have also become involved in the "new partnerships." Several have established relationships with universities. Joint research is also being undertaken. Projects range from small scale dual-party agreements to the creation of the Microelectronics & Computer Technology Corporation, a ten-company cooperative effort to develop a broad base of technologies for use by members. How such arrangements will affect personnel policies for E/S, if at all, remains uncertain.

CHEMICAL INDUSTRY

The chemical industry is dependent on R&D for growth and continuing competitive advantages. Research has been described as the lifeblood of a chemical company—leading to new processes, new products, new applications for old products, etc. Chemical companies employ large numbers of E/S. Engineers are typically involved in process maintenance and development and usually work in manufacturing facilities, although some engineers are involved in research. Scientists are concentrated in research laboratories, although some work very closely with manufacturing processes. The desired outcome of personnel policies in this industry is the creation of an ideal organizational climate. The development and maintenance of an environment which encourages innovation and creativity is a major challenge. One method frequently used to create the desired atmosphere is the establishment of a dual or multiladder career-pathing system. Administration of such systems is particularly difficult, because continuous monitoring is necessary.

The goals of research facilities tend to be long term. Conflicts often arise between R&D organizations and operating companies concerning research orientation and the applicability of results. Several firms have integrated their R&D planning with corporate strategic planning. Research coordinating committees, which frequently have distinguished scientists from outside the organization as members, are also common.

In past years the chemical industry has had trouble recruiting chemical engineers because it could not match the salaries offered by petroleum companies. The recent economic downturn in petroleum has, however, reduced the intensity of this problem. The chemical and petroleum industries currently spend the highest percentages of payroll on employee benefits of all industries.

The chemical industry has been affected by government regulation in several ways. The representation of women in chemistry has historically exceeded that of women in engineering. Most firms indicated that they had no problem recruiting women. Practically all firms in the chemical industry, however, have had difficulty recruiting black engineers and scientists because of their low representation in the required disciplines. Therefore, many large chemical firms have become actively involved in programs to encourage pre-college minority students to pursue careers in math and science. Some of these firms participate in national programs, others in regional ones, while still others have established their own local programs. Occupational safety and health legislation also affects the chemical industry, particularly where individuals work with hazardous chemicals or where pregnant women may be exposed to materials that can damage the fetus.

Our study found several interesting programs providing for professional recognition and development in the chemical industry. For example, many firms offer awards for outstanding achievement, patents, significant contributions, publications, etc. These awards may be tangible or intangible. Group awards are also presented to project teams for attaining productivity goals or meeting project milestones. Presentation of group awards may prevent intracompany competition which may develop if too much emphasis is placed on individual contributions.

Conflicts between the employee's professional needs and expectations and those of the company seem especially intense in the chemical industry. These conflicts can intensify over issues such as the publication of proprietary material and participation in professional societies. The American Chemical Society (ACS) has been outspoken concerning issues related to professional treatment. The ACS Professional Employment Guidelines have received a great deal of criticism from industry, particularly concerning the section on termination procedures. To ease the professional-organizational conflict, some firms allow certain individual contributors to choose the direction of their research. Distinguished scientists have also become involved in strategic planning for the R&D function.

One problem related to the above conflict, which was frequently mentioned during field interviews in the chemical industry, was the difficulty that new graduates have in making the transition from academia to industry, or in adjusting to industrial careers. Several firms have established a series of rotational experiences for new graduates. These assignments create a transitional bridge for the new employee. In general, positive experiences with such programs have been reported.

The importance of research makes advanced degrees more important in the chemical and pharmaceutical industries than in other industries included in the study. The caste system that develops in the research laboratories frequently creates problems with bachelor degree level employees. These individuals perceive a lack of opportunity for advancement and may develop motivational problems. Providing alternate career opportunities for such employees has proved a good answer.

The chemical industry has helped to pioneer the development of partnerships with universities. This industry relies heavily on basic research, and universities perform a substantial percentage of the basic research in the United States. Furthermore, the universities need funding while chemical companies have funds available for R&D. Thus, a symbiotic relationship exists. The details of partnership arrangements vary and are still being worked out, but the potential benefits to both parties are significant. E/S both in academia and industry can profit by the interaction. Moreover, E/S employed by industry usually regard such association with favor.

PHARMACEUTICAL INDUSTRY

The pharmaceutical industry is one of the most research oriented in the country. Most of its professionals are scientists working in laboratories. The development process is a long one that is materially lengthened, if not inhibited, by costly government regulation. Successes can be extraordinarily profitable, but they must also pay for the many failures. The pharmaceutical industry manufacturing process is done in a clean, pleasant environment, labor conditions are usually good, and the rewards are high. As a result, unions are rarely successful.

The need for sophisticated research in the pharmaceutical industry creates a demand for quality E/S. Professionals with advanced degrees are common in this industry. Scientists generally work in research while engineers work in both research and manufacturing. As in the chemical industry, a caste system frequently develops in the laboratory. Rotation between jobs is uncommon because individuals typically have had highly specialized training. Alternate opportunities, therefore, need to be created for bachelors and masters level employees who may find their career progressions limited by their degrees. If "escape routes" are not built into a career development plan, these employees are likely to become frustrated, which can lead to a decrease in productivity. Since, however, most doctoral scientists, and also many scientists with bachelor's and master's degrees, remain in research throughout their careers, many firms have designed comprehensive multiladder systems.

Opportunities for professional recognition and reward are also widely available. Several firms have peer review programs to ensure that individuals receive recognition from associates, a form of intangible reward. In addition, many companies organize lectures and symposiums where internal and external research projects are discussed. Seminars which encourage professionals to remain current in their fields are also common. Also, most companies have awards for distinguished scientists. Those who receive the highest distinction in the laboratory may participate in charting the future direction or orientation of the research facility. Their ideas on how to integrate the projects in the technical arena with the firm's general strategic plan may be sought. Participation in professional societies is generally encouraged, although proprietary information must be kept confidential.

Shortages of pathologists, toxicologists, genetic engineers, and others with specific skills are reported. These shortages, however, usually refer only to deficiencies of one or two key individuals. In some cases there are only a handful of professionals in the country qualified for these jobs. Thus, recruiting critical skills in the pharmaceutical industry occurs in a small community atmosphere, often by word of mouth. This situation is significantly different from the shortages of electrical engineers and computer scientists reported by other industries. When many openings requiring similar skills exist, it is clear that other methods of recruiting are required. In particular, publicity is very important. Open houses generally draw many applicants. Few pharmaceutical companies have problems hiring women, but blacks and Hispanics are apparently difficult to recruit.

The salaries paid by pharmaceutical companies tend to be quite competitive with those of other industries. To improve salary potential, one firm recently uncapped compensation levels on the individual contribution career progression. Benefits, as measured by percentage of payroll, are also above average. Quite a few pharmaceutical companies sponsor special health-related programs for all their employees. Some concentrate on physical fitness while others address mental health problems, as well as alcoholism and drug addiction.

As noted, the product-development process in this industry is lengthy. It takes many years before a new drug becomes available to consumers, if it is introduced at all. The development process is characterized by high uncertainty in terms of experimental outcomes, and it involves many people, extensive testing, and regulatory reports. Patents are extremely important, but given the number of years spent on product development, seventeen years of protection is deemed too short by the industry.

Technology has affected the pharmaceutical industry in several ways. Industry boundaries are becoming blurred as some electronics companies diversify into the health field through medical electronics products. Production processes are also affected by changing technology. One company has established a technical resources group. This central engineering department monitors new equipment introductions and searches for process applications throughout the firm's many locations. It was established because the company found that when engineers were isolated in individual plants, it was difficult for them to maintain state-of-the-art knowledge. Increased interaction and reduced span of technical control has improved equipment upgrading. New devices called intelligent analytical instruments have the potential to enhance productivity in research laboratories. These microprocessors can simulate experiments and predict outcomes.

There are no known unions composed primarily of pharmaceutical research scientists. This is in part attributable to the sense of professionalism instilled in the scientist via the education process, and in part to the excellent conditions under which they work. Many scientists believe that professionalism and unionism do not mix, and much of a scientist's work is done independently in a pleasant environment. It is unlikely that a union will attain the support of a large proportion of scientific professionals in a pharmaceutical research facility in the near future. The quality control workers at a few firms are, however, unionized. Many of these individuals have college degrees. Technicians in laboratories, frequently bachelor's degree holders, have also been targeted by unions, but as yet not successfully.

PETROLEUM INDUSTRY

The petroleum industry offers an excellent example of the manner in which shifts in the economy can affect human resource programs. In particular, it illustrates how external forces can shape personnel policies. As we have noted in previous chapters, when this study began, a major problem in the petroleum industry was the recruiting and retention of petroleum engineers, geologists, and geophysicists. Small independent firms were pirating engineers and scientists from larger organizations. These larger companies liberalized their compensation packages in response. Company cars were introduced as perquisites. A few of the larger companies tried to match the little independents who offered "piece of the action" programs by instituting deferred bonus and phantom stock plans. Although special perquisites for a limited group may achieve their intended purpose in the short run, several corporate respondents mentioned that engineers and scientists in other disciplines began complaining of inequitable treatment. Programs developed in response to critical skill areas, therefore, can create problems throughout the organization.

Because the petroleum industry historically has been highly profitable, oil companies have often paid salaries at a premium over those offered by firms in other industries, and spent a very high, if not the highest, percentage of payroll and the highest absolute dollars on benefits per employee. The magnitude of the total compensation package including salary, benefits, and perquisites has, as noted, created difficulties for industries that compete for chemical engineers.

Since petroleum engineers were in such short supply, some petroleum companies started hiring civil engineers. Although civil engineering does not require identical skills to petroleum, they are transferable. These firms established training programs which utilized the existing engineering base and then expanded upon it by introducing additional material.

Most of the oil companies that participated in our study supported large research and development efforts. Most offered multi-ladder career progressions. Research coordinating and/or steering committees were common. In several cases E/S were encouraged to flow between the research facility and various operating companies.

Since OPEC has lost price control, and energy consumption has stopped growing so quickly, the labor supply situation described above has practically become reversed and there has been a turnaround in the demand for earth scientists. Individuals who left to join independent energy companies began flocking back to the majors. At the same time, however, many of the perquisites introduced when oil was deemed in short supply are still in effect, as is the resentment stimulated by these plans. Those petroleum engineering students who have graduated since 1983 have found that their skills are no longer in such high demand, although at the time that they entered college, new graduates in this discipline commanded the highest starting salaries among all fields.

Exogenous economic changes are always likely to create imbalances between supply and demand. When such changes are not anticipated, those who have made such a substantial progression in their education that they cannot transfer disciplines, as well as those who have narrowed their career opportunities, are likely to become victims. Nevertheless, such imbalances do become adjusted. For example, a higher percentage of graduates are likely to pursue advanced degrees. Other individuals adjust by seeking employment in related industries, such as chemicals, pharmaceuticals, or forest products. Some graduates choose to work outside their field of study. Fewer incoming students select chemical engineering and earth science as majors. Individuals who remain current in their fields and do not become too narrow can be the most flexible and are therefore in the best position to deal with economic swings. Companies willing to invest in retraining can utilize such development to solve their staffing problems.

PAPER INDUSTRY

Paper making has historically been an art. Today, the forest products industry is recognized as cyclical and mature. Companies are being forced, by competitive pressures, to bring in people with greater technical expertise because of advances in technology associated with paper production.

Engineers are typically found in three business areas: (1) mills or production facilities, (2) corporate engineering, and (3) research and development. Scientists usually work only in R&D. The type of work performed varies significantly between areas. Engineering positions in mills are production oriented and range from process administration to general management. Corporate engineering is design and application oriented, while research and development ranges from basic research to new product development.

In recruiting engineers, the paper industry must overcome hurdles created by its unglamorous image, reputation for unpleasant working conditions (at mills), and facilities found in adverse locations. Several firms also mentioned that they experienced particular difficulty in recruiting minorities. To attract and retain engineers, some firms are reevaluating their selection procedure and renovating their personnel policies. To attract individuals to isolated areas, most firms have become heavily involved in recruiting from local universities. Others try to match individuals with isolated locations based on hobbies (such as fishing or hunting) and lifestyle preferences. Several firms have created detailed career development programs. Experience in all three business areas is usually encouraged for those who aspire to move up through the corporate hierarchy. One company has recently designed an integrated career progression document which illustrates the variety of paths which are available. Through career planning sessions, breadth of experience (particularly mill experience) is encouraged. Because of the manner in which the progression is presented, the E/S can see "over the hump" of isolation at a mill to a more prestigious position within the firm after a series of experiences has been completed. Through counseling sessions, engineers' goals are meshed with those of the organization. Individuals can then be provided with tools to progress along the chosen path.

Individuals involved in both corporate engineering and research and development must stay current in their fields. Participation in professional societies is one method of keeping current, but for historical reasons, engineers in the paper industry must be careful not to violate antitrust laws when attending technical meetings. Another problem for technical personnel desiring professional recognition is the growing tendency towards secrecy. The paper industry used to be very open and it was not unusual for companies to share information. As managers trained in other industries came into the paper industry, there was a move towards the protection of proprietary information. Companies now want to maintain their competitive advantages as long as possible, and tend to discourage publication. For the young E/S eager to establish a professional reputation, the inability to publish can make a career in the paper industry unattractive.

OTHER MANUFACTURING INDUSTRIES

Representatives from a number of companies in mature industries were interviewed for our study. These study participants were involved in a variety of areas such as printing and the manufacture of such products as farm equipment, tires, and automobiles. These firms felt the effects of the 1982 recession severely and were undergoing extensive internal change throughout the study period. They were retrenching, both physically and organizationally, frequently concentrating on revitalizing their corporate structure. Some firms, with the objective of improving labor productivity, were in the process of reducing their white-collar staffs. Thus, E/S who had worked loyally for the same firm for many years suddenly were faced with the threat of layoffs. Many firms froze professional salaries, and some even reduced professional compensation levels.

The revitalization process also included increased attention to productivity and distribution. Existing processes were upgraded or new techniques introduced. The impact of computers and related products on these companies was apparent. Those firms that had implemented automated manufacturing, or had become involved in computer control processes, found that they were competing with the more glamorous industries for electrical engineers and computer scientists to which graduating E/S were clearly more attracted. Individuals with electronic and computer skills were sought while those with more traditional skills were being terminated. Obsolescence was clearly a factor, and was largely brought about by the failure of some companies to encourage retraining and upgrading in past years.

Engineers in such industries frequently have more managerial responsibilities than those in the high technology businesses. These managerial duties include running operations and, often, the supervision of blue-collar workers. Traditional industries are sometimes unwilling (or unable) to compete with ECC industries in salaries. Several strategies have, however, been developed to surmount recruiting problems. Retraining is a common tactic. Engineers already working in these companies are trained in electronics. Rather than offering high salaries, firms may try to retain computer scientists by creating challenging projects and by providing formal career progressions. Several of the companies studied were attempting to move computer engineers through career paths quickly with the hope that as these engineers became managers and obtained a broader view of the business, they would have more incentive to stay with the firm.

In the more traditional industries, personnel policies had remained status quo for a long time. Recently, the need to attract and to retain electronic and computer engineers forced several companies to revise their personnel policies for specific skill groups. Once experiments with new personnel policies prove successful for one skill group, or simply for the sake of equity, changes often follow for other personnel within the company.

Few firms studied had implemented innovative programs for broader groups of E/S, although several interesting concepts had been developed. One problem was that funds were not yet available to launch or support the new programs. For example, one firm had redesigned its professional compensation package, increasing opportunities for recognition and reward. This package provided for individual tailoring of compensation based on performance. Another firm redesigned its corporate engineering center with special emphasis on creating an organizational climate to encourage creativity and innovation.

The combination of professional layoffs and pay freezes during the 1981–1982 recession and the increasing threat of obsolescence created an environment characterized by turbulence and uncertainty which undoubtedly adds to the recruiting problems of these companies. Unions, however, were unable to capitalize on these problems.

CONSTRUCTION INDUSTRY

Construction is basically a service industry. Since the work is project oriented and jobs are often performed on site, changes in location are frequently required. Some projects may be done in remote areas or in unpleasant environments. Either temporary living quarters are obtained or complete relocation occurs, depending upon project length. This may imply separation from family for time periods of varying lengths. Sustained periods of overtime may also be required. In some areas, engineers working on location must deal with tough construction unions. This industry seems to have developed a "macho" image which has made it difficult to recruit female engineers. Yet recruiting in general is not a major problem. Construction firms recruit primarily civil engineers although they also employ mechanical, electrical, and chemical engineers. They do not as a rule compete directly for individuals in critical skill areas such as electronics and computers.

Although numerous project bids may be submitted at any given time, the actual bids that will ultimately become jobs usually cannot be identified. Thus, future projects are not always known far in advance. Because of this uncertainty in future workload, engineers may be hired only for the duration of a single project. If an opportunity to utilize their skills exists upon project completion, they will be kept on. It is difficult for management to identify or to define specific career paths. Human resource development is limited by the projects that are available for engineers to work on. Flexibility is essential, and relocations are both common and expected as part of the job. Lateral transfers are more common than promotional relocations. When viewed in this light, the stability and security offered by other industries are forfeited when one enters the construction industry.

In this industry, a common form of organizational structure is the matrix. Engineers are members of both functional departments and project teams. Functional managers are responsible for maintaining technical expertise in a given area. When a project is organized, the required specialists are selected from their functional departments and assigned to a team. Human resource data base systems are helpful in team development. A matrix organization creates a challenging environment for the development and administration of performance appraisal systems.

Construction firms are very conscious of their client relationships. Because they are essentially service organizations, in many respects the product sold is the collective expertise of the engineers. Large construction firms have one of the highest ratios of engineers to total number of employees. The need to assure clients of technical competency may encourage malutilization, or the use of engineers who are overqualified for the job required. For example, licensed engineers may be used where experienced draftsmen are sufficient. Professional certification is encouraged, and sometimes required.

Since work is done on a contract basis, overhead spending is typically kept to a minimum. Consequently, resources available for training and development tend to be tightly controlled.

Managers of large construction firms realize that certain skills, such as those related to project management, are necessary for continued success. These skills must be tailored to individual company style and are often developed from within through a series of planned project rotations. Some firms have invested in the development of good project managers, and retain engineers with these skills regardless of temporary business troughs.

Most projects involve only design and construction. Research and development activities are uncommon. Where proprietary processes are involved in construction projects, customer technology is frequently used. Few scientists are employed by construction firms. Unlike companies more dependent upon research, these organizations need only limited dual ladders. Elaborate programs to recognize and motivate technical innovation are unusual.

CAD can be used to enhance engineering productivity in this industry, but several firms indicated that software improvement is necessary before substantial savings can occur. CAD has been used to reduce manpower fluctuations because of changing workloads.

As in the aerospace industry, periodic layoffs are expected in the construction industry. It is, however, recognized that business usually picks up again. Hence, even if employees must be terminated, most firms make an effort to administer the process carefully in an attempt to ensure that top engineers will return when new projects are obtained. Economic swings can affect the entire industry (except perhaps for firms with special market niches or those concentrated in specific geographic locations). Laid off engineers typically do not find that they can work for a competitor down the street or across town as they can in the aerospace industry. No industry assist programs were uncovered, but they are potentially feasible if one firm needs engineers to work on projects while another has surplus engineers. Despite the environment of project uncertainty, lack of training, and threat of layoffs, engineering unions are rare in this industry.

UTILITIES INDUSTRY

In contrast to the electronics, communications, and computer industries, employment in this industry has historically been characterized by stability and security. This has changed recently, however, as the demand for energy has failed to grow and resistance to price increases has stiffened. Although there have been periodic technological innovations, the business is basically mature and not driven by the same forces or changes which characterize other industries. Apparently there has been a shift in the thrust of an electrical engineering education over the past decade. The emphasis on electronics has caused a few respondents to mention that they had experienced difficulties in recruiting new graduates in the traditional fields of power transmission and distribution. Several companies offer cooperative positions to encourage college students to pursue careers in utilities.

The stability of the industry has encouraged investment in training programs. Formal career planning is also possible. There are limits, however, to the resources that can be devoted to organizational development. Because utilities are regulated, their expenditures are examined by regulatory agencies and consumer groups. Since utilities do not want to appear as if they are wasting money, they must be cautious in introducing innovative personnel techniques or unusual benefit programs. Consequently, most have refrained from doing so. Most programs and policies are standard. Engineers in a few utilities are organized, but no new waves of unionization have occurred in recent years.

CONCLUSION

Personnel policies toward E/S are thus clearly affected by the structure of a particular industry. Such distinctions both hinder and assist E/S recruitment and retention. Regardless of the industry in which it operates, a company must compete for E/S with companies in other industries as well as those within its own. Programs developed by one company in an industry are likely to be adopted by others therein if such programs achieve their purposes. Such programs do not, however, spread as rapidly to other industries. If the programs are adopted widely, they are likely to be modified to conform to the needs of diverse companies. The pressures on each group resulting from structural and business needs determine the response. Part of that pressure comes from the relative scarcity of E/S and the necessity for companies in many diverse industries to attract and to retain these key personnel.

PART FOUR

Concluding Remarks

CHAPTER XIII

Summary and Conclusion

It is difficult to summarize the numerous personnel policies and programs for engineers and scientists (E/S) adopted by a multitude of companies in various industries. The information in the preceding chapters does, however, provide a number of insights into the nature and usefulness of many such policies, the most important aspects of which are delineated in the following sections. Moreover, a number of trends uncovered in this study suggest the direction which future developments will take.

THE INSTITUTIONAL ENVIRONMENT

There are no strong indications that there will be any fundamental changes in the institutional environment. The supply of E/S continues to expand but also continues to be outstripped by demand. Given the significance of the defense budget, the rise of high technology companies, and the need of all industry to automate and otherwise to apply engineering and scientific skills, it is difficult to foresee any lengthy cutback in the demand for E/S, or even a serious diminution of the upward trend in demand. Future recessions, however, could again create a temporary oversupply of various specialties. In addition, critical skills are likely to always be in very short supply and other specialties overabundant.

When shortages of skills occur, ways to improve methods of work and utilization of professionals are usually found. The almost universal agreement of our interview respondents was that there was considerable room for improvement in E/S productivity and utilization. For this reason, one can be more sanguine that large and serious shortages of E/S may not come to pass despite problems in the colleges and universities concerning faculty and equipment shortages. On the other hand, the age and currency of faculties may result in future quality problems which would require more industry training and retraining.

Women and Minorities

In recent years women have made significant gains in the engineering and scientific professions; the progress of blacks has, however, been slower, in part because of their small participation rates in the fields prior to 1970. Affirmative action to alter this situation has resulted in some gains, but the problem will not be solved for many years.

Government Role

The federal government plays a major role in the engineering and scientific community. It is a major employer of E/S, a tremendous contributor to research and development (R&D), and an increasing force in regulating the labor market. The government's affirmative action requirements are in no small part responsible for the gains made by women and blacks in the engineering and scientific professions. In recent years, the Age Discrimination in Employment Act (ADEA) has been a very significant force in limiting the coupling of age and obsolescence, and in forcing companies to develop new programs designed to retrain older E/S. Unfortunately, the ADEA has also been used by employees who are laid off for legitimate reasons but are within the age brackets as defined by the act. Assuming, as we must, that compulsory retirement is outlawed, industry must greatly improve its appraisal system if the truly incompetent and obsolete are to be distinguished from those workers who would benefit from retraining. Few appraisal systems were believed, either by human resource or E/S executive managers interviewed for this study, to be administered as satisfactorily as is required for optimum results.

Professional Societies

Professional societies play an important role in the lives and work of E/S and should continue to do so. In particular, their educational programs are both significant and valuable. There remains, however, a fundamental conflict between the advocations of the societies and the needs of industry. The ideal perpetuated by these societies is of the individual E/S, responsible only to himself and his client in a one-to-one relationship. In practice, most E/S are employees and as such cannot realize this ideal. Too often neither their education nor their professional society relationships prepare them for the organizational realities associated with employment.

Attempts of professional societies to establish work standards are also negatively received by companies. Although the societies emphatically reject this notion, any discussion with them in regard to professional employee standards of compensation or working conditions would constitute a form of bargaining. In addition to the fact that companies desire to avoid such a relationship, possible violation of the National Labor Relations (Taft-Hartley) Act could be involved because the memberships of the societies include managers as well as employees, and because there is no proof that any society truly represents a majority of any one company's professional employees.

Unions

Unions represent only about 2 percent of the E/S employed in industry, and for the most part are weak, local organizations. The desire of companies to operate nonunion, insofar as E/S are concerned, gives these unions a role beyond their size because the management of many companies carefully consider in advance the impact any policy may have on the employees' propensity to unionize. The fact that the unions failed to gain any significant new bargaining units during the severe cutbacks of the early 1970s and early 1980s would seem to indicate that unions remain unattractive to the bulk of E/S.

If the attitudes of E/S toward unions change, one can expect the professional societies to attempt to establish bargaining units. Virtually the only point on which professional societies and unions agree is that there is no room for both in a given field. The rivalry between the National Education Association (NEA) and the American Federation of Teachers, as well as that between the American Nurses Association (ANA) and various unions attempting to organize hospital nurses, are cases in point. This same situation occurred among engineers and chemists in the period 1935–1947 before separate bargaining units were mandated for professionals. At that time, various societies promoted unions of their own creation to prevent regular unions from gaining a foothold in the field.[1] Society-related unions are more likely to gain the allegiance of professionals who object to being led by, or affiliated with, organizations of blue-collar workers. The result, however, as evidenced by the NEA and ANA experience, would be that the professional societies would cease to function as societies per se, and instead become unions themselves.

PERSONNEL POLICIES

It is clear from the information presented in Part Three of this study that industrial corporations by and large recognize the impor-

---

[1] See Herbert R. Northrup, *Unionization of Professional Engineers and Chemists*, Industrial Relations Monograph, No. 12 (New York: Industrial Relations Counselors, Inc., 1948); and Northrup, "Collective Bargaining by Professional Societies," in R. A. Lester and J. Shister, eds., *Insights into Labor Issues* (New York: Macmillan & Co. 1948), pp. 134–62.

tant role that E/S play in the continued growth of their businesses, and that they therefore strive to institute policies that will permit them to retain and to motivate such personnel. There have been many different policies implemented to achieve this end, some of which have been more successful than others.

Recruiting

Most companies handle recruiting quite well. Those with long and deserved reputations as good places to work have a distinct advantage in recruiting. In addition, those companies in industries that E/S consider exciting, or that are located in preferred places to live, have inherent advantages. Most companies that employ a sizable number of E/S spend considerable sums on recruiting. Perhaps the most frequent shortcoming of recruitment practices is that more is promised to the college recruit than can be delivered, not necessarily because the recruiter exaggerates or is dishonest, but because the training at universities does not usually include sufficient education in understanding organizations or economic realities. Therefore, unreal expectations of rapid rises in the hierarchy or individual assignments of one's own choosing can easily be read into the recruiter's glowing account of the company being touted.

Orientation, Training, and Development

Companies' orientation policies are often less professionally advanced than their recruiting policies. It is easy for an individual to become lost or pigeonholed in a large company. Supervisors and managers vary tremendously in their human relations skills and can often frustrate the best of policies. As in all jobs, turnover is the highest for E/S in their early months or years of employment with a company. The concerns that have the best and most carefully directed orientation and early career development programs have the least turnover of newly recruited E/S.

Training and development policies vary tremendously among companies. In the fast moving technology of the current era, both E/S and the companies they work for have a very real and necessary obligation to maintain currency and to develop within the special fields with which they are associated. The companies that budget amply for personnel development are likely to be the leaders in their industry; the E/S that make company development a personal priority are the ones that continue to advance.

Many companies provide career planning assistance to E/S. Failure to do so can reduce retention and encourage discontent. The dual-ladder approach accommodates both the potential E/S manager and the individual contributor. Providing proper incentives and opportunities to the latter is a difficult task that many companies have not done successfully. Companies which have overcome such hurdles, however, have been very satisfied with the contributions which E/S who remain in their professional fields have made to their company's success.

Productivity and Utilization

As we have already noted, the productivity and utilization of E/S offer considerable potential for improvement. Interview respondents generally agreed that more effective use of para-professionals and clericals is necessary to achieve this aim. Improved organizational relationships between R&D and manufacturing could improve productivity in some companies. Perhaps most important of all, computer aided design (CAD) and computer aided manufacturing (CAM), which are gaining adherents, offer enormous possibilities that some companies have been slow to explore.

Salaries, Benefits, and Recognition

E/S are quite well paid and receive standard to generous benefit packages. Problems of compensation include compression—the tendency of rising starting salaries to outstrip advances for experienced E/S or of the E/S earnings differential over blue-collar workers to lessen; and the relationship between the salaries paid to E/S who are working in their specialty fields and those paid to E/S who become managers. The problem of compression has been somewhat mitigated recently by the decline in inflation and the use of carefully constructed compensation programs. The failure of some companies to differentiate between general increases as a means of offsetting inflation and merit increases for individual performance, however, caused problems during the 1970s that still need further analysis and correction.

Overtime work has become a problem because of its impact on the blue collar-E/S earnings differential. The most successful approach to this problem seems to be providing bonuses for extended overtime duties without making such payments either automatic or by formula. Otherwise, overtime is likely to be created by those who will profit by it.

The compensation relationship between E/S who become managers and those working in their fields has been handled best by those companies that have created dual ladders with carefully constructed career paths and an equally carefully constructed compensation system. Even with such policies and programs, difficulties can arise, but having a program provides the means for the solution, or at least mitigation of problems.

Intangible rewards and recognition designed to motivate E/S play a very important part in noting achievement and in giving achievers important satisfaction. For very little effort and expense, companies have won in this manner considerable loyalty and support from E/S employees.

Communication

Communication exists in all companies, but it is all too often in spite of company policies rather than because of them. Traditionally, American industry has been better at making products than communicating with people, including its own employees. Moreover, E/S by nature are typically not expansive communicators. Unless communication permeates the whole organization, policies can be misunderstood, opportunities lost, and productivity lessened. The few companies that understand this thoroughly seem to profit immensely.

Communication must, however, be understood not to mean loose discussion of proprietary matters. On the other hand, excessive secrecy can be self-defeating by preventing understanding of essential factors needed for intracompany cooperation.

Obsolescence and Retraining

Obsolescence comes on slowly and usually manifests itself only when it has grown for a considerable period. It is likely, but not necessarily, correlated with age, but using age as a criterion is both intellectually and legally wrong. Combating obsolescence requires the cooperation both of the individual E/S and the company he works for. A variety of retraining methods are available to companies. No matter what methods are utilized, however, obsolescence in this dynamic, technological world must be continually attacked and offset. Some innovative retraining practices which serve both to combat obsolescence and to supply needed critical skills are described in Chapter IX.

Retention and Layoffs

Given the fact that the labor market for E/S does not adjust perfectly, or sometimes quickly, at the micro or macro level, there will always be some shortages and oversupplies of particular specialties.

Companies, therefore, give considerable attention to policies designed to reduce turnover and to mitigate workforce reductions. Without doubt, concern and action to improve orientation, to encourage development, to assist in career planning, to provide opportunities for advancement, and to communicate these policies and others effectively are the keys to effective retention.

Companies work assiduously to avoid layoffs of E/S, but in industries such as aerospace and construction, the dynamics of contract winning, cancellation, and completion often require layoffs. In a depressed situation, such as that which affected metal manufacturing concerns, layoffs are also extremely difficult to avoid. The Lockheed program of "lending" E/S (presented in Chapter X) is an interesting example of a program that avoids layoffs to the benefit of E/S and company alike. Although layoffs do indeed occur, the unemployment rate for E/S, even in the worst of times, is considerably below the national average.

The Research Laboratory

Managing a research laboratory is a unique experience. The typical laboratory is a complex, hierarchical organization based upon degree level. Often such laboratories are located in attractive settings and provide very comfortable quarters. The investment is great, as is the risk. The organizational problem consists of integrating the work of E/S involved in R&D, who often tend to consider their role as being similar to that of an academician, with the practical needs of the operating organization. All the policies discussed above must be carefully considered and applied in this situation so that optimum relationship and productivity can be achieved. In particular, a certain autonomy regarding their work and recognition for their accomplishments seem extremely important to R&D personnel.

Recently, corporations have found it wise to establish cooperative relationships with universities and government research laboratories in order both to gain from the knowledge of personnel in institutions and to support these institutions. E/S in industry R&D usually applaud this commingling as a valuable way to exchange information and expand their knowledge of new developments.

Differences Among Industries

Different industries require policies that comport with their needs and structures. Moreover, while different industries may pursue the same general policies, the applications are often quite different because of structural constraints. Our interviews uncovered a host of varied personnel policy applications for E/S resulting from different environments. The preceding chapter recounts the ways in which environmental and structural constraints both hinder and assist E/S recruitment, retention, rewards, etc.

CONCLUDING COMMENT

Engineers and scientists are a key to the successful defense and growth of the United States. In the fierce competition of the final two decades of the twentieth century, the work of E/S will play a major role in determining whether this country remains free and vibrant. Managing E/S is, therefore, a key role, not only for industry, but for the country as a whole. The personnel policies which have been developed for this significant group of employees are in general well thought out, but as always in large organizations, often less well executed. By highlighting the issues and the considered solutions to problems, it is hoped this book can contribute to the development of superior policies and to their effective execution.

APPENDICES

Appendix A

OUTLINE OF INTERVIEW QUESTIONNAIRE

by
Herbert R. Northrup, Director
and
Margot E. Malin, Research Associate

OBJECTIVE

The purpose of this study is to explore the current personnel policies used by various industries in the management of engineers and scientific professionals.

These policies will be reviewed and their effectiveness will be evaluated.

Attention will be called to especially meritorious programs and recommendations will be made to improve programs that have demonstrated shortcomings.

Individual cases may be cited as examples showing positive or negative features, but company names will not be utilized except by permission.

Engineers and scientific professionals are defined in this study by job function. This includes personnel in areas of industrial and scientific research, design, development, manufacturing, operations, information systems, technical sales, and other related areas. In particular the following engineering fields will be included: electrical, mechanical, civil, aeronautical, and other miscellaneous disciplines. The scientific fields include organic, inorganic and physical chemistry, life sciences, biology, geology, physics, and others which may be pertinent to a particular industry. Computer scientists are also included, but not keypunch operators or other technicians. Engineers and scientific professionals by training and education who currently hold management positions, or who have moved into other job functions such as human resources or finance are not included.

The attached outline has been designed to cover a broad base in an effort to facilitate adaptation to a variety of situations. It is perceived that the environment in an industrial research laboratory is significantly different from situations engineers and scientists are involved in daily operations (production, design, manufacturing, etc.). Additionally, the relationships among professionals may vary. These differences will be explored and implications analyzed. The flow and spirit of the outline should be clear although not every section is applicable to each company.

It is also recognized that the role of engineers and scientists may vary significantly among industries. Preliminary research indicates that computer scientists and software engineers present special problems. These factors will receive special attention in the analyses in order to provide accurate, meaningful results.

The study will cover an assortment of industries including, but not limited to, the following:

Industries

1. Electrical
2. Electronic
3. Chemical
4. Petroleum
5. Aerospace
6. Paper and Wood Products
7. Computer and High Technology
8. Automobiles
9. Other Metals
10. Others to be chosen

TOPICAL OUTLINE

Broad categories are defined. Each one is then detailed. Sample topics in each category are suggested.

I.   The Job and the Individual Engineer
I(a).   Industrial Research Laboratories (special section)
I(b).   Software Engineers and Computer Scientists (special section)
II.   Compensation
III.   Innovation
IV.   Professional Societies
V.   Legislation: Effects and Impact
VI.   Management Structure in the Company
VII.   Productivity/Utilization
VIII.   Location
IX.   The Crisis in Engineering Education
X.   Unions

I. *The Job and the Individual Engineer*
 A. Classification of Engineers and Scientists
  1) Definition of traditional job functions: research, development, applications, design, industrial production
  2) Who else may be included in this study?
  i.e., engineers in sales, marketing, management
  3) Are engineers considered professionals or labor by the company?
  4) Scientists: i.e., chemists, physicists, geologists, etc. In determination of who is an engineer or scientist, three viewpoints must be considered:
  a. the individual engineer's or scientist's
  b. management's
  c. the researcher's
 B. Specialization Versus Job Rotation
  1) Does the company encourage diversity or specialization?
  2) Does the engineer get a "broad picture" including economics, market development, etc.
  3) What is done by the company to prevent pigeonholing?
  4) What is done to prevent obsolescence?
 C. Social Awareness and Responsibility
  1) Are engineers encouraged to be active in the community?
  2) Politics?
  3) Assisting or providing information for government policy formation?
  4) What about press coverage, editorials, and opinions?
 D. Registration and Licensing
  1) Does the company require/encourage:
  a) EIT—Engineer in Training?
  b) PE—Professional Engineer?
  2) Are certificates displayed at work?
  3) If engineers are licensed do they have a chance to "sign their work"?
  4) Will the company reimburse the engineer for the licensing fee?
  5) Will a license enhance an engineer's opportunity for promotion?
I(a). *Industrial Research Laboratories*
What are the differences between engineers and scientists who work in the lab and those in operations, as perceived by management?

A. Motivation
   1) What is used to motivate scientists?
   2) Are there any special rewards for this group?
   3) Is there a motivation problem for those who have "reached their level of competence"?
B. Goals
   1) Is research considered basic or directed?
   2) How are the objectives of the company integrated with the scientists' personal, professional goals?
   3) How is the direction of research decided?
   4) Who ultimately selects which projects to pursue?
C. Hierarchy
   1) Is there an informal "caste" system?
   2) Is an advanced degree required for promotion?
   3) What are the perceptions of the scientists as to their position in the company (are they appreciated)?
D. Environment
   1) Is the lab perceived as an academic environment?
   2) Does the management of the research group have scientific backgrounds and experience?
   3) Is the environment specifically designed to stimulate creativity?
   4) Is there one central R & D facility, or are they decentralized?
E. Communication
   1) Is the lab an isolated entity or does it interact with other divisions?
   2) Is there a link between the lab and the ultimate customers so there may be some feelings as to potential projects?
   3) What kind of feedback does the lab get from corporate management?

I(b). *Software Engineers and Computer Scientists*
   A. Are there special problems in hiring or retaining these professionals?
   B. Job progression/career paths?
   C. Is there an in-house training for individuals with related degrees, with general degrees?
II. *Compensation*
   A. Salaries (money wages only)
      1) Methods of evaluation
      2) Types of increases
         a) COLA

       b) Merit
       c) General
       d) Combination
    3) Frequency of reviews
    4) Overtime compensation
       a) Do the engineers punch time clocks?
       b) Fill out time cards?
    5) How does the company deal with compression?
    6) Method of salary administration (personnel, engineer, management, etc.)
    7) Salary system used
       a) Grid
       b) Grades
       c) Curves
       d) Other

B. Benefits
    1) What percent of total compensation does this represent?
    2) At what rate are benefits increasing in relation to money wages?
    3) Cafeteria style plans: are they used?
    4) Vacation
    5) Personal days
    6) Sick days
    4), 5), 6):
       a) Are they accrued year to year?
       b) Are engineers paid if this time is not taken?
       c) Amount received
       d) When does their coverage begin (time period)?
    7) Medical
    8) Dental
    9) Legal assistance
    10) Optical
    11) Disability
    12) Life insurance
    13) Retirement provisions
    14) Pensions:
       Length of time required for vesting
    15) Savings plans
    16) Stock plans
    17) Profit sharing

C. "Perks"
   1) Van pooling (transportation)
   2) Child care
   3) Placement for employment of spouse
   4) Housing—is it company sponsored? Is the engineer subsidized?
   5) Physical fitness programs
      a) Track, gym, pool, showers "in house"
      b) Separate company-owned club
      c) Group membership discount to health club
   6) Involvement and concern for family
      Is a return to paternalism predicted for the future?
   7) Extras:
      i.e., turkeys at Christmas, bonuses, etc.
   8) Flextime: hours of work
      a) Number per day
      b) Number per week (i.e., four ten-hour days vs. five nine-hour days)
   9) Coffee and donuts
   10) Company-sponsored parties or dinners
   11) Company food facilities
       a) Cafeteria
       b) Microwave oven
       c) Refrigerator
   12) Other: company cars, royalty sharing, etc.

   What has been the trend in these perks? If the company has found it difficult to meet their demand for engineers, have they found that increasing "perks" helps? If not, what is being done to meet increased demand?

III. *Innovation*
   A. Patents
      1) Who gets the title?
      2) Compensation
         a) Bonus
         b) Award
         c) Dinner
         d) Other
   B. Publications
      1) Is there a limitation on what can be published?
      2) Compensation or bonus
      3) Is there a consultant who can assist in editing (English grammar)?
      4) Internal publications

C. Presentations
   1) Are new and innovative inter(intra) company develop-
      ments presented?
   2) Does the engineer make management presentations?
   3) Are there presentation workshops to improve those
      skills?
D. Continuing education—What are the policies applying to
   continuing education?
   How strongly is it encouraged?
   1) In-house (during work or after hours)
      a) By other employees or management
      b) By outside consultants or professors who are hired
         to teach seminars at the company location
   2) Tuition reimbursement for university courses
      a) Are advanced degrees encouraged?
         What type: MBA, MSE, or J.D.?
      b) What is the reimbursement policy?
      c) Scope and breadth of courses covered?
      d) Must a course lead to a degree?
      e) Are books covered?
      f) Will an advanced degree enhance the opportunity
         for promotion?
      g) Is an advanced degree required for promotion?
      h) Do the majority of the managers of engineers and
         scientists have advanced degrees?
   3) Seminars given by professional societies or universi-
      ties
      a) Are engineers reimbursed for attendance?
      b) Is time granted or is this time spent considered
         vacation?
IV. *Professional Societies*
A. Company's viewpoint
   1) Is the company aware of: "Guidelines of Professional
      Employment for Engineers and Scientists" by the
      EJC and "Professional Employment Guidelines" by
      the ACS?
   2) If so, do they comply with them?
      What are the attitudes toward them?
   3) Does the management of the company "hear" the pro-
      fessional society and the individual engineer's empha-
      sis on professionalism?
   4) Does management attend professional society func-
      tions?

5) What percentage of the engineers and scientists belong to professional societies?
6) Of the above group, how many participate actively?
7) Does the threat of antitrust legislation or former problems with antitrust limit the involvement of professionals in professional societies?

B. A comprehensive look at the professional societies
   Unique programs of the societies addressing:
   1) Ethics and professionals
   2) Engineer/management communications
   3) The education crisis
   4) Unions
      a) Their attitudes
      b) Alternatives
         A look at:
         The American Association of Engineering Societies (AAES)
         American Chemical Society (ACS)
         American Society of Civil Engineers (ASCE)
         American Society of Chemical Engineers (AIChe)
         Institute of Electrical and Electronic Engineers (IEEE)
         National Society of Professional Engineers (NSPE)

V. *Legislation: Effects and Impact*
   A. Age and discrimination
      1) Old age and retirement
      2) Retraining: How to keep older employees alert and motivated
   B. Handicapped
   C. Veterans
   D. Minorities
      1) Hispanic
      2) Black
      3) Oriental
   E. Women
      Is there a policy for a spouse simultaneously working for a company?

The following topics will be examined for the above groups:
   1) What special programs are there to attract these segments of the population? (recruiting, on the job training)
   2) What special "tracking" systems are there for these groups once they are hired?

3) Are there special training programs to help them enter into management and receive promotions?

4) What is the history of retaining these engineers, compared to others? (attrition rate)

VI. *Management Structure in the Company*

The following are programs and policies which must be developed by the management:

A. Training

1) Are there established training programs or is it basically on the job?

2) If established, what is the format, the progression? What is the intent?

3) Are there programs received periodically?

4) Is there a feedback mechanism for engineers?

5) Who is responsible for the individual engineer's progression?

B. Career paths

1) Is there a "dual ladder"? If so, does it work?

a) Opportunities for continuing in engineering

b) Opportunities for becoming management

This is the career progression from management's perspective. What is the ideal flow of talent?

2) What about engineers switching into other fields?

a) Marketing

b) Sales

c) Strategic planning

Is there a flow of engineers into these other fields?

3) For the engineer does promotion also mean moving to another company location? (headquarters to plant, etc.)

What has been the best method for developing a broad base of engineers in any one location?

4) What is the career path/progression as perceived by the engineer? Is it clear what the opportunities are?

C. Performance appraisal

1) Frequency

2) Who has the responsibility for evaluating the engineers?

3) Feedback mechanisms

4) Is the engineer aware of the company's expectations of him?

5) Does the company use a program like Management by Objectives?

D. Management techniques of communication
    1) Visual (Video)
        Group meetings, frequency of:
        a) Seminars
        b) Brainstorming
        c) Updates
    Newsletters
    Company literature, magazines or newspapers
    Where are they distributed?
        a) At work
        b) Mailed home
    2) General management communication
        a) Does management communicate its overall objectives and plans?
        b) Is the engineer informed of company's overall competitive position in the market? Financial performance?
        c) What modes of feedback are there?
        d) What procedures exist for an engineer to express dissatisfaction or voice a grievance?
        e) Intergroup communication
           Do engineer groups interact with each other? Do they interact with other employees: sales, marketing, production, etc.

E. Recruiting
    1) Methods
    2) Techniques
    3) What does the company look for in an engineer?
    4) How are engineers screened? (selection criteria)
        a) Qualities
        b) Education
        c) Personal characteristics
    5) New graduates
        a) Cooperative programs with universities
        b) Summer or vacation opportunities
        c) Campus recruiting
        d) Where within the engineer class should they recruit? (realistic approach)
        e) Do they recruit both:
           i) Top people
           ii) Middle-of-the-road and have different progressions for the two?
        f) At which universities should the recruiting be concentrated? Local or well-known?

g) If they hire the middle-of-the-road group, is supplemental training required?
6) Experienced engineers (from universities or other companies)
   a) Employee bonus for "add-a-friend"
   b) Headhunters (recruiting firms)
   c) Advertising
      —trade journals
      —local newspapers
7) What are the best predictors of performance?
8) Does the company conduct exit interviews or surveys, and if so, what information have they learned from them?
9) What is the turnover rate for engineers and scientists? Is it satisfactory? How does it compare to the industry rate?
10) Are attitude surveys taken periodically?
11) Minorities (see Section V)

F. "Pre" recruiting/development of talent
1) Are there any programs aimed at high school students to encourage them to enter math and science related fields?
2) Are there programs which explain the careers of scientists and engineers to junior high and high school students?

G. Layoffs
1) Is the nature of the business cyclical?
2) What selection criteria are used to determine who will be laid off?
3) Are there any programs aimed at maintaining a constant level of professionals: intraindustry borrowing, intracompany borrowing, subcontracting, alien hiring etc.?
4) In the event of a mass layoff, does the personnel department work as an outplacement service or clinic?

VII. *Productivity/utilization*
A. Productivity
1) Are there any current policies to improve productivity in this employee group?
   a) CAD/CAM
   b) Information systems; examples of new technology
   c) White-collar quality circles

        d) Group projects (synergy)

        e) Quality of work life seminars

     2) Are there any devices or techniques used to measure engineer productivity?

  B. Utilization

    1) Support staff

      a) Clerical

      b) Technicians

      c) Cooperative students

Using the established definition of an engineer, a look into two other populations:

    1) Technicians

    2) Associate engineers

Does the company employ engineers with no degrees (those who have worked their way up from technician)? Are there people working as engineers with nonengineering degrees (i.e., industrial engineers)?

    2) How are jobs set up?

      a) Projects

      b) Individual

      c) Piecemeal

      d) Groups

VIII. *Location*

  A. Geography, cost of living, urban vs. suburban

  B. How to attract and hold engineers in "adverse" areas

  C. Does the company offer mobility?

  D. Is there more than one location for engineers?

  E. If so, can they transfer from place to place?

  F. Is it feasible for some engineers to operate remotely?

    1) From another city

    2) From home

  G. Does the company use housing perks?

  H. Is there any travel required of the engineer on the job?

  I. What is the relocation policy?

IX. *The Crisis in Engineering Education*

This problem is well-documented in "Report to the White House" which appeared in *Professional Engineer* magazine. Does the company have any specific plans developed to address this situation:

  A. Donate data equipment

  B. Allow the use of their equipment (students or faculty use after working hours)

  C. Encourage engineers to give seminars or teach part-time at local universities

D. Sabbatical leave to engineers for teaching
E. Subsidizing professors' salaries to make them more equitable with industry
F. Industry/education cooperation: employ professors during the summer
G. Establish fellowships for graduate students

X. *Unions*

This topic will include a section on the history of engineering unions. Current engineering unions will be reviewed as well. Much of the background material used will be from Geoffrey Latta's research and his current article appearing in *Industrial and Labor Relations Review* (October 1981)

Companies interviewed will also be asked for their response on the following:

A. Company general attitudes
B. Is there currently an engineering union?
   1) Yes:
      a) Who is included in the bargaining unit?
      b) What is the membership total?
      c) What is the percentage of engineers who belong?
      d) Is membership compulsory?
   2) No:
      a) What procedures have been followed to prevent or avoid union formation?
      b) Have any "middle-ground" approaches ever been tried?

Appendix B

PROFESSIONAL SOCIETIES
AND SOME OF THEIR POLICIES

There are professional societies for ever conceivable subfield of engineering and science. In addition, several others have been created to coordinate the activities of existing societies. The *Encyclopedia of Associations* takes 115 pages to list such societies, their memberships, fields, and principal duties. Some of those listed do not conform to the objectives described below of a professional society; others are in social science or in subprofessional callings. Most, however, are truly professional groups. In this appendix, the material on such societies (summarized in Chapter III) is elaborated. Emphasis will be upon those societies listed in Table III-2, which include the most active ones in the economic as well as in the engineering and scientific fields.

PROFESSIONALISM AND THE SOCIETIES

"The terminology of professionalism is fundamentally eulogistic."[1] Members of a profession are assumed to possess special knowledge and to perform work not easily comprehended by a layman. Since professionals provide special services that consumers cannot easily judge as to quality, it is assumed that consumers must be protected by a code of ethics to which professionals adhere. Such codes, however, can also be used to protect the economic interests of the professionals: for example, by including in the work reserved for professionals much of what can be safely and accurately performed by subprofessionals. Moreover, since such codes of ethics are frequently written into law and administered by members of the profession involved, the line between monopolizing work and protecting the public can be easily transgressed.

It is quite natural that persons trained for and working in the same profession seek to join together to support their profession, to enhance their knowledge, and to improve their economic well-being.

---

[1]Oliver Garceau, *The Political Life of the American Medical Association,* Harvard Political Studies (Cambridge, Mass.: Harvard University Press, 1941), p. 5.

Thus, professional societies came into existence and have flourished performing these functions. It is also very understandable that, in a world in which corporations are the principal employers of their members, professional societies should seek to serve these members in their relations with their corporate employers, and that corporate management should in turn find it wise to limit any such outside "interference." Finally, it is not surprising that professional societies should consider unions "unprofessional" organizations that are intruding into the territories of the societies and utilizing distasteful tactics, such as bargaining over conditions of employment and striking.

As noted in Chapter III, professional societies today play an important role in the fields of science and engineering. In this appendix the interaction of professional societies and industrial corporations will be explored. Specific attention will be paid to the components of the forces which professional societies exert on corporations and examples will be given of the policies of key societies.

GENERAL FOCUS OF SOCIETIES

Professional societies have historically had a primarily technical orientation through activities such as sponsoring continuing education programs, publishing technical journals, organizing symposiums, setting standards, and preparing policy statements. They fulfill an important role by offering methods of combating obsolescence, providing various means by which an engineer or scientist (E/S) can maintain currency in a particular field. This may include participation in professional development programs, articles in professional journals, sponsorship of courses, or even cooperation with particular companies to develop special courses.

In addition to strictly technical activities, professional societies have periodically involved themselves in economic and employment issues pertinent to science and engineering. For example, following the enactment of the National Labor Relations (Wagner) Act of 1935, several societies, but particularly the American Society of Civil Engineers (ASCE) and the American Chemical Society (ACS), helped to establish separate local unions for E/S in order to keep them out of bargaining units dominated by blue-collar workers.[2] Then when the amendments to the Wagner Act were being considered, most professional societies lobbied hard and successfully for

---

[2]For society actions during this period, see Herbert R. Northrup, *Unionization of Professional Engineers and Chemists,* Industrial Relations Monograph, No. 12 (New York: Industrial Relations Counselors, Inc., 1946).

the inclusion of what became known as the "professional proviso" to section 9(b) of the Taft-Hartley Act of 1947. The proviso states in part that "the Board shall not (1) decide that any unit is appropriate for [collective bargaining] if such unit includes both professional employees and employees who are not professional employees unless a majority of such employees vote for inclusion in such a unit. . . ." Section 2(12) of this law requires that the National Labor Relations Board (NLRB) use the following definition of professional employee in administering the section 9(b) proviso:

> The term "professional employee" means—
> (a) any employee engaged in work (i) predominantly intellectual and varied in character as opposed to routine mental, manual, mechanical, or physical work; (ii) involving the consistent exercise of discretion and judgement in its performance; (iii) of such a character that the output produced or the result accomplished cannot be standardized in relation to a given period of time; (iv) requiring knowledge of an advanced type of a field of science or learning customarily acquired by a prolonged course of specialized intellectual instruction. . . . [3]

After this victory, the professional societies' interest in promoting separate local unions for E/S virtually disappeared, and E/S interest in such unions also declined. As will be noted below, several societies do, however, have a definite opinion on the appropriateness of collective bargaining for E/S. The societies also continue to give serious attention to such related matters as professional ethics, industrial employment practices, and lobbying on behalf of legislation pertinent to E/S both as individuals and in regard to their chosen fields of employment. Professional societies have also commenced to advocate cooperation between industry, academia, and the government as an approach to strengthening the nation's technological infrastructure. They support the formation of "partnerships" between entities aimed at sharing resources, improving conditions, and upgrading equipment and faculty at professional schools and universities. The societies have also supported efforts to expand the number of minorities and women admitted to educational institutions and given opportunities in their professions.

Because of the diversity of their activities, professional societies exert pressures on companies in two ways. External forces are applied through direct involvement with corporations. For example, the publication and distribution of employment guidelines through-

---

[3]See John E. Abodeely et al., *The NLRB and the Appropriate Bargaining Unit*, rev. ed., Labor Relations and Public Policy Series, No. 3 (Philadelphia: Industrial Research Unit, The Wharton School, University of Pennsylvania, 1981), pp. 210-14, for the legal application of the professional proviso.

out various industries, which is discussed more fully below, constitute one component of this force. In addition, internal forces are
applied indirectly through company employees who are professional
society members. These internal forces can take many forms. For
example, employees may learn about innovative programs at a competitor's facility through attendance at a conference. Also, an individual's need for recognition and reward on the job may increase
through participation in professional society activities. Employees
may also become dissatisfied as a result of divergencies between
company practice and a professional society's pronouncements.

Factors Limiting Society Activities

Although the collective arenas in which professional societies are
involved are diverse, there are several factors which limit the range
of their individual activities or effectiveness. One is the diversity of
member interests within each society. A random sample of members
of a major society would include individuals from different occupations, working in different sectors, and situated on various rungs of
a career ladder, or on different levels of an employment hierarchy:
professors, technical managers, individual engineers and scientists
employed by industry, engineers and scientists employed by government, self-employed individuals, etc.

This diversity of membership has created internal conflicts when
professional societies have attempted to determine their appropriate
stances on specific topics, and when they have attempted to decide
upon their levels of involvement in certain issues and on future direction. The societies' involvement in professional activities and
employment practices has been often either considerably less or considerably more than some members would like. In other words, the
magnitude of the forces exerted by professional societies on corporations represents at best a compromise among their collective memberships' opinions.

Tax Classifications

Since the professional society needs assets to operate, it must register with the U.S. Internal Revenue Service as an organization or
association. Revenue to a society comes from membership dues,
standards testing, sale of publications, and related areas. The tax
status that the society selects dictates the amount of lobbying in
which it can engage, and thus influences its activities. For example,
the ACS, the ASCE, the American Institute of Chemical Engineers
(AIChE), the American Institute of Mining, Metallurgical, and

Petroleum Engineers (AIME), and the American Society of Mechanical Engineers (ASME) have all selected a tax status of 502(c)(3) which limits the extent of their lobbying activities. On the other hand, the National Society of Professional Engineers (NSPE) and the Institute of Electrical and Electronics Engineers (IEEE) have selected a tax status of 501(c)(6) which does not require that they refrain from influencing legislation.

The tax status classification determines whether the majority of activities offered must be educational and technical. No substantial funds may be used to influence legislation by 501(c)(3) registered societies. The programs which they sponsor to influence legislation dealing with unions, pensions, or employment conditions for their members are thus effectively limited. The NSPE and the IEEE, however, both have offices in Washington, D.C. and employ lobbyists. The lobbying of professional associations can affect company policies in a number of ways. For example, regulations or laws can result which dictate specifications or personnel utilization, particularly of subprofessionals. At the state or local levels, such lobbying is often concerned with license requirements. Although licensing (or registration) is advocated as a protection for the consumer, it also limits the market and in some cases can prohibit a company's employees, however qualified, from performing work.

Organization Structure and General Activities

Diversity of membership and tax status are two important determinants of society activities in controversial, nontechnical matters. A society's principal function relates to the technical aspects which are best understood by a brief review of the typical society organization and structure.

The national unit of all societies is composed of local chapters throughout the United States. (Some of the societies also have international representation, but in this study only domestic units are examined.) Local chapters sponsor general meetings with speakers, and technical groups are organized in exploration of particular topics. Lectures are very common in the local chapters. The national unit has staff members with different responsibilities: education, membership, public relations, etc. The national unit organizes seminars and conferences on particular topics. Annual meetings are also held with different subcommittees giving reports. Some societies have very active standards and testing groups. These standards are published and used throughout industry. In certain cases, task forces are organized to explore a particular topic and make policy recommendations to the board of directors. Members of the task force are volunteers and are usually supported by a national staff member. Task forces and subcommittees often publish reports and recommendations. Each society has a monthly magazine and/or newspaper. Conference proceedings are also available.

Many professional societies also have active student chapter programs. Through these programs, students are exposed to working engineers and scientists and to the applications of theories learned in school. These student chapters perform an important service by helping to bridge the gap between industry and academia. Students who actively participate in local chapters develop a more realistic view of the workplace. The student chapters also contribute to the development of professional standards for students, and present the opportunity for students to understand how these standards may be applied to the workplace. The societies also encourage interaction between student chapters of different schools through activities such as design competitions and paper presentations. These activities encourage students to continue participation after graduation.

A relatively new program, developed jointly among societies, has created a limited number of summer internships for engineering students in Washington, D.C. The students selected as interns have the opportunity to interact with government officials. The intent of this exposure is to increase the student's awareness of the government sector, specifically the activities involved in policy formulation.

Opportunities for involvement in continuing education programs are varied, including lectures, technical study groups, update courses, etc. Participation in professional society activities is one method by which a diligent engineer can combat obsolescence. Many of the professional societies encourage licensing and registration and some offer study courses to prepare individuals for the required tests.

The professional societies collectively represent an enormous stockpile of technical knowledge. They are often asked by Congress for assistance in preparing policy statements or reports on technical subjects. In addition, members may be called upon to testify as professional witnesses on technical issues. Through activities such as these, E/S have the opportunity to contribute to their social responsibilities as professionals.

Association Coordination

The engineering societies have long cooperated, and the ASCE, AIChE, ASME, IEEE, AIME, and ASM (or their predecessors) were members of the Engineers Joint Council (EJC). The need for a more active and more inclusive cooperating group led in 1980 to the formation of the American Association of Engineering Societies (AAES) which originally included thirty-nine societies. Since then, some of the societies have dropped out, but more remain. In addition to replacing the EJC, the AAES also took over the functions of the former Engineering Council for Professional Development, now the Engineering Accreditation Commission, and the Association for Cooperation in Engineering (ACE). The AAES has a very active manpower group, the Engineering Manpower Commission, which performs statistical manpower studies and gathers manpower data for different groups—data that have been very useful for this study. Some of the other objectives of the AAES are to

> Facilitate intersociety communication; provide a forum for joint society actions; provide a forum for consideration of issues; identify opportunities for service; recommend studies and research to engineering institutions; undertake activities the member societies could not individually do as well; and foster interaction between the engineering community and other segments of culture.[4]

THE SOCIETIES AND THE EMPLOYMENT RELATIONSHIP

In 1973 the EJC published the first set of "Guidelines to Professional Employment for Engineers and Scientists" (GPEES) which were revised in 1978. These guidelines have been endorsed by twenty-eight societies. The formation of the GPEES was really a monumental step: a united venture by the endorsing societies on a controversial topic with which many societies had previously avoided involvement. The stated objectives of the GPEES were set forth as follows:

> The endorsing societies, with their avowed purpose to serve the public and their professions, recognize clearly that, in order to make their maximum contribution, it is necessary for professional employees and employers to establish a climate conducive to the proper discharge of their mutual responsibilities and obligations.
>
> The prerequisites for establishing such a climate include:
>
> 1. A sound relationship between the professional employee and the employer, based on mutual loyalty, cooperation, fair treatment, ethical practices, and respect.
>
> 2. Recognition of the responsibility to safeguard the public health, safety and welfare.
>
> 3. Employee loyalty and creativity in support of the employer's objectives.

---

[4]K. A. Godfrey, Jr., "New Umbrella Society for Engineering Is Taking Shape," *Civil Engineering,* Vol. 49 (May 1979), p. 64.

4. Opportunity for professional growth of the employee, based on employee's initiative and the employer's support.

5. Recognition that discrimination due to age, race, religion, political affiliation, or sex should not enter into the professional employee-employer relationship. There should be joint acceptance of the concepts which are reflected in the "Equal Employment Opportunity" regulations.

6. Recognition that local conditions may result in honest differences in interpretation of, and deviations from, the details of these Guidelines. Such differences should be resolved by discussions leading to an understanding which meets the spirit of the Guidelines.[5]

Recommendations are made to both the employer and employee in regard to (1) recruitment; (2) employment; (3) professional development; and (4) termination and transfer.

Although the publication of the guidelines was a major achievement for the EJC, their impact on industry did not meet expectations. No uniform method of distributing or encouraging compliance with the guidelines was either apparent, or even possible. Some societies pushed more actively than others for industry acceptance. Some individual members took it upon themselves to distribute the guidelines throughout their companies. Some approached management requesting compliance because no methods for forcing or even encouraging compliance were included with the GPEES. It does appear that if the true intent was to encourage compliance, the effort was both naive and totally lacking in understanding of the needs and psychology of industrial management.[6]

The interviews performed for this study indicated that most large firms are now aware of the GPEES, but few either endorse them or give them any official recognition. Several firms mentioned that they were introduced to the guidelines in a rather hostile and militant manner by "activist types," and therefore had a very negative initial reaction. Some of this negative reaction has mellowed to the indifference with which many companies greeted the GPEES. A minority of those interviewed for this study are both aware of the GPEES and endorse them. Those that endorse them also claim that they comply with them, but few, if any, modified their prior policies specifically to conform. In general, industry response as measured by study participants, was hostility or indifference, in either case motivated by a strong reluctance to share management policy formulation with an outside organization.

---

[5] *Guidelines to Professional Employment for Engineers and Scientists,* 2nd ed. (New York: Engineers Joint Council, 1978), p. 3.

[6] This is a general consensus opinion of nearly all respondents from industry who were interviewed for this study.

Managerial opposition to the GPEES is motivated by more than a reluctance to share responsibility with an outside organization. Although the societies vehemently deny the connection, recognition of the GPEES could be the first step toward a collective bargaining relationship. Discussion of these guidelines between a committee or group of E/S and a management is clearly very close to negotiating. Since, however, there is no proof that those promoting such discussions represent a majority of the professionals involved or that they have been selected as official bargaining agents pursuant to the National Labor Relations (Taft-Hartley) Act, management is on sound legal and practical grounds to deny all official recognition of the GPEES or any relationship to professional societies in regard thereto.

Collective Bargaining: ASCE's Typical Policies

Since the effort during 1935-1947 to sponsor independent local unions as a means of forestalling the "swallowing" of E/S by blue-collar dominated organizations, most engineering societies have taken a neutral, or at least circumspect attitude toward membership participation in collective bargaining. The NSPE, as discussed below, is a notable exception. Typical is the position of the ASCE, the leading pre-World War II sponsor of society-related local unions. Its Committee on Employment Conditions issued a booklet in the mid-1970s which discusses the pros and cons of unionism, and then tells engineers how to form a union and go about gaining recognition through the procedures of the NLRB. The ASCE policy statement 1) affirms the right of professional employees who so desire to form unions and to bargain collectively; 2) emphasizes that such employees should not be forced to affiliate with, or become members of a bargaining group which includes nonprofessionals; and 3) declares that "no professional employee should be forced, against his desire, to join any organization as a condition of his employment, or to sacrifice his right to individual personal relations with his employer in matters of employment conditions."[7]

The first two points of the ASCE policy conform with the law of the land. The third however, is debatable. Compulsory union membership can be legally negotiated in thirty of the fifty states; there is no exception for professionals. One can regard such compulsion as inappropriate, as the authors of this study do, but whether it is

---

[7]*Collective Bargaining and the Civil Engineer: A Reference and a Guide* (New York: Committee on Employment Conditions, American Society of Civil Engineers, [1976]), p. 5.

appropriate, to advocate a policy that has no legal standing in thirty states is questionable if not unrealistic.

The other aspect of the ASCE's third point is an illustration of the society's attempt to please all views. Collective and individual bargaining are basically incompatible. Moreover, for an employer to deal directly with an E/S so desiring it when the employer is required to bargain *exclusively* with a legally chosen bargaining agent pursuant to the Taft-Hartley Act, would seem to be a violation of Section 8(a)(5) of the Act. Reconciling divergent views on controversial subjects is a severe problem for the societies.

The ASCE is active on the other fronts which can affect personnel policies. For example, the society believes that engineers who belong to unions should be active, become involved, and make the union work for them. In addition to publishing technical journals and transactions, the ASCE publishes *Issues in Engineering* which deals with ethics, but often has economic implications. The ASCE encourages the passage by states of "Little Taft-Hartley" laws which contain the professional proviso.

OTHER INDIVIDUAL SOCIETY POLICIES

In addition to the ASCE, a number of societies have taken positions on collective bargaining and employment conditions which have potential implications for company personnel policies. A few of these are summarized in the following sections.

NSPE

The National Society of Professional Engineers (NSPE) was formerly composed only of registered engineers, but it is now possible for a nonlicensed engineer to gain membership. As previously mentioned, the NSPE has a 501(c)(6) Internal Revenue Code classification and therefore can engage in lobbying activities. The NSPE believes that it is very important for an engineer to have an active political voice along with keen social consciousness if he is to be recognized by the government.

The NSPE has, from the outset, taken a very strong stance against collective bargaining for engineers. This is apparent in its policy statement:

> Collective bargaining for professional engineers is in conflict with the basic principles of a professional individual.
>
> The individual responsibility and independent judgement required of a professional engineer are incompatible with the regimentation fundamentally inherent in unionization.

Collective bargaining divides the members of the profession into hostile groups and promotes discord among members of the same profession.

Constructive relations between professional engineers and management, and the full development of professional engineers can best be accomplished through programs in cooperation with all elements of the engineering profession.

More than twenty years of experience and experimentation demonstrate conclusively that the individual engineer and the engineering profession are best served through reliance upon the professional concept of solidarity in service to the public welfare and avoidance of collective bargaining.[8]

In fact, the NSPE has an ongoing task force on collective bargaining which continues to publish periodic booklets on the subject. But whereas the NSPE opposes collective bargaining, it espouses "collective action" in which E/S come together and discuss their problems with or without managers present.[9] Such organizations do exist in various forms in General Electric, Bell Telephone Laboratories, and a few other companies, but most companies interviewed for this study believe that such organizations could well turn into full-fledged bargaining agents, and therefore do not sponsor them.

The NSPE has also supported the EJC guidelines. Thus, in 1978 the NSPE established an "Employer Recognition Program." The program was established to "give public recognition to those employers of engineers with employment practices generally consistent with the philosophy of the [GPEES]."[10] This program is part of a "multi-faceted thrust by NSPE to encourage employers to give closer attention to the needs of their professional engineering employees and to provide visibility and recognition to those who do."[11] Other examples of the NSPE's involvement in the workplace are the regular publication of the NSPE *Professional Engineers Income and Salary Survey* and of NSPE's *Recommended Income Ranges*.

ACS

The American Chemical Society membership consists both of chemists and chemical engineers. Congress granted the ACS a

---

[8]"Professional Responsibility vs. Collective Bargaining," NSPE Publication No. 1425 (Washington, D.C.: Professional Engineers in Industry, A Functional Section of National Society of Professional Engineers, 1966). This policy of the NSPE remains in effect.

[9]*Collective Bargaining v. Collective Action* (Washington, D.C.: Task Force on Collective Bargaining, National Society of Professional Engineers, 1973).

[10]Gayle N. Wright, "NSPE's Employer Recognition Program Lists 100 Firms for Employment Practices," *Professional Engineer,* Vol. 48 (November 1978), p. 9.

[11]*Ibid.*

national charter in 1937. The society is a nonprofit and educational association. The ACS does not endorse the GPEES. Instead, it has developed its own set of "Professional Employment Guidelines," adopted in 1978. The ACS's guidelines are stricter than those developed by the EJC, especially on terms of layoff conditions and severance pay, although they follow the same general format. Included in the Professional Employment Guidelines is a definition of multiple termination:

> A multiple termination occurs when the employment of three or more chemists or chemical engineers is terminated within a six-month period for reasons other than: 1) continuing evidence of previously documented inadequate performance, 2) completion of a contract, or 3) cause. The academic chemists or chemical engineers must be tenured or in a tenure-leading position.[12]

The ACS Committee on Professional Relations (CPR) investigates all multiple terminations which are brought to their attention by members. It sends surveys both to the terminated employees and the employer involved. The responses are compiled and published in detail in *Chemical and Engineering News*, the society's magazine (unless a respondent wishes to remain anonymous, then the partial report is published). Increased attention to the profile of employees terminated has occurred in recent years as a result of an escalation in the number of members' allegations of age discrimination received by the CPR. One of the interesting results of this practice is that members, when contemplating employment with a particular firm, may call ACS to find out its termination history. Negative publicity concerning layoff history and policies can adversely affect a firm's recruiting capability.

When the EJC issued the GPEES, they became available to members of the endorsing societies. As indicated previously, there was not an active push by any society to industry to comply. It was expected that due to the diverse membership, management would become aware of the guidelines. The ACS took a different approach. Some sections of the society actively contacted industry, and visited some companies to make them aware of the ACS guidelines and encourage them to comply.[13] Today, if a company has a policy that the ACS feels is particularly exemplary, the Committee on Professional Relations will send the appropriate unit a letter of commendation.

---

[12]*Professional Employment Guidelines* (Washington, D.C.: American Chemical Society, 1978).
[13]Several companies interviewed received such visits.

The ACS also provides a "member assistance program" for employees who either believe that they have been terminated inequitably, or are involved in employment positions which they believe do not afford a proper professional environment. Assistance on this program must be requested formally by means of a signed waiver authorizing the society to contact all parties involved so a thorough inquiry can be conducted. This waiver absolves the society of liability, and ensures that cases will be treated with confidentiality. This program is coordinated through the office of professional relations at ACS headquarters. Requests for assistance are processed through that office and then submitted to a subcommittee where suitability for study is judged. If it is determined that a case is within the member assistance guidelines, and within the scope of the committee's expertise, it is accepted and an investigation is carried out. The investigation is usually performed with the assistance of one of the three consultants who are available to assist the committee. "In all cases, the subcommittee seeks remedial action by discussions and through correspondence in an attempt to achieve a mutal understanding and an equitable and professional solution to the particular problem." The society has no legal authority, and therefore, depends upon voluntary cooperation. Moral suasion is its strongest tool although for unusual cases in which ethical violations or unprofessional conduct are clearly documented, the subcommittee can resort to citations on the ACS council floor and in *Chemical & Engineering News*. Such citations are rare.[14]

The ACS attempted to establish an "Employer Recognition Program" for employers complying with the Professional Employment Guidelines, modeled after that of the NSPE. It did not receive positive feedback from industry, however, and was therefore abandoned.

The ACS has gone farther than most societies in establishing programs related to professional treatment for members. It actively approaches employers while most other professional societies take a passive role. Several firms interviewed described the ACS as militant. Of all the professional societies, the ACS most clearly approaches a union in its policies.

This raises the question of whether there is potential for a professional society, like the ACS, to become a bargaining agent. Although it might seem unlikely that this will occur, given the diversity of membership and the history of technical orientation of the ACS, it is not without possibility, particularly if unions appear strongly on the

---

[14]Phillip S. Landis, "The ACS Member Assistance Program," *Chemical & Engineering News,* January 18, 1982, p. 85.

scene. The ACS staff appears to lean toward this direction, but it may well be restrained by the membership.

IEEE

The Institute of Electrical and Electronics Engineers is also a 501(c)(6) classified Internal Revenue Code society. It employs three active lobbyists. The IEEE, the largest of the engineering professional societies with over 210,000 members, also endorses the GPEES. It has a wide range of professional programs, most of which are administered through its Washington, D.C. office, although its headquarters is in New York City. (See Table B-1.)

On October 22 and 23, 1981, the IEEE sponsored a career conference entitled "What's Working to Enrich Engineering Careers." The program included industry representatives, professional society members, and representatives from academia. One of the sessions dealt specifically with sounding boards, unions, and traditional supervision.

AIChE

The AIChE seems to be the least active of all societies interviewed in addressing the nontechnical aspects of engineering through task

TABLE B-1
IEEE Task Forces Related to Professional Development

1. Patent Rights Task Force—Improve patent rights of employed inventors.

2. Manpower Task Force—Evaluate manpower needs versus resources in the electrical engineering field by IEEE studies as well as by participation in the AAES Manpower Commission, the NSF Post Census Survey activity, joint SMC/EMC meetings and the like. Obtain data and recommend solutions to special manpower problems such as the alien engineer issues, localized unemployment, etc.

3. Committee on Professional Opportunities for Women—Promote principles of equality hiring and advancement of women in the electrical/electronics engineering profession, identify and address special problems encountered by women in engineering.

4. Age Discrimination Task Force—Inform IEEE members and employers of laws and legal process that affect employment practices regarding discrimination based on age.

5. Employment Assistance Task Force—Maintain and publicize the quarterly unemployment survey of members. Assist members seeking jobs.

6. Occupational Handbook Task Force—Interact with the Department of Labor, Bureau of Labor Statistics, to ensure that those sections of the Occupational Outlook Handbook pertaining to electrical and electronics engineering present a valid image.

7. Ethics Task Force—Invite and analyze members' opinions on preferred language of Code of Ethics.

Source: *IEEE Handbook,* U.S. Activities Board Program Plan, 1981, pp. 9–10. © 1981 IEEE.

forces and specific programs, although its literature (*Chemical Engineering Progress,* for example) contains many articles on ethics and professionalism. AIChE endorses the GPEES. It annually publishes a confidential membership salary and benefit survey. This survey is sent to the members at no charge, but is not available to nonmembers. Members' opinions on various topics are included in the benefit section. It was stated in one of our interviews that the 1981 survey of chemical engineer members of AIChE found that only 1.3 percent belonged to unions.

AIChE also publishes an employment newsletter which lists situations wanted and positions available for their members. This is mailed monthly. During annual meetings which are held in various cities in the United States, executive lunches are sponsored. Industry leaders are invited to attend and interact with the society members.

ASME

The ASME has several interesting programs. Most of its activities in the professional development field are carried out by the member services and field services groups. The latter act as regional offices in several major cities. One of this group's functions is to visit industries in their area to encourage interaction with the ASME. Ideally, a two-way communication channel could develop through these offices to enable the ASME to be more responsive to industry's needs. In turn, industry would encourage its engineers to be active in the ASME functions. The field service locations provide the headquarters with feedback on regional industry.

Summary

Rather than taking a firm stance on the collective bargaining issue, most professional societies, in general, seem to choose an indirect approach. They sponsor educational seminars which deal with manpower and personnel techniques. Through these seminars the subject is is approached indirectly. The societies seek to develop better employee relations and conditions through the education of industry leaders. Through their programs they heighten the awareness of commendable working environments among both employers and employees. Outstanding or innovative professional development programs may be used as examples or models during seminars. The speakers at such functions are usually involved in the administration of professional development or recognition programs which they describe. The ACS is the most aggressive in pushing its concepts of personnel administration; the NSPE is the most outspoken foe of collective bargaining. In a more unionized environment, both the ACS and NSPE, ironically, could become bargaining agents or union sponsors.

INDUSTRY'S RESPONSE TO SOCIETIES

The fact that the professional societies exert forces on industry should not imply that the forces are always, or even necessarily, hostile. Neither is it true that industry response to the societies is consistently negative, even though the employment guidelines were not, and probably could not be, embraced by industry. Many corporations encourage their E/S to participate in professional society activities. Indeed, some provide an incentive to participate by paying membership dues either partially or completely. In addition, E/S are usually granted time and given expenses to attend pertinent technical conferences. Participation in professional society activities can help an individual combat obsolescence. Current research and design techniques are discussed in technical meetings. Even if the meetings are not attended, information is often contained in publications available through the societies. Interaction with peers provides an opportunity for professional recognition.

One could also argue, however, that the professional-organizational conflict is fueled by participation in professional societies. If this is true, it would be most detrimental to those firms which offer no internal opportunities for intangible reward. Participation in society activities can supplement a company's intangible rewards but should not be considered a substitute.

The corporate interviews for this study indicate that industry regards the professional societies as providing an important technical service. Moreover, industry executives do not object *per se* to professional development activities. They object only when they infringe upon areas that have traditionally been exclusively under management's control, and attempt to set conditions or to establish control over working conditions and personnel policies.

Appendix C

UNION ORGANIZATION AMONG ENGINEERS: A CURRENT ASSESSMENT

GEOFFREY W. LATTA*

This article presents a study of a number of campaigns conducted since 1968 by unions seeking to organize professional engineers. The author draws on the results of interviews with union and management representatives to describe four major causes of the relative failure of unions on this front: employer opposition, the attitudes and values of engineers, the lack of bargaining power of engineers, and union attitudes and organizing policies. The author discusses the way in which these four factors interact to thwart engineering unionization, focussing on the manner in which strong resistance to unionization by employers can draw on a value system in the United States that is not supportive of unionization. He concludes that the short-term prospects for further unionization of this occupation are very limited.

THE decline since 1958 in the percentage of the American labor force that is unionized can be attributed partially to the difficulty unions have had attracting white-collar employees in the private sector. In their efforts to counteract stagnating membership levels, particularly in the early 1970s, a number of unions have sought to organize engineers and scientists. The results have been very disappointing so far, from the unions' standpoint. Few groups have been successfully unionized and some that voted for union representation later decertified their unions.

This article outlines the history of the attempts to organize engineers and scientists in the private sector in the 1970s, analyzes the reasons why attempts to unionize this key group have not met with significant success, and discusses how the situation could change in the future. The research for this study was conducted through interviews with company and union officials and with representatives of professional societies and other relevant groups. A total of forty-two persons from twenty-six organizations were interviewed between June 1978 and May 1979. The companies and unions selected were known to have been involved in organizing campaigns. In most cases, cooperation was given freely, but representatives of two unions and one company refused to be interviewed.

*At the time this research was conducted, the author was a research specialist at the Industrial Research Unit of the Wharton School at the University of Pennsylvania. He is now affiliated with a consulting firm. He would like to thank Herbert R. Northrup and Janice R. Bellace for their comments on this paper and the Pew Memorial Trust for their research grant.

Industrial and Labor Relations Review, Vol. 35, No. 1 (October 1981). © 1981 by Cornell University.
0019-7939/81/3501-0029$01.00

305

The History

The first serious attempt to organize engineers was made by the American Association of Engineers (AAE), which was founded in 1915.[1] In the following decades, unions affiliated with the American Federation of Labor (AFL) and the Congress of Industrial Organizations (CIO) competed for the allegiance of engineers against independent unions, which were affiliated with neither the AFL or CIO and which drew membership from only a single company. Neither type of organization achieved major success, although the years between 1943 and 1948 were the most fruitful period of organizing. The modest growth of engineering unionization in that period reflected the wider trends that encouraged union membership in the years following the passage of the Wagner Act. By 1948, independent organizations of engineers had established a firm foothold in such companies as Westinghouse, RCA, Lockheed, and Boeing.

The major AFL and CIO unions regarded the single-company independents as pale imitations of real trade unions, although some of the independents were sometimes quite aggressive in the sphere of collective bargaining. The independent at Westinghouse, for example, conducted a three-week strike against the company in Pittsburgh in 1945.[2] The skepticism of affiliated unions toward the independents reflected the fact that the latter were sometimes established as a defensive reaction by engineers against organizing campaigns launched by AFL or CIO unions. At other times the formation of an independent was encouraged by the professional societies that represent engineers and scientists.[3]

In 1952, a number of the independents united to form a federal organization called the Engineers and Scientists of America (ESA), which by 1955 had fifteen affiliates representing about 50,000 employees.[4] In the late 1950s, however, ESA experienced pressures from three different directions. First, several major independents affiliated with AFL-CIO unions. The Engineers Association of Arma and the Engineers Association of Sperry both joined the International Union of Electrical Workers (IUE), for example, and the Federation of Honeywell Engineers affiliated with the United Automobile Workers (UAW). These moves created internal conflict within ESA, as a number of the affiliates objected to any affiliation with AFL-CIO unions. At the same time a battle raged between independents that sought to restrict their membership solely to professional employees and those that opened their membership to technicians. The third pressure arose from the decertification in 1960 of ESA's largest affiliate, the Council of Western Electric Professional Employees. As a result of these problems, by 1961 ESA had only five member associations with about 9,700 actual members,[5] and so it was dissolved in March 1961.

Between 1961 and 1968 union-organizing efforts among engineers were limited; the Sperry engineers decertified the IUE in 1962, and the Western Electric independent lost an election in 1963.[6] In 1968 – 69, however, the IUE won back its Sperry unit and was selected as bargaining agent by a unit of 700 engineers at Western Electric in Kearny, New Jersey. These victories seemed to usher in an era of greater promise for engineering unionization. Data on the major private-sector elections among engineers in the period between December 1968 and December 1980 are presented in the table below. Although the period 1968 – 80 witnessed more elections per year than had the previous decade, unions only won four

---

[1]William G. Rothstein, "The American Association of Engineers," *Industrial and Labor Relations Review*, Vol. 22, No. 1 (October 1968), pp. 48 – 72.

[2]"The AWSE Story," *AWSE Reporter*, Vol. 7, No. 9 (September 1948), pp. 5 – 6.

[3]Herbert R. Northrup, *Unionization of Professional Engineers and Chemists*, (New York: Industrial Relations Counselors, Inc., 1946), pp. 15 – 20.

[4]Donald W. Jarrell, *A History of Collective Bargaining at the Camden-Area Plants of the Radio Corporation of America with Special Attention to Bargaining Power* (Ph.D. thesis, University of Pennsylvania, 1967), p. 87.

[5]Ibid., p. 90.

[6]George Strauss, "Professional or Employee-Oriented: Dilemma for Engineering Unions," *Industrial and Labor Relations Review*, Vol. 17, No. 4 (July 1964), p. 521.

UNION ORGANIZATION AMONG ENGINEERS

Table. Representation Elections in Private Sector Units of Over 100 Engineers, December 1968 to December 1980.

Date		Company	Location	Union	Vote		Percentage	
					For Union	Against Union	For Union	Against Union
December	1968	Western Electric	Kearny, N.J.	IUE	373	294	55.9	44.1
July	1969	Sperry Gyroscope	Long Island, N.Y.	IUE	827	492	62.7	37.3
May	1971	North American Rockwell	Cape Kennedy, Fla.	MEBA	98	124	44.1	55.9
August	1971	Amoco Chemicals	Napierville, Ill.	MEBA	44	131	25.1	74.9
October	1971	Western Electric	Kearny, N.J.	IUE (decertification)	349	356	49.5	50.5
June	1972	Lockheed	Sunnyvale, Calif.	MEBA	1,618	2,690	37.6	62.4
June	1972	Boeing Vertol	Philadelphia, Pa.	SPEEA	354	436	44.8	55.2
June	1972	North American Rockwell	Cape Kennedy, Fla.	MEBA	93	100	48.2	51.8
November	1973	General Electric (Knolls)	Schenectady, N.Y.	KASE	423	629	40.2	59.8
November	1974	General Dynamics (Convair)	San Diego, Calif.	NEPA	607	468	56.5	43.5
July	1975	Leeds and Northrup	North Wales, Pa.	PESA	138	117	54.1	45.9
August	1976	General Dynamics (Convair)	San Diego, Calif.	NEPA (decertification)	334	462	42.0	58.0
February	1977	Rohr Industries	Chula Vista, Calif.	NEPA	160	277	36.6	63.4
August	1977	North American Rockwell	Los Angeles, Calif.	NEPA	2,866	3,192	42.6	57.4
August	1977	North American Rockwell	Tulsa, Okla.	NEPA	28	81	25.7	74.3
June	1978	North American Rockwell	Los Angeles, Calif.	NEPA (rerun)	2,161	2,690	44.5	55.5
June	1979	Boeing	Cape Kennedy, Fla.	MEBA	86	59	59.3	40.7
May	1980	Boeing Vertol	Philadelphia, Pa.	SPEEA	281	373	43.0	57.0

Source: National Labor Relations Board data.

major certification elections, and in two of these units they lost decertification elections within three years of their initial victories.

One factor inhibiting organizational success has been the absence of a union that has been concerned primarily with organizing engineers. In theory one might think that the AFL-CIO affiliated International Federation of Professional and Technical Engineers (IFPTE), founded in 1918, would be the focal point of the attempt to unionize engineers, but this union, which has about 15,000 members, consists largely of technical employees. (The IFPTE has also concentrated its attention in the public sector, and therefore its largest recent success, which came in 1972 when it was chosen to represent a unit of 1,614 professional scientists and engineers at the Marshall Space Flight Center in Huntsville, Alabama, falls outside the scope of this study.[7]) In the five years between 1975 and 1979, the union participated in only fifteen NLRB elections, mainly in technical units, and won representation rights for only 105 employees in five units.[8]

A number of other unions have been active in seeking to organize engineers, with the IUE, UAW, and the Marine Engineers Benevolent Association (MEBA) taking the lead. The tactics adopted by different unions have varied. Both the International Association of Machinists (IAM) and the International Brotherhood of Electrical Workers (IBEW) undertook some campaigns among engineers, most of which did not reach elections. These two unions, as well as the IUE, relied on traditional organizational tactics, with an effort made to sign up individual employees. Both MEBA and, later, the Teamsters were more inclined to attempt to secure the affiliation of existing independent organizations of engineers. In 1969 – 70, for example, MEBA secured the affiliation of independents at Pacific Gas and Electric in San Francisco, at the Shell Development Company in Emeryville, California, and at Amoco's facility in Whiting, Indiana. At

North American Rockwell, MEBA took over the Aerospace Professional and Technical Association (APTA), which had fought an unsuccessful election in the Autonetics Division in 1969, but a campaign by MEBA-APTA in 1971 petered out. MEBA seemed to have secured a major victory for its policy in 1971, however, when the executive board of the Southern California Professional Engineering Association (SCPEA) at McDonnell-Douglas recommended affiliation to MEBA; a membership ballot, however, narrowly rejected this proposal.[9] After 1972, MEBA's organizing initiative lost momentum, although the union later won an election at Bechtel Corporation in San Francisco (in a unit of fewer than 100 employees and therefore not shown in the table), and in 1979 its affiliate, the Florida Association of Professional Employees (FAPE), was selected as bargaining agent by 190 professional engineers at Boeing Services International in Cape Kennedy.

The Teamsters followed a similar strategy and in 1975 gained the affiliation of SCPEA at McDonnell-Douglas. The company refused to recognize this affiliation, and a period of maneuvering ensued during which officials of Teamsters Local 911 were able to appear at SCPEA negotiations as "consultants," only. While the Teamsters filed unfair labor practice charges against the company, the company announced that it would only accept the link with the Teamsters if the union would go through an NLRB election to change the certification.[10] The company was confident that the Teamsters lacked sufficient support among the engineers to contemplate this course of action. It appears to have been right, for in December 1978 SCPEA disaffiliated from the Teamsters, reportedly with 84 percent of its members voting in favor of disaffiliation.[11]

The UAW chose a different strategy by

[7]Bureau of National Affairs, *Daily Labor Report*, No. 244 (December 18, 1972), p. A-2.

[8]Bureau of National Affairs, *Bulletin to Management*, No. 1587 (August 7, 1980), pp. 4 – 6.

[9]Interview with union official, Los Angeles, July 24, 1978.

[10]Interview with company official, Los Angeles, July 24, 1978.

[11]Southern California Professional Engineering Association, *SCPEA: An Independent Union*, (Los Angeles: SCPEA, January 1979).

UNION ORGANIZATION AMONG ENGINEERS

creating a separate section for engineers in 1975, called the National Engineers and Professionals Association (NEPA). This body owed its origins to the affiliation to the UAW in 1972 of an organization of the same name that had been established at North American Rockwell, and that had been building up its membership in order to file for an election.[12] NEPA sought both to organize directly and to take over independents. Its greatest victory occurred in 1974 when it was selected as bargaining agent for a unit of 1,300 engineers at General Dynamics' Convair Division in San Diego.

In other attempts to organize directly, NEPA fought several elections, such as that at Rohr Industries in California in 1977 and at Rockwell in both 1977 and 1978. In its attempt to organize through taking over independents, it secured the affiliation of the Professional Engineers and Scientists Association (PESA) at the Leeds and Northrup Company in North Wales, Pennsylvania. It suffered a major blow, however, when it was decertified at General Dynamics in 1976. Thereafter its continuing lack of success led to a reevaluation by the UAW, and in 1978 NEPA informed PESA, its only affiliate with bargaining rights, that NEPA could no longer provide it with bargaining support. PESA then reverted to independent status.[13]

Among engineering independents, the aim of establishing a national federation remained alive and the Association of Professional Engineering Personnel (ASPEP), the independent at RCA in New Jersey, took the lead in discussing federation with an organization that had been established in California, the Council of Engineering and Scientific Organizations-West (CESO-W). As a result in 1968 a national CESO was formed.[14] CESO enjoyed a rather checkered history as several major independents disaffiliated from it for varying periods of time. By 1979, however, it seemed to have established a stable base, with eleven affili-

ated members.[15] In contrast to the situation in ESA, CESO affiliates adopted a less hostile attitude to mainstream trade unionism and admitted into membership both NEPA in 1977 and the IFPTE in 1978.

In terms of organizing, ASPEP was the only independent actively to seek new members in companies different from those in which it had traditionally organized. In 1972 it fought an election in a unit (too small for inclusion in the table) at Lockheed Electronics in Plainfield, New Jersey, but it was defeated; several other ASPEP organizing campaigns, including one at Allied Chemical in Morristown, New Jersey, proved abortive. The largest independent union of engineers, the Seattle Professional Engineering Employees' Association (SPEEA) at Boeing, adopted a different growth strategy, seeking to extend its membership within the company. In 1971, it won an election in Seattle for a technical unit, which marked its movement away from a purely professional membership. This evolution was further emphasized in May 1980 when SPEEA fought an election in a professional and administrative unit in Seattle. The union lost by a vote of 2,333 to 1,440. At the same time, SPEEA unsuccessfully fought an election in a unit of Boeing Vertol in Philadelphia, where it had lost a previous election in 1972.

In summary, except in the unusual circumstances of the 1940s, engineers have never been very susceptible to union organization. Between 1968 and 1980, however, it looked as though the situation might have altered and, in fact, that period saw more major elections per year in the private sector among engineers than had taken place in the previous decade. Despite the number of elections, however, union victories were scarce, and as the 1980s commence, the little momentum the unions had achieved is slowing markedly. The following sections will try to explain why the number of elections increased in recent years and also why the unions were usually unsuccessful.

[12]Bureau of National Affairs, *White Collar Report*, No. 773 (January 7, 1972), p. A-6.

[13]Interview with company official, North Wales, Pa., April 19, 1979.

[14]Bureau of National Affairs, *White Collar Report*, No. 611 (December 21, 1968), p. A-9.

[15]Bureau of National Affairs, *White Collar Report*, No. 1149 (May 11, 1979), p. A-2.

INDUSTRIAL AND LABOR RELATIONS REVIEW

Unionization Campaigns

One means of assessing the attraction of unionism to some groups of engineers is to examine the issues raised during union-organizing campaigns. In many cases these issues are not dissimilar to those one might have expected in any union campaign. Job security occupied a high place in a number of campaigns, for example, especially after 1968 in the aerospace industry. Elections were not concentrated in the period between 1968 and 1972, however, when employment fell sharply in aerospace, but in the years after 1972 when employment remained static. Organization was thus not an immediate response to layoffs, but a longer-term effort to prevent the recurrence of the conditions of the 1968 to 1972 period. Although it was not always apparent what unions could do to halt the layoffs, unions such as NEPA at Rockwell and Rohr often cited past layoffs as reasons for organizing. In part this was an attempt to offset company appeals for loyalty by reminding engineers that the company was not always so solicitous of their interests.

The union criticism of employers on this issue usually centered on the method of selecting individual employees for layoff. Unions rarely pushed for seniority to be the sole factor in determining layoffs, but they would also not accept management's unfettered right to decide on a "skill and ability" basis. The potency of this issue had been illustrated by ASPEP at RCA, which in 1967 conducted a 77-day strike largely on the question of selection for layoff. The SPEEA contract with Boeing currently includes the provision of a "retention index," which determines selection for layoff. Length of service is an important component, although not the sole one, in this index.[16] Unions have dealt carefully with this issue in campaigns, both for fear of alienating shorter-service engineers and because they realize some engineers do not regard strict seniority as compatible with a professional role.

The remuneration of engineers relative to other groups of employees was also a common campaign theme. At Electric Boat Company, an organizing campaign by the IUE followed the granting of wage increases to draftsmen and technicians, who were unionized, in excess of those given to engineers. Both union and company personnel agree that this was a major factor in the campaign.[17] Similarly, in the Convair Division of General Dynamics, merit increases for engineers in 1971 were less than the pay increases achieved by unionized employees in the company, and that disparity provided the initial impetus to a union-organizing drive that led eventually to NEPA's victory in 1974. In many other cases, even absent specific instances, there seems to have been a feeling by engineers that they were being left behind by unionized groups.

Many of the company and union officials who were interviewed during the course of this study asserted that engineers embraced unionism partly as a response to a perceived decline in their status relative to other groups of employees. This situation seemed to arise most frequently where engineers worked in large units. Although status is always a somewhat nebulous concept, campaigns often drew on specific instances of managerial action, such as attempting to tighten up on engineers' coffee-breaks. The following comment of one manager is typical of many managers' views:

Professional engineers feel a significant loss of status during the last decade. . . .[They] do not feel they are part of management and in fact they feel isolated from the mainstream of management decision making.[18]

While, as might be expected, union officials did not always agree with managers about the reasons for engineers' interest in unionization, the comments of the two groups on status concerns were often similar. As one union official put it:

Professionalism is not fully utilized by management. . . .They don't bring them into

---

[16]"Collective Bargaining Agreement Between the Boeing Company and the Seattle Professional Engineering Employees Association (Engineering Bargaining Unit), Article 8," (February 1, 1978).

[17]Interview with union official, Washington, D.C., April 25, 1979. Interview with company official, St. Louis, Mo., June 22, 1978.

[18]Interview with company official, San Diego, July 25, 1978.

UNION ORGANIZATION AMONG ENGINEERS

the decision-making process so the engineers get frustrated at their non-involvement; they think management "doesn't give a damn," and if the employer won't adequately recognize their professionalism, professional engineers may go the collective bargaining route therefore, since they can't get recognition as individuals.[19]

In the campaign at Rohr Industries, the company claimed that a vote for NEPA would endanger the engineers' role as part of the management team. The NEPA response was clear:

The company suddenly "claims" us as a part of management . . . going so far as to infer we will lose our "management" standing if our union is certified. The question is, how can we *lose* something we *do not* have?[20]

The nature of engineers' work could also be an underlying campaign issue, especially at times when economic conditions reduced employment opportunities for engineers. As one manager expressed it, "Engineering work used to be glamorous, but then that fell apart. There was less R and D work and more routine maintenance."[21]

This problem was linked to the obsolescence of engineering skills, sometimes mentioned by managers. The notion was that sometimes older, longer service engineers tended to be in the forefront of union organization because they were no longer able to keep pace with rapid changes in technology and knowledge and so sought to find in union activity an interest their own careers had ceased to provide. In addition, it was claimed that skill obsolescence made engineers more fearful of layoffs, thus encouraging unionization. Also, the lack of potential for career progression may encourage unionization, independent of the argument about obsolescence: those engineers who both aspire to managerial jobs and have a realistic hope of attaining them are probably less receptive to unionization than those who neither seek nor expect such advancement.[22]

The argument for this managerial view may be treated with some skepticism. The evidence is highly subjective, not least because it is difficult in practice to define an "obsolescent" engineer. Also, other evidence from management itself contradicted this view. Many managers pointed out that often the major supporters of unionization campaigns were highly-skilled and well-respected engineers. In a number of cases these people were subsequently promoted to managerial positions. The organizational ability required to take a leading role in a union-organizing campaign would suggest that the more able engineers would be involved. The fact that the leading unionization campaigners were older is also not entirely surprising, because the more experienced group would probably be the ones who received the highest respect from their colleagues and would therefore be more likely to act as leaders of their peer group.

Union officials were usually not prepared to accept the validity of the argument about skill-obsolescence. They typically would argue instead, "They are not obsolescent. Management doesn't give older engineers sufficient opportunity to maintain their skills."[23]

The importance of the lack of career progression received some support from union officials, although they pointed out that management frequently misled engineers about the potential scope for career advancement. Many union officials also agreed that the leading internal supporters of unionization were often the most skilled engineers.

The issues raised in engineers' election campaigns serve mainly to show that most engineers were similar to other employees in the reasons that attracted them to organize. The key issue is why the initial interest in unionization so rarely bore fruit for unions. This study suggests that the reasons for union failure fall into four categories: employer opposition, the attitudes and

---

[19]Interview with union official, Washington, D.C., April 25, 1979.

[20]National Engineers and Professionals Association—San Diego, California, Chapter No. 3001, Handbill (January 20, 1977). (Emphasis in original.)

[21]Interview with company official, St. Louis, Mo., June 22, 1978.

[22]Henry S. Farber and Daniel H. Saks, "Why Work-

ers Want Unions: The Role of Relative Wages and Job Characteristics," *Journal of Political Economy*, Vol. 88, No. 2 (April 1980), pp. 364–65, supports this finding.

[23]Interview with union official, Washington, D.C., March 15, 1979.

values of engineers, the lack of bargaining power of engineers, and union attitudes and organizing policies.

Employer Opposition

Those four categories are merely analytically distinct, of course; in practice they are closely intertwined. Nevertheless, the first two reasons appear to be the most important causes of the union defeats. This study suggests that although engineers' attitudes tend to make them wary of unions, they would probably have voted to unionize in many of the cases studied if employer opposition had not been present. In these campaigns, management often adopted a subtle approach, drawing heavily upon the engineers' own ambivalence about unions, contrary to the more normal, fairly direct antiunion propaganda employers generally rely on.

All the union officials interviewed believed that strong employer opposition was the major cause of union defeats. One union official who had worked as an organizer for both a major public sector union and one that was primarily in the private sector, provided the following comparison:

The reasons for wanting to organize are identical [in the private and public sectors]; the problems are identical. The big difference is employer attitude. . . .In the public sector employers are basically neutral.[24]

It might be argued, of course, that union officials seek to blame employer opposition for defeats, both as a way of avoiding the possibility that engineers merely do not want unions and as a means of deflecting attention from the unions' shortcomings. Thus the nature of employer campaigns requires some attention.

In all the elections studied, employers waged active campaigns against unions. One aspect of the employers' strategy was usually an effort to remedy some of the grievances that had led to union activity. In one company, for example, the immediate response to an organizing campaign was the introduction of a dental plan, previously

limited to unionized employees, and the raising of meal and mileage allowances.

While one aspect of the company response was thus to woo engineers with concessions, company propaganda also involved an undercurrent of threat, stressing the negative results that could occur if engineers voted for unions. The use of the argument that a barrier would be created between management and engineers was very common. Companies frequently asserted that engineers would no longer be able to complain as individuals, but would have to follow a formalized procedure. The cost of union dues was usually raised, along with the loss of "professional status" from joining a union. One issue that surfaced in every company campaign was the argument that voting for a union would inevitably lead to engineers being forced into taking strike action. Union officials in general corroborated management's view that engineers were hesitant to be seen as potential strikers.

In addition to employer opposition during election campaigns, a tough policy usually followed either an election victory or a union takeover of an independent. A classic instance was the tough management bargaining that led NEPA to lose support and be decertified at General Dynamics' Convair Division. Management tactics were geared to the belief that it is an essential weakness of engineers' unions that strike action is unpopular among their members and would probably be ineffective in any case. The company negotiators at Convair believed that if NEPA called a strike, engineers would provide insufficient support to make the strike viable. The union began bargaining in June 1975 and a year later had still not obtained an agreement. Although the membership voted in February 1976 to authorize strike action, NEPA officers refrained from actually calling a strike, preferring to continue to negotiate rather than risk an ineffective strike. This suggests that willingness to strike is a less important constraint than the perceived inability to damage the employer significantly.

Without an agreement with Convair after a year of bargaining, however, NEPA found itself faced with a decertification petition in June 1976. During the decertification cam-

---

[24]Interview with union official, Washington, D.C., April 25, 1979.

UNION ORGANIZATION AMONG ENGINEERS

paign, the employee group opposed to NEPA attacked the union for not achieving results and depicted the union's final demands as a sellout. The basis for the latter charge was that the union's initial demand for a one-year agreement with a "substantial," though unspecified, wage increase had been pared down to a final offer to accept a three-year agreement providing increases of 5.5, 4, and 4 percent. Thus the union was blamed for the results of managerial intransigence and lost the decertification election held in August 1976. In November Convair awarded their engineers merit and promotional increases averaging 13 percent.[25]

Not only was the issue of bargaining power relevant to the decertification vote, but it surfaced in later NEPA activity. At Rohr, an employee group opposed to NEPA distributed a handbill in 1977 saying:

In order to negotiate a contract which provides more than we are currently receiving requires some power at the bargaining table. The *only* power a union has is the threat of a strike. . . .The union did not accomplish anything at Convair because they did not have any *bargaining power*.[26]

Thus Convair's award of large pay increases to engineers after decertification carried a simple but effective message to engineers in other companies.

These tough management tactics are only a variant on the common theme of increased employer hostility to unions in recent years. Employers in these cases generally felt that engineers were more susceptible to management arguments than were blue-collar workers, and the employers were sophisticated enough to avoid unfair labor practice charges being filed against them. At Convair, for example, there were fifty-seven negotiating sessions with NEPA, during which company negotiators were careful to make some concessions. In election campaigns, a number of companies used management consultants who spe-

cialize in union election campaigns. This practice seemed to ensure that threats and promises were made in a manner that almost entirely precluded challenges before the NLRB.

Engineers' Attitudes and Values

Although it is clear that engineers as a group are not highly receptive to unionization, the focus in this study has been on those situations in which engineers had overcome their distaste for unions sufficiently to make a campaign viable. The attitude of engineers toward unionism can be illustrated partially by a study of the role of those professional societies to which engineers belong.

Until the 1970s the professional societies maintained · a generally hostile attitude toward unions. The recession of 1970 and the resulting layoffs of engineers provoked membership demands for greater involvement in the employment field. The involvement manifested itself mainly in attempts to draw up employment guidelines companies would then be encouraged to follow. The interest in guidelines is an example of the degree to which many engineers felt that fair treatment from their employers was not dependent on unionization and that employers could be persuaded to act reasonably on a unilateral basis.

The use of employment guidelines was not new, but to avoid the proliferation of possibly conflicting guidelines, the National Society of Professional Engineers (NSPE) took the initiative in bringing together twenty different societies, which agreed in 1973 on a set of guidelines.[27] The guidelines proposed standards to govern employers' recruitment and professional development activities and urged that an engineer's salary should be "in keeping with his professional contribution."[28] They also recommended a notice period for layoffs of one month, plus one week per year of service.

Although the guidelines were mild and

---

[25]This account of events at Convair is based on interviews with a company official, St. Louis, Mo., June 22, 1978, and a union official, Washington, D.C., March 13, 1979.

[26]Al Alter and 45 others, "Look at the Big Picture," —Handbill (February 3, 1977). (Emphasis in original.)

[27]Twenty Engineering Associations, *Guidelines to Professional Employment for Engineers and Scientists*, (Washington, D.C., 1973).

[28]Ibid., p. 9.

stressed loyalty to the employer, they aroused considerable opposition from aerospace employers on whom the layoff notice provisions could have had a definite effect. Whether as a result of employer opposition or not, the guidelines do not seem to have had a great deal of impact. Hoffman's 1976 survey of 172 companies showed that only 25 percent claimed to have received the guidelines and only about half of these to have reviewed them.[29] The lack of impact reflected both the generalized manner in which the guidelines were written and the absence of any mechanism for enforcement. The reliance on guidelines is a good example of a certain degree of naivete in engineers' views about employee relations.

It has sometimes been suggested that the professional societies might develop into something resembling unions, paralleling the evolution of the National Educational Association. In practice, however, this seems a remote possibility, and Hoffman has cogently pointed out the barriers to such a transformation.[30] One major factor is that society dues are too low to finance a wide range of union services. In addition, most societies have a disparate membership that includes employees, employers, and self-employed. Even among the employees, there is a lack of common interest among those employed in government, teaching, and private industry. The NSPE, for example, has 80,000 members, but only 22,000 of these work in private industry.[31] The NSPE brings together engineers from different specialties and has regarded the study of employment conditions as part of its role. It has consistently opposed trade unionism among engineers. In 1972 a task force, established in response to membership pressure, concluded that:

The National Society of Professional Engineers believes, on the basis of extended experience and study over a long period that collective bargaining is not a desirable, effective or appropriate

mechanism to achieve the objectives of professional employment practices.[32]

The NSPE argues that unionism and professionalism do not mix. Its Code of Ethics depicts participation in strikes by engineers as unethical.[33]

A study of the attitudes of engineers, as expressed through their professional organizations, illustrates some of the factors that inhibit the growth of union membership. Companies have regularly argued that unionism would undermine the engineers' professional status. Unions in response argue that doctors and lawyers believe in self-organization and that engineers should follow suit. Both sides agree that engineers seem very conscious of any challenge to their professionalism. Engineers appear less confident of their status than doctors or lawyers, a reflection both of public perception of their position and of the fact that most engineers are employees. The 1970 census data showed that only 3 percent of engineers were self-employed, compared to 59 percent of lawyers and 60 percent of physicians.[34] The absence of a strong central professional body on the lines of the American Medical Association or the American Bar Association is probably also a factor. One result of the engineers' status consciousness is that independents like SPEEA at Boeing, which also organize technicians, have been careful to place the latter in separate bargaining units. Others have not wished to go even that far and have turned away potential recruits. In one case in 1960, the inclusion of nonprofessionals in a unit led engineers at Western Electric to surrender their NLRB certification and file for an election as a new, carefully defined, purely professional unit. The independent lost this election.[35]

Several empirical research projects have illustrated that engineers may fear that un-

[29]Eileen B. Hoffman, *Unionization of Professional Societies* (New York: The Conference Board Inc., 1976), p. 33.

[30]Ibid., p. 48.

[31]Interview with a society official, Washington, D.C., March 13, 1979.

[32]National Society of Professional Engineers, *Collective Bargaining v. Collective Action,* Report of Task Force on Collective Bargaining (Washington, D.C.: NSPE, 1973), p. 41.

[33]Ibid., p. 34.

[34]Data cited in Hoffman, *Unionization of Professional Societies,* p. 2.

[35]Strauss, "Professional or Employee-Oriented: Dilemma for Engineering Unions," p. 526.

UNION ORGANIZATION AMONG ENGINEERS

ionism will undermine their professional status. A study of federal government engineers by Manley and McNichols is a case in point.[36] There is, however, an apparent lack of consensus among researchers on this point. Kleingartner's research in the late 1960s showed that three-quarters of the two hundred engineers interviewed saw no conflict between unionism and professionalism, and those whom he defined as the "highest" professionals were least likely to see such a conflict.[37] In this context, he defined the degree of professionalism in relation to the level of education, the professional's self-image, and his occupational commitment. Kleingartner concluded that the argument about professionalism was really an employers' argument about unionism and not one put forward by engineers.[38]

It is not impossible to reconcile these apparently divergent results. Kleingartner's study was carried out in two unionized aerospace companies. It seems likely that experience with unionization serves to reduce professionals' fears of potential conflict, and also that engineers, like other employees, have an interest in not defining their own situations as involving conflicting roles. This does not mean that fear of such conflict is not an important force in reducing the attraction of unionism to unorganized engineers. Many union officials felt that engineers were unrealistic in their belief in their status. Although they are often in the same objective situation as other employees in relation to their employer, the engineers' perception is that there is a difference.

Some managers have argued that engineers are often not seriously interested in union membership but are seeking, rather, to attract the attention of management. Even some union officials expressed a certain cynicism about the degree to which engineers really wished to accept the ob-

ligations of union membership. The evidence on this point is mixed. On the one hand, early concessions by employers often seemed to erode the unions' initial support. On the other hand, the degree to which employers resorted to tough tactics suggests a greater amount of tenacity among engineers than a mere desire to attract attention would entail.

Bargaining Power

The concept of relative bargaining power is an important one in looking at engineers and unionization. Slichter, Healy, and Livernash defined bargaining power as "the ability to induce the other side to make concessions that it would not otherwise make. It means more than the mere fact of obtaining concessions."[39] In this context, most groups of engineers cannot immediately paralyze the employer's operations and in an industry like aerospace, with long production lead-times, strike power may not be very great. As the protracted negotiations at Convair illustrated, union officials are conscious of this lack of bargaining power. Thus, even if an engineering union wins an election, it may have difficulty achieving significant gains in the ensuing negotiations.

It might seem that bargaining power is a relevant factor only after an election has been held. Most of the campaigns studied, however, also drew attention to the difficulty engineers would face in applying sanctions against their employers. It is here, particularly, that the ambivalence of engineers toward strike action becomes a significant factor, because strike action would often need to be protracted to prove effective.

Bargaining power is also influenced by the engineers' individualistic orientation. Kuhn has pointed out that engineers, like some other white-collar employees, have opportunities for individual bargaining that are not available to most blue-collar employees.[40] Even when engineers are

[36]T. Roger Manley and Charles W. McNichols, "Attitudes of Federal Scientists and Engineers Towards Unions," *Monthly Labor Report*, Vol. 98, No. 4 (April 1975), pp. 57–60.

[37]Archie Kleingartner, "Professionalism and Engineering Unionism," *Industrial Relations*, Vol. 8, No. 3 (May 1969), p. 229.

[38]Ibid., p. 235.

[39]Sumner H. Slichter, James J. Healy, and E. Robert Livernash, *The Impact of Collective Bargaining on Management*, (Washington, D.C., The Brookings Institution, 1960), p. 918.

[40]James W. Kuhn, "Success and Failure in Organ-

INDUSTRIAL AND LABOR RELATIONS REVIEW

organized, for example, both sides attest to their relatively low use of the formal grievance procedure, which reflects both the engineers' ability to use other channels to solve problems and their unwillingness to be seen to be in a conflict with management.

Union Attitudes and Organizing Policies

One important issue for international unions in campaigns to organize engineers was the balance they should strike between appealing to engineers' professional interests and to their desire to be represented by an effective union. It seems clear that unions that projected a strong blue-collar image felt it was necessary to stress their ability to adapt to the special interests of professionals. On the other hand, a blue-collar image could sometimes be identified with effectiveness, even by the engineers themselves.

This issue arose most directly in relation to the links between the engineers' groups and the international unions. Most major unions apparently accepted the view that engineers wanted some distance between themselves and the blue-collar members. The establishment of NEPA within the UAW was a specific instance of this attempt to provide separate representation. In its campaigns, NEPA stressed its independence from the UAW hierarchy of locals by pointing out that it reported directly to international headquarters. The Teamsters similarly offered SCPEA considerable autonomy as an inducement to affiliate.

Companies certainly seemed to believe that it benefitted them during campaigns to identify NEPA as closely as possible with the UAW and to stress the extent to which membership dues would not be retained locally. Unions made no effort to play down the relationship, however, and frequently cited access to professional advice in bargaining and legal and research services, as well as to the additional resources available from a union should a strike occur. On balance, it does not seem that the issue par-

ticularly hurt NEPA, not least because the UAW could not be attacked as undemocratic or corrupt. The company campaigns against the Teamsters and MEBA played more heavily on a perception of "corruption." That this tactic had an effect need not be left to management to attest. After its disaffiliation from the Teamsters, SCPEA issued a notice that pointed it out:

SCPEA has a tremendous rebuilding task. Our membership is now below 30% from a high of 70% prior to affiliation with the Teamsters. SCPEA knows there are a number of eligible candidates who are hesitant about rejoining because of their feelings toward Teamsters.[41]

The moral is probably the relatively unspectacular one that unions cannot escape from their general image and that engineers may be more concerned about the problem of corruption than are blue-collar workers.

Conclusion

Not for the first time in the history of engineering unionization, it is tempting to write an epitaph for an unsuccessful period of organizing. It is sobering to reflect that in the period since July 1969—when 1,300 Sperry engineers voted for the IUE—only about 2,500 private sector engineers have unionized, and the largest group of these, at General Dynamics, voted within two years to decertify the union. By any criterion, the unions cannot regard their efforts in organizing this occupation to be successful.

In part, the lack of union success in organizing engineers is another instance of the broader problem of union organizing at present in this country. The continuing decline in the unionized percentage of the labor force and the recent increase in union decertifications are two obvious examples of this problem. It is clear that there are certain common elements that affect unions in organizing all types of workers. Private sector employers in the United States have generally shown a particular aversion to white-collar unionism and there are signs among some employers of an increasingly hostile attitude toward all unionism. This

izing Professional Engineers," in Industrial Relations Research Association, *Proceedings of the 16th Annual Meeting* (Boston: IRRA, December 1963), pp. 194–208.

[41]Southern California Professional Engineering Association, *SCPEA: An Independent Union.*

UNION ORGANIZATION AMONG ENGINEERS

employer response is one that would not be socially or often legally acceptable in many Western European countries. The hostility to unions flourishes because a significant section of American society is imbued with values drawn from individualism, free-market capitalism that are no longer widely espoused in Europe. The greater acceptance of the role of unions at all levels in Europe than in the United States means that there even employees who tend to identify with management see only limited objections to unionization.

Employer propaganda against unions finds a much more receptive audience in this country than in Europe. In the United States, white-collar workers in general, and engineers in particular, are likely to accept management criticisms of unions. Studies of occupational choice suggest that those who select engineering as a profession may be more individualistic and less willing to join any organization than those in most other occupational groups.[42] This view received support from several union officials, including one who was himself an engineer.[43] Even in the United Kingdom, where white-collar unionism is far more extensive than in the United States, engineers have been a more difficult group to organize than other white-collar employees in the private sector.[44]

For engineers willing to unionize, there arises the practical problem that they often lack significant bargaining power. This is particularly important in the United States,

where unions are judged by their members and potential members on strongly practical criteria and where they lack the underpinning of ideological support on which European unions can draw. In the United States, members tend to see their unions more as external service organizations than as the embodiment of the collective will of a group of employees. The corollary of this attitude is that a union that fails to deliver tangible benefits may be rejected. Thus, with limited bargaining power, engineers' unions often are unable to resist aggressive management tactics and are seen as failures by their members.

In this context it is tempting, but unfair, to blame unions for being the authors of their own misfortunes. The argument that unions have become inflexible and conservative and unable or unwilling to respond to problems with innovative solutions is common. The evidence from this study, however, shows that a number of unions, especially the UAW, have adopted a flexible approach to organizing engineers. In addition, it is difficult for anyone familiar with the British trade union movement to believe that British unions have been any more flexible or innovative than American unions, yet in the United Kingdom the organization of white-collar employees in the private sector has expanded significantly during the 1970s.[45] The problem for American unions is basically not internal; it arises because they are operating in a political and social environment that is not supportive of their role and because they are subject to a high degree of management opposition.

If this argument is valid, the extent to which unions can improve their position is limited and gains in organizing engineers are unlikely. Naturally, major economic or political changes could alter this picture, but the higher levels of inflation of the 1970s have not resulted in significant increases in union membership. In the political sphere, the failure to enact the innocuous Labor Reform Bill in 1978 offers little hope of developments in the legislative arena that

---

[42]Ann Roe, "Early Determination of Vocational Choice," *Journal of Counseling Psychology*, Vol. 34 (1963), p. 357.

[43]Interview with union official, Washington, D.C., March 15, 1979.

[44]The author here draws on his experience in 1975–77 as an organizer for the major union of professional engineers in the United Kingdom, the TUC-affiliated Engineers' and Managers' Association (EMA). See, also, Council of Engineering Institutions, *Professional Engineers and Trade Unions*, (London: CEI, 1975). For the most thorough recent estimate of white-collar union density in the U.K., see Robert Price and George Sayers Bain, "Union Growth Revisited: 1948–1974 in Perspective," *British Journal of Industrial Relations*, Vol. 114, No. 3 (November 1976), p. 347. These authors estimated that 39.4 percent of white-collar workers belonged to unions in the U.K. in 1974.

[45]Price and Bain, "Union Growth Revisited," pp. 339–55; Trades Union Congress, *Annual Report 1977* (London: TUC, 1978), pp. 610–22.

will aid union organizing.

This conclusion may seen unduly fatalistic. The key questions from several of the campaigns studied are why engineers, a majority of whom had signed authorization cards, voted against the union and why engineers who voted union later voted for decertification. In both cases the simple answer is that management arguments often swayed sufficient engineers to vote against unions in the first place and that lack of bargaining success later provoked decertification. In the short term, it is difficult to foresee circumstances in which engineers suddenly develop greater bargaining power or become less receptive to management persuasion. In the long term these two issues are linked. Bargaining power is not a totally objective phenomenon; it depends in part on employee attitudes. Engineers have so far not generally been willing to face the protracted battles . that might be required to prove their bargaining power. Only when American unions can persuade engineers to do so will the potential for engineering unionization be translated into reality.

Index

Racial Policies of American Industry Series

Order from: Kraus Reprint Co., Route 100, Millwood, New York 10546

STUDIES OF NEGRO EMPLOYMENT

Order from University Microfilms, Inc.
Attn: Books Editorial Department
300 North Zeeb Road
Ann Arbor, Michigan 48106

* Order this book from the Industrial Research Unit, The Wharton School, University of Pennsylvania, Philadelphia, Pennsylvania 19104.